PRAISE FOR KATRIONA O'SULLIVAN

'Soaring with compassion, intelligence and hard-won wisdom, this standout book confirms that O'Sullivan is arguably Ireland's most important contemporary voice'
Louise Kennedy

'Utterly compelling, deeply moving and brilliantly written, Hungry is a raw, insightful look at women's complex relationship with their bodies. Every woman needs to read this book. Every man needs to read this book'
Edel Coffey

'O'Sullivan is such a vivid, empathetic storyteller who writes so beautifully not just about the correlation between the body and poverty and abuse, but the intersection between sex, body image, culture and dieting. I doubt there's a woman alive who won't immediately see herself in these pages'
Tanya Sweeney

'Hungry is more than a book: it's a song, a map, a journey. I couldn't put it down'
Elaine Feeney

'A raw and brutal account of one woman's battle with her own body, as profound and honest as anything I have ever read'
Liz Nugent

'One of the most remarkable people you will ever meet'
Guardian

'A beautiful telling of determination despite the odds'
Irish Times

'Raw and remarkable'
Irish Independent

'Moving, uplifting, brave, heroic'
Nuala McGovern, Woman's Hour, BBC

Dr Katriona O'Sullivan is a professor of psychology and the bestselling author of *Poor*, winner of Biography of the Year and Newcomer of the Year at the 2023 Irish Book Awards. The memoir has been translated into seven languages, adapted into a sold-out play at Dublin's Gate Theatre, and remained in Ireland's top-ten non-fiction chart for two years. A regular commentator on the BBC and across Irish and international media, she has spoken at Westminster, the UN and UNESCO.

Born in Coventry to Irish parents, Katriona's early life was marked by poverty, addiction, teenage pregnancy and homelessness. In 1998, she moved to Dublin, where she entered Trinity College through the Access Programme and went on to earn a PhD in psychology. Now a professor at Maynooth University, she directs the National Centre for Inclusive Higher Education and leads the award-winning STEM Passport for Inclusion, which has supported over 10,000 young people from underserved communities into higher education and high-status careers.

HUNGRY
A biography of my body
KATRIONA O'SULLIVAN

WILDFIRE

Copyright © 2026 Katriona O'Sullivan

The right of Katriona O'Sullivan to be identified as the Author of the Work has been asserted by her in accordance with the Copyright, Designs and Patents Act 1988.

First published in Great Britain in Hardback in 2026 by Wildfire
An imprint of Headline Publishing Group Limited

'Babylon'. Words and Music by David Gray. Copyright © 1999 BMG Rights Management (UK) Ltd. All Rights Administered by BMG Rights Management (US) LLC. All Rights Reserved. Used by Permission.

1

Apart from any use permitted under UK copyright law, this publication may only be reproduced, stored, or transmitted, in any form, or by any means, with prior permission in writing of the publishers or, in the case of reprographic production, in accordance with the terms of licences issued by the Copyright Licensing Agency.

Cataloguing in Publication Data is available from the British Library

Hardback ISBN 978 1 0354 2777 2
Trade Paperback ISBN 978 1 0354 2773 4

Typeset in Garamond by Bookends Publishing Services, Dublin.

Printed and bound in Great Britain by Clays Ltd, Elcograf S.p.A.

Headline's policy is to use papers that are natural, renewable and recyclable products and made from wood grown in well-managed forests and other controlled sources. The logging and manufacturing processes are expected to conform to the environmental regulations of the country of origin.

Headline Publishing Group Limited
An Hachette UK Company
Carmelite House
50 Victoria Embankment
London EC4Y 0DZ

The authorised representative in the EEA is Hachette Ireland,
8 Castlecourt Centre, Dublin 15, D15 XTP3, Ireland (email: info@hbgi.ie)

www.headline.co.uk
www.hachette.co.uk

This book is for seven-year-old me – 'I've still got you!'

All the names within this book – apart from Dave, John, Sean, Tadhg, Noel, Steph, Tony and Tilly – have been changed.

Contents

Prologue: July 2022   *1*

PART ONE
Mine
1   Hungry   *11*
2   'She's Good ... For a Girl!'   *27*

His
3   Teacher   *41*
4   Chosen One   *48*

Hers
5   My Mum   *59*

Them
6   You Are Bad!   *73*

Theirs

7	You Made This Happen	*93*
8	Jace	*97*
9	Just for the Sex	*106*
10	John's Birth	*114*
11	Weight Watching!	*124*
12	All of the Men	*141*

PART TWO
What Am I Made For?

13	The Rutland Centre	*159*
14	Dylan	*179*
15	I Am Normal After All	*189*
16	Whack-a-Mole	*195*
17	May the Maypole	*200*
18	A New Hunger	*210*
19	A Break	*216*
20	A Kind Man	*218*
21	What I Was Made For	*233*
22	Just Like My Dad	*248*
23	Motivation	*253*
24	Achievement	*257*
25	Before-and-After Pictures	*260*
26	Tadhg	*265*
27	A Wedding	*268*
28	A Funeral	*271*

29	Driven *275*
30	Gastric Solutions *283*
31	Gastric Lies *295*
32	This Is Not Right *307*
33	Healing *316*
34	Cleaning Up the Piss – and My Body *326*
35	Unravelling in Turkey *332*
36	Meltdown *338*

Mine – Ours

| 37 | Summer 2025 *345* |

Epilogue *350*

Acknowledgements *357*

Prologue

July 2022

The room is a mess, clothes everywhere. I have tried on every dress I have with me, and I hate everything. The sun is beating down outside. Perched on the edge of the bed, sweat-beads rolling down my back, I cry. Deep tears.

I hate myself.

I hate my fucking body.

Three weeks in Turkey, three weeks of half-naked people, three weeks of bikinis, bodycon dresses, shorts, vests, shoulders, arms and legs. Three weeks of comparing. Every slim, beautiful woman feels like a direct attack on my self-esteem. Three weeks of watching his eyes; looking where he is looking, thinking I am not sexy enough, skinny enough, full enough to fulfil his needs.

He never says that.

He doesn't need to.

'Babe, I don't want to go out for dinner tonight ... I'd rather stay in with the boys than face going out ... You could head into Centrum and pick us all up kebabs?'

My voice sounds tense despite my best efforts to sound easy-breezy.

He knows what is wrong.

He has always known.

Those first few months when we got together, when I felt on top of the world, I was well able to hide this from him: the doubts, the body hate, the hurt. Eighteen years on, and there is no hiding now. He has seen it all. He has seen me cry, laugh, dance, get surgery, get sick, hurt myself, hurt him. He knows it all.

And he stays.

'You are beautiful, babe.'

He means it. I can see it in his eyes. In the way his body responds to me when I lie next to him at night. It's clear from the way he has adapted himself for me. He means it.

And, somewhere deep down, I know this.

I know I am beautiful.

I know I am enough.

Since starting with my therapist, Máire, last year, I have been feeling much better. I have seen the glimmers of light that healing brings. I have a new voice developing, one that says 'you are enough' really quietly.

But being here in Turkey, where the food is cheap and luscious, where there are half-naked, beautiful bodies everywhere, where I know that somewhere, just five minutes away from me, some Irish girl is getting a gastric sleeve fitted – it's hard. Three weeks without my home, my foundation, my wardrobe, my comfort clothes, my friends, my therapy, my network, and I'm slipping. Everything I had been working through with my therapist is fading. The gastric band hasn't worked for me, but the illusion of another miracle weight-loss solution grows brighter and brighter with every day that I'm here.

'Babe, look at this picture of Leigh she just posted on Facebook. Look how well she looks.'

I am starting something.

He knows.

I know.

'Yes, she looks great. I preferred her with a bit of meat on her bones, though, love ... and hasn't she been sick all the time since she got it done?'

He knows.

I know.

'Yes, she had sepsis, but that was from an infection. The problem with Leigh is that she hates vegetables and salad. I love all that food.'

He knows.

I know.

'It's very expensive though, isn't it? Like, you paid so much for the gastric band and look how that turned out – you still get sick now from that.'

He knows.

I know.

'The gastric sleeve is so cheap here in Turkey, though, babe. I was enquiring on the website, and they could do it all for less than five grand: remove the band *and* do the sleeve. That's a bargain ...

and I'm going to have to get the band out anyway at some point!'

He looks at me with the slow realisation that this is a done deal. I'm not asking, I'm telling. Inviting him into the decision – after it has been made.

'Don't say anything yet, babe,' I go on quickly. 'I know you're going to think it's impulsive, but I've been thinking about this for years now, and they said they can fit me in before we go home, which means I can go in tomorrow morning and be out on Thursday to fly back to Dublin ...'

Disappointment and fear cloud his face.

'I cannot do a holiday like this again ... where I hate myself and the way I look. I can't do this again!'

Tears roll down my face. I want to tell him that sometimes I want to cut off my hair. To remove a limb. To end everything. Sometimes, the shame of failing, of looking like this, of feeling like this, makes every other thing in my life feel pointless. I want him to be me. To feel this.

Him, with his black-and-white thoughts and his black-and-white feelings.

Him, with his unwavering commitment to running and working and loving me.

I want to shake him for reflecting his love on to me, for showing me that I am more than this. So much more.

He takes my hand. 'Babe, I love you no matter what you look like. If you think this is going to make you happy, I will support you. I will always support you.'

Even though he's saying the words, I know he's disappointed. This past year has been better in so many ways. My commitment to myself and my therapy has brought a truth to us that wasn't always there. I've told him about the deep hurt – he knows about the sexual abuse, how I was used by men, how my body feels alien to me sometimes. He sees how it has affected me sexually. I've told him I perform for him. I put him first. I've shared about Bob, about being suffocated by grief. And he has held me in ways he never did before.

This gastric sleeve obsession is a step backwards for me and for him. And I can feel that.

But I bulldoze ahead.

I bulldoze over his fear and his doubts.

The hunger is so strong that even love cannot stop it this time.

PART ONE

Mine

Hungry

Sitting, aged seven, at the window of our house, staring into the darkness of a council estate in the middle of England, waiting for my mum to come home. Waiting for the food she went searching for hours ago. My little body unsure of how to cope with the incessant noise of its hunger.

Matthew, my little brother, born hopeful, is smiling at me, making my heart melt.

'Come on, Kat. Let's go downstairs – see if there's anything to eat.'

He is six, and my best friend in the whole world.

'What time do you think it is?'

My mum went out at 6pm to get us dinner. It's hours later, and she isn't back yet. My hunger is urgent now.

'It's dark.' He pulls my hand towards the door.

'OK, OK, I'm coming. You better not cry if there is nothing there.'

We sneak down the stairs, avoiding the familiar creaks on the thirteen uncarpeted steps that lead down to the 'back room'. Our house, a three-bed semi in the middle of Vine Street, has a front room, a back room and a small scullery kitchen. A tiny bathroom, with its faded lime-green wall tiles and dark black ring around the top of the bath, is at the very back. The back room has brown velvet curtains that are never opened, a frayed brown carpet on the floor and a round table under the window with a misty glass top. Remnants of Rizla and tobacco form a pattern across the table's surface, and four unused chairs sit tightly around it.

Our house is a mess. Clothes everywhere, rubbish flung on the floors, bags of cans, old papers – drug paraphernalia. The carpet has cigarette burns; the Artex walls are stained yellow. A painting of a little girl with short hair and a tear rolling down her left cheek hangs on the wall. I make up stories about why she's crying. Maybe her dad is in prison too; maybe her mum, too, is ignoring all the bad things that are happening to her.

Matthew climbs the countertop and opens the cupboard; there is a loaf of bread, a bag of sugar and some sauces. He looks at me and smiles. 'Sugar sandwiches?'

'Yes! My favourite!'

Matthew is built like the Sugar Puff Monster. Short, square, stocky, and he chases sugar everywhere he goes. I check the fridge for butter – I wish! There's an empty plastic marge container and three eggs. A glass bottle of milk stands in the door, and a green stain sits at the bottom – mould grows out of old food. The fridge light flickers. I open the marge, take out the wrinkled sheet of protective paper, and wipe it over the four slices of bread. Not a scrap of marge on the sheet, but it makes me feel better. As if we are having a proper sandwich.

Matthew gets a teaspoon and puts it into the bag of sugar. 'One spoon or two, *madame?*' He is using his fake posh voice.

'Two, please, sir,' I say, grinning. Nobody is better to be around than our Matthew. No matter how sad and hard things get, he has the brightest heart and the funniest laugh.

He heaps two spoons of sugar on to one of my slices of bread, and does the same for one of his. We put the bag back in the cupboard and look at each other.

'*Bon appétit, madame.*' He bites hard into his sandwich, sugar spilling out of both ends of his big smile.

I laugh at him as I take a bite out of my own. Sugar sandwiches are our staple diet.

'Mmmmm.' I laugh, the sugar melting on my tongue. The joy of food. The joy of having something sweet to eat. When something is rare, it's nicer. And food is rare in our house, especially as my dad is in prison.

These are memories of growing up poor. All the families on my road were poor. But poverty is not the same for everyone. It has layers, slices of difference, reasons why some survive and some don't. I was a hungry poor kid: starved of love, desperate for nourishment and hungry for the most basic need – food.

'Hurry up, Sheila, time to get ready for school, luv.' As Matthew and I head past the Kellys', en route to school, I hear Mrs Kelly call my best friend Sheila to get out of bed. Her Irish lilt reminds me of my grandma back home in Ireland. The faint smell of sausages wafts as I spy through the net curtains; she smiles as she cleans the embers of last night's warmth from the old wrought-iron fireplace.

In Hillfields, Coventry, the council estate where I grew up, some of the families were what I call 'rich-poor', and some of the families were 'poor-poor'. All struggling to make ends meet; all doing their best to survive. But most of the families were rich-poor. They had stuff – just never enough stuff.

The Kellys are rich-poor and my mouth waters as I pass on my way to school; my heart aches for the sustenance they have in their house. Mrs Kelly walks back into the kitchen, her shadow moving quickly now. I imagine her cooking breakfast, putting bread and butter and red sauce out on the table, waiting for her three girls to emerge from their dreams. They are fed well in the Kelly house. Mrs Kelly packs snacks for her girls so they won't go hungry throughout the school day. Jam and butter and bread. A bit of cooked ham from the night before. On Sundays, they sit around the table and eat a Sunday roast. Mr Kelly cuts the wings and legs off the chicken, sharing them equally between the girls, saving the white meat from the breast for his wife. My dreams are pretty simple. I want, more than anything else in the world, to be a Kelly girl!

Their dad is Irish, too. He works with his hands on a building site. He goes out at 7am and gets home at 6pm every evening. He carries his packed lunch in an old bread bag. He loves a smoke; he loves a drink of a Friday after work. I sometimes put my ear to the wall to hear Mr and Mrs Kelly fighting because he has spent too much of his wages in the pub. His Friday thirst puts Mrs Kelly under pressure to keep the house going for the week.

I want to be a Kelly.

I want to be rich-poor.

But we are poor-poor – hungry for food, for hugs, and for safety.

'Matthew, Matthew, you should put him over there, so he's higher up than everyone else. That's where the king would be standing.'

My brother and I are huddled under the blankets, playing imaginary games. He's always a king, reigning over a kingdom, and I am either the queen, the princess or the joker. But Matthew, my Matthew, is always the king.

'No! No, Katriona! The king is here with everyone around him. They can all see him here.' Matthew stands his ground, holding the cheap little green soldier he has decided is the king in the middle of all the other identical-looking cheap little green soldiers.

The soldiers are a Christmas gift from Social Services. Matthew got soldiers; I got a doll. Social Services supplement Santa Claus for poor-poor kids who have nothing.

'The king demands the attention of everyone!'

The sheet feels warm over our heads, playing his game of king and the king's men. I let him lead. He is better at this than I am. I follow along blindly, happy he has agreed to stay with me in my little bed, in my little bedroom. I make up the dances and the songs while he makes up our games.

'Now, Kat, you bring the queen and her ladies down towards the king. Make them bow to him as they arrive.'

Matthew watches intently, making sure every character plays their part. We laugh into the night, all part of the king's court.

I snuggle closer to him. The heat and the lingering smell of piss in our makeshift den are making me tired. Since my dad went to prison, I have taken to sleeping in with Matthew or getting him to sleep in with me. Matthew is my comfort blanket, my very own teddy bear. I watch his face, hoping he can read my thoughts. I want to make sure he'll be here when I wake up – that I am not left alone.

'Shall we go to sleep now, Kat?'

Connected. I don't have to tell him.

'Can we?'

I smile as he pushes the soldiers to the end of the bed and lies down next to me. I spoon in behind him, grabbing on to his soft, round belly. He laughs as I tickle him a little. I keep one eye on the half-open door. One eye on the moonlight that shines on to the side of his face.

The house is quiet.

No parties tonight.

Nothing to fear, Katriona.

'G'night, Kat. I love you,' he whispers into the darkness.

'I love you too.'

And then it happens.

In the midst of our safe dreams, a warm rush fills the bed. Hot piss feels good for a short minute, until it doesn't. Like a warm hug that ends with a cold slap. One of us has pissed.

We are both bedwetters.

We are both afraid.

We don't know who has done it.
And we never, ever, talk about it.

'What time is it, Kat?' Matthew isn't properly awake yet; his eyes the size of two blackened peas. 'Is it morning yet?'

I laugh at him. 'Yes, it's morning. Come on, get up and we can go in early. We can get extra time on the climbing frame.'

I am always awake before him. Most nights I sleep half-awake, listening for the creak of the stairs, for the door handle to move, for someone to enter. My eyes open as soon as the sun pops through the long wooden-framed window in my bedroom. The damp bed from our pissfest isn't the nicest place to doze.

So, I watch him sleep.

Not wanting to break the spell of sweet dreams.

Not wanting to wake him to our shared nightmare.

'Come on, Matt, up, up, up! If we get there early enough, we might see Miss Holby arriving.'

We both know what this means: food. Miss Holby is the headmistress of the school, and some mornings, when she finds us there before her, she gives us something sweet – a biscuit or a Jaffa cake – something to fill the swilling sound of our empty bellies. Matthew races out of bed, the thought of food like a rocket up his six-year-old arse, into the boys' bedroom to search for his clothes among those strewn about the room. Everything is too small or full of holes.

The clothes I own are gifted from neighbours, from Social Services or from the lovely Ms Atkins, my teacher, the one I pop in to most days for a little hug and an iced bun. I am wearing her daughter's dress today, the one with the pink and red and purple squares and the huge collar. I long for some patent-leather shoes like the other little girls or some tights with little bows on the ankles like Laura Harris has.

I stand at the top of the stairs and smooth my dress down over the still-wet pants. 'Matt, will you hurry up? I want to go down.'

I won't go on my own, afraid of who or what I will find down there.

He pulls my hand and leads the way.

No fear in my Matthew.

Not yet, anyway.

She is lying ragged on the brown sofa in the back room, her denim skirt around her waist, blue-grey knickers covering where we came from. Bright pink pin-marks decorate her groin and ankles, reminding me of the dot-to-dot books we received from Social Services last Christmas. Her white skin is see-through; purple and blue veins throb through her legs. Her eyes are sunken into dark pools; even in her sleep she looks troubled by the ghost of heroin, the ghoul that chases her through our nights and days.

'Mum ...?' Matthew touches her face so gently that a tear bounces into my eye. He tries his best not to startle her. 'Muu-uummm ... are you OK?' His voice comes from somewhere sore.

'She's OK, Matt, look!' I roughly pull her eye open. Her pupils contract inwards and outwards beneath my small fingers. She tries to focus on us. 'She's fine!'

I act cockier than I feel. I know his thoughts, his fears – I want to rescue him from them. To stop him from saying what we both think.

Dead.

Is she dead?

'Come on, we'll go and get to school before everyone else.' I grab him now as he stands over her, willing her to wake. To be our mum. To hug him, or me, or us both. 'Let's go, kid. We can play kings and queens along the way!'

The idea of being the king always works on Matthew. I leave knowing that when I return home, my mum, Tilly, will still be imprinted on the brown, blood-stained sofa.

'Miss, I'm not sitting next to Katriona. She smells!'

Simone Garrison sticks her tongue out at me as she shouts this. My heart beats in my ears. Red rushes from my toes to my frown. Fists clench.

'Fuck you, Simone, you bitch.'

'KATRIONA! Do not use that language!'

I am moved to the 'relaxation' table. Matthew is always sitting at this table. Or else he is in Miss Holby's 'special' room – the room for kids who throw things and hit teachers.

That is Matthew: the thrower, the hitter.

Me, I am the swearer. I am pissy.

'But, miss, Simone is always calling me names. It's not fair, and she never lets me play any of the games!'

Simone Garrison is my nemesis – from day one at primary school, she has hated me. Every chance she gets, she pulls my hair and calls me names. She lives in one of the fancier houses near us, and, for no reason, she hates me.

It may be because I am an easy target. Or maybe it was because my mum is 'working' from the corner of her road, selling herself for the price of a bag of gear and chips for her starving kids.

Whatever the reason, I don't understand it. I am fun, outgoing. I can run, chase and laugh like everyone else. Yet, she hates me to be part of things – and, because she is strong and big, the others follow her. I am left out.

Pissy pants.
Nitty Nora.
Smelly Kat!
These are my names.
Kids are cruel.
She is cruel.

The worst part is, I know what she's saying about me is true. I am smelly; I have nits; I have pissy knickers. But I also know that there is nothing I can do about it. In the middle of the playground, with the kids surrounding me singing 'pissy pants, pissy pants', I know I can do nothing. My body is letting me down, and I cannot control the most basic bodily function.

'OK now, fingers on lips, children. Fingers on lips, please!'

The noise of twenty-seven seven-year-olds gets louder before 'shushing' sounds come from the good kids, and we are all settled at our little desks holding our fingers over our lips.

This is the special reading and writing class that has been put on for children who show potential with reading, or for kids who just love books and stories. Every day, for one hour, a group of us go to Ms Atkins' classroom and read, write or make up stories together. It's my favourite hour of the school day.

'Now, we have all been working really hard, and it is that time of the week again where we celebrate one of your achievements.'

Ms Atkins smiles down at us like the sun. Her dark-brown hair curls tight to her head in a Joan Collins sort of way. Her sweet Irish voice reminds me of jam and bread and hot milk and all things comforting.

She picks up one of the pictures or stories we submitted to the writing boxes and holds it close to her chest.

'This week, we have had the most amazing story submitted to the Student of the Week box. The words and the pictures made the other teachers and me laugh and cry. Such talent in my little class!'

Every one of us grows a little in that moment. Shoulders straighter, smiles brighter. She does that to you, my Ms Atkins. She puts things inside you that never leave. Love, hope, heart – and for some of us, those of us who are hungry, she gives us food and extra hugs.

'This little girl is one of the brightest buttons. She has an amazing future ahead of her, and, when she focuses her mind on something, she cannot be beaten.'

Everyone's face rises in anticipation, hoping to be picked, hoping for her light to shine on them.

'This week's student of the week is ... Katriona O'Sullivan.'

Me ... ? Me! I can't believe it! She beckons me up to the front of the class, holding out her tanned hand with the sparkly rings that decorate every finger. I walk towards her, dazed, the fizzing of love and joy inside of me making me dizzy.

'Katriona, your story was so wonderful. Could you do us the greatest honour and read it out to the class, please?'

She pulls me in close to her smooth knees, her blue dress shining in the afternoon light. Her eyes soft, smile warm. She hands me the story I wrote.

Imagining Simone's face somewhere in the class, I waver, the nerves taking over.

'You can do this, now – you are the best at reading out loud,' she whispers to me. 'You are such a wonderful girl. This story made us all so proud.'

Ms Atkins knows me. She stays standing beside me, takes hold of my hand, smiling down at me, radiating warmth and support – all of it seeping into me as if by osmosis, filling me up.

I look down at my story and smile. This one I am proud of. This one I based on *The BFG*. For a fleeting second, I know without any doubt that I am good at something, and, as long as Ms Atkins thinks I am good at something, I will be OK.

'Katriona! Katriona, come here!'

Our classrooms are open-plan – little squares of students fill the large room of our primary school. Instead of walls, the border of each 'class' is a line of colourful masking tape. I can see Matthew every day, smashing things, hitting people, fighting. This day, though, I have been moved to the only separate classroom, separate from the big, shared room, doing arts and crafts. I missed the commotion. I only realise something is wrong when Michelle opens the door and shouts.

'Katriona, Simone has locked Matthew in the coat room! She's put the brush in the handle so he can't get out.'

Her words hit the back of my head. I am already running to the back of the big classroom towards the gang of kids huddled around the cloakroom, laughing. Simone is standing there, smirking, looking at me. She knows she can get to me through him. I never care what they do to me. They can say what they want about me. I don't care. But Matthew – he is off limits.

Don't fuck with my little brother. Don't fuck with my heart!

'Where is he? Where is he?'

'KAT, KAT! I'M IN HERE! LET ME OUT!'

The fear in his voice, the crowd of faces, her smirk – I lose it. I yank the brush out of the door handles to let him out and turn on her. The smirk leaves her face as the brush comes crashing down on the top of her head. 'You won't fucking hurt him! You won't hurt him!' I hear myself screaming, and then the brush leaves my hand and hits her straight between her eyes.

'Katriona ... Katriona ... KATRIONA, ARE YOU LISTENING TO ME?'

Mrs Cowes is shouting now. I have no idea what she said or what I did. She's my teacher this year, and she's always shouting. As she marches towards me from behind her big wooden desk at the front of our classroom, I feel my gut wrench, my heart race. The sound of my hunger fills everything. It's after noon and I've had nothing to eat since yesterday. Even the fear of what she is about to say or do is dampened by my incessant need to eat.

'Katriona, STAND UP!' Mrs Cowes towers over me. Her dry, curly hair looks like a burst of black worms sitting on the top of her fat face, on top of her even fatter body. The sweat stains under the armpits of her brown corduroy dress look like one of the continents on the map on our classroom wall.

I push my chair back slowly and stand up, scraping its feet along the floor. I know she hates the sound.

She glares down at me. For a minute, I think she is going to hit me.

'Katriona, can you explain to me, and the rest of the class, why you are not answering my questions? Why have you decided that what I have to say is not important to you? WHY ARE YOU STOPPING EVERYONE IN THE CLASS FROM LEARNING?'

Her spit sprays me as she raises her voice. I stay quiet. There is nothing to say when she is like this. Just let her have her say. She will send me to the headmistress, Miss Holby, soon enough.

'WHY IS IT THAT THE O'SULLIVAN FAMILY THINK THEY ARE BEYOND LEARNING? You and your little brother, who has no sense and no capacity to learn, ruin every class you are in. CAN YOU EXPLAIN TO ME, OR THE CLASS, WHY THAT IS? WHAT IS WRONG WITH YOU?'

I want to scream at her. I want to open my mouth and sink my big, beautiful teeth into her face to show her how hungry I am, how I have nothing left to give her, how I didn't hear her, how I never hear her, how I *can't* hear her when I have nothing inside of me. I want to pull Mrs Cowes' hair, scratch her horrible beady eyes out of her head and put them inside my own head, to let her feel what it is like to be me for one minute: the shake of my hand, the drip, drip, drip of thoughts that focus only on my empty tummy. I want her to see and feel this, to know that her words can't hurt me, that I am already fucking broken apart – that watching my mum slowly dying in front of me, without anyone to help me, has taken every ounce of concentration from me. I want her and her fat fucking belly to sit in my shoes. To feel what it is like to have nothing to eat.

I am a good girl really. I read books incessantly. *The Children's Bible*, which sits next to my bed, sets me up for sleep: stories of Noah and Jonah and Lot and Ruth instil ethics and care into me. I live through Judy Blume and Roald Dahl – they provide hope and heart to me. I can do the work Mrs Cowes prescribes. I can do more than most – I am bright and good and capable.

Just not when I am hungry.

Ms Atkins tells me to come to her for a bun every morning. But when I don't see her, if she isn't at school before lessons start, I spend the morning empty. We have food in our house sometimes, but it is sporadic. Drugs come first. On payday – when the welfare arrives – my mum goes to the big supermarket and buys a large bag of potatoes and a big packet of eggs. Egg and chips is our staple diet. If we're lucky, she buys cheap baked beans or frozen peas to go with it.

I am bright and capable, just not when the loudest part of me is screaming for sustenance. Mrs Cowes' class this year has been the worst so far in school. The screaming happens every day. I am distracted. I am vacant. I am empty. She is right, but it's not because I am bad. It is because I have one thought that dominates every other: the thought of food – the need to eat. I am hungry. I am *hungry*. Why can't she see this?

'Go to Miss Holby's office immediately. Tell her I cannot teach you anything, that you are naughty, that you do not deserve to be in my classroom ...'

I scrape the feet of my chair along the floor as I go to leave. Watching her wince once more feels like a small victory. I walk towards Miss Holby's office, every step taken slowly, steadily. I pass the canteen, listening to the sound of the lovely canteen ladies working hard behind the silver shutters to make our hot lunches. Like Pavlov's dog, I salivate at the sound of the hatch opening. I memorise the weekly menu – Thursday, my favourite day, roly-poly pudding day! My heart pounds, my lips wetted. In twenty-five minutes, I will eat what might be the only meal I will have that day. Fuck Mrs Cowes, fuck school, fuck learning. All I care about is eating.

'She's Good ... For a Girl!'

'She's not playing, is she?'

His eyes dart from me to my brothers to me again. They flank me: Michael on my right shoulder, James on my left, Matthew at the back.

Undeterred, Steve McVeigh keeps talking. 'How old is she? She isn't even old enough to be out at this time of the day, let alone playing a *proper* match. Are you Sullies mad or what?'

He's laughing at me now, eyeing the crowd around him, encouraging his lads to join in. His body shakes; his shit-stain-tanned neck contrasts with the white rim of his shoulders, sticking out of his Coventry City jersey. A real street kid. Tan stains on legs and faces and hands and arms. We have no sunscreen in the 1980s. You play out and you get brown or you get burned. The extent of the tan stain will be revealed at Sunday-night bathtime when the outline of your clothes becomes clear for the world to see.

The other kids join in with Steve's joke, laughing at the idea of a little girl playing in a match between Vine Street and the Hartlepool

Street crew. This is the biggest rivalry in our area, and the Vine Street lads want a girl to play! No one can believe it.

Steve is the self-appointed leader of their estate. Hartlepool Street is five minutes from Vine Street, and he is the oldest of their crew. Like my brother Michael, Steve decides what games we play, who can play and, more importantly, who can't. He is in the same class as Michael in Sidney Stringer. They are not friends, but they have a solid respect for each other, neither wanting to come to blows with the other, neither confident of who would win.

'Steve, look, mate, can we just have her play this time? We have to bring her everywhere we go. The old lady will kill us if we leave her out, especially since she got hit by that car that time. Don't worry, we'll have her on our team. You won't even know she's here!'

Michael works his magic with every word. Steve relaxes his stance, watching the lads around us, checking that his tough man status will remain intact if he backtracks.

'OK ... OK, fuck it, she can play ... but don't come crying to me if we get too physical for you, little girl.' He watches me as he walks away, hoping I will react. I keep my face blank. *I'll show this fucker on the pitch!*

'James, James, pass it, pass it, I'm free.'

I am playing on the right wing, the wind in my hair; my feet are light. I'm on fire – it is nil-nil; it's only a matter of time before we score. I am playing the best football I have ever played. Even the grit from Sidney Stringer's gravel pitch is on my side today: the slip and slide underneath my worn-out trainers go in my direction. The mid-term temperature is perfect for winning – not too hot, not too cold; no rain, but no shine either.

None of the Hartlepool lads can get near me.

They have underestimated me, as all boys do. They leave me to sit out on the wing on my own, wide open, unmarked. *She's only a girl!* This blinds them to my skill. I've been playing ball with my three brothers since before I could walk. My skill is innate, my physical build perfect for the rough and tough of the game, my determination the icing on the cake. The Hartlepool boys are too busy chasing down players they assume are better than me.

'JAMES, JAMES! Over the top. I'm free ...'

James looks up. He sees me, he smiles, he knows. He scoops his right foot under the ball, chipping it over the heads of five players. I watch it float through the air, every player's face turned upwards. I pull my foot back – loading up – feel my foot hit the ball perfectly, on the volley. I watch as it glides past their keeper and into the back of their net.

I take off, looking for James. The wind in my hair, arms in the air, screaming at full tilt. 'YYYYYAAAAAAYYYYY! One-nil! One-fucking-nil.' James grabs me, lifts me up, spins me in the air. The rest of our team gathers around us. Squishing into us, patting me on the head, slapping James on the back.

'What a fucking goal, Kat!'

'Some volley, Kat!'

'Lovely chip, James!'

I feel it.

The freedom.

The potential of my body, of what it can do.

The connection to my team, my brothers, my community, the Vine Street crew. I am part of them, and they are part of me.

The afternoon continues like that. I am on fire. The drive to show Steve what I can do outweighs everything. *Fuck you, Steve. Fuck you, Steve. Fuck all of you boys! I am good enough. I can do what any boy can do.* I score again. We win. Five-nil. We have never beaten them by so much. My heart and soul are full. Cheeks red, feet sore, arms warm from hugging my team, my brothers.

'Great game, Kat – you've never played that good.' Michael pats me on the head as he walks by. I grow.

'Kat, you were so good today, so good!' Matthew keeps hugging me. Always my champion.

Steve eyes me as I'm about to head home. 'Hey, Kat.'

I stop, stare up at him, waiting for another jibe, preparing to tell him to go fuck himself.

'Great game today, Kat. You're a good player, really good ... for a girl!'

These memories of my body are good, filled with joy. I could run, jump, skip and fight. Big gangs of kids out on our street, playing war until it was too dark to see each other. Finding hiding spots under the flashing streetlights; keeping the games going until the dead of night.

All day, every day, I played out.

All day, every day was an adventure.

My mum and dad's addiction meant I was kicked out early and not let back in until late. Vine Street was my playground: a long line of red-brick houses down one side and a huge secondary school on the other. Sidney Stringer Academy catered for over three thousand working-class students from the surrounding area, all of them surviving, very few thriving. The Foresters pub sat at the foot of Vine Street while the Queen's sat at the top. Arriving home to an empty house, with an empty belly, always meant one of three things: they were in the Foresters or the Queen's, or they had been arrested.

'Come on, Matt, let's go up the road and see if we can get ourselves a few sweets.'

Matthew knows what I'm saying without me saying it. He laughs.

'Kat, the last time we got chased for miles ...' The spark in his eye tells me he is plotting. 'Maybe this time, you go in the shop before me and pretend like you're going to get sick, act like proper sick or something and, when his back is turned, I'll grab some stuff for us both.'

He is being dead serious. He wants me to distract Mr Rakesh, so that he can rob sweets for us. My heart pounds thinking of pretending to be sick while Matt fleeces the shop. That feels like hell to me.

'No, Matt, I'm not getting sick. Fuck off with that! You get sick, and I will grab stuff. I can't lie like you can. You do it, Matt ... please.'

He laughs as we walk the short distance from our house to the sweet shop, which sits right next to the Queen's pub. He grabs my hand, fingers cold from the November air, no gloves or jacket.

'I won't let anything bad happen to you.' He is sincere now. 'You're better at the acting up than me, Kat. You do all the drama and stuff in school, in all the plays and everything. I wasn't even picked to be a snowman this year in the nativity play because of how bad I am at acting.'

He knows how to get to me. Tell me I am good at something, and I'll do it twice over. Tell me I'm good at acting or singing and you will get a full show for the night. My dream is to be on the stage. Doris Day, Sandy in *Grease* – I would even play Rizzo if it meant getting to be seen, to be heard. To sing for people.

'You didn't get picked to play anything because you are always in Miss Holby's office, Matt. You can't do as you are told!'

The little sweet shop looks ominous at dusk; the black Labrador collection box with its faded words, 'Guide Dogs for the Blind', threatens now, guarding the door against would-be robbers.

Matthew smiles at me and nods towards the door. 'Go on, Kat, do your best *Carry On Sick* act for Mr Rakesh. I'll be right here.'

I walk in, holding my tummy, bent over slightly, one eye on the door, the other on the counter. Shit, it isn't Mr Rakesh. It's his wife, the old bag. There is no getting anything past her.

'What do you want?' She eyes me immediately; this game has long been played. The O'Sullivan kids are known for their hunger, for their swiping hands. 'Show me your money before you come any closer into the shop.'

She won't take any shit from me today.

'I ... errrr ... fell over outside ... and I have the worst pain in my stomach. Can you help me?' My sick voice comes out all wrong – it sounds as if I'm mimicking her Indian accent.

She crosses her arms, using her large breasts as a makeshift shelf for them. Her red sari shimmers as she chuckles.

'Sick, sick? You are not sick, little girl. *I* am sick – sick of you and your brothers stealing from our shop!'

Shit. Shit. She knows.

'Honestly, I feel really sick. Can I come in and show you?' I put on my best acting face, eyes squinting with feigned pain, hand holding my tummy. I've even produced a sheen of sweat across my tanned brow.

She wavers. A frown of concern flashes across her face. I have her.

'OK, OK, come here. Sit down.' She beckons me to the chair behind the glass-topped counter she stands behind. The rows and rows of penny sweet jars look like Christmas presents under the bright lights. My mouth waters as Matt darts into the shop behind me. My eyes stay focused on her face. My heart is loud in my ears. I wonder if she can hear it too.

She hasn't seen him.

Or heard me.

'Come, come, sit ... you can have a drink. Come, come.'

I stand straight. Smiling. Heart slows to a song, 'Food, Glorious Food', mouth watering at the thought, as Matt grabs.

'Actually, I think I feel better now. Yeah. Yeah. The pain has gone.'

I back towards the door. Her eyes dart from me to the shop

door and back to the shop. The slow realisation that she has been duped by the O'Sullivan kids again washes over her. Anger replaces care.

'Get out! GET OUT OF MY SHOP!'

Her words hit the back of my head as I run as fast as my legs can carry me to Matthew. He is standing at the corner of our street under the flickering streetlight, his too-small jumper swollen in the centre where he has shoved our goodies.

'Good job, Kat. You'll make it on to the stage yet!'

I grab his hand, and we run together, laughing into the night.

Michael, my older brother, unpacks the food delivery from Social Services. 'More tinned peas. I'll keep those for later in the week ...' Taking each can out of the brown box, he checks the contents and plans when we'll use what and how long it will all last. He sorts out the tinned beans, tinned peas, tinned meat and tinned pies. A plethora of tinned food to fill our empty bellies. Michael, our surrogate parent, makes sure we have just enough to get through the dark hours of my dad's sentence.

Back then, during the chaos in our home and the hunger and cruelty of school, my brothers, Michael, James and Matthew, were my safety net. My heroes. They buffered the hurt; they were the heart of me. I did everything with Matthew. There was no difference between us. We played the same games, watched the same shows – we were nearly the same person.

While being poor-poor meant that we didn't have a lot, it couldn't steal the love we had. In some ways, it strengthened our bond. We were in the trenches together. Hunger bound us. Michael would lead the charge, taking the place of Mum and Dad, his daily mission to find food for his fledgling family. He tried to make sure we got something each day. Leaving school aged thirteen to work in a butcher's shop was one of many sacrifices he would make for us, swapping books for the blood and guts of animal carcasses. Bringing home meat and potatoes and the odd pig's eye to pop on to one of our dinner plates was his gift to our hungry souls.

My brothers and I were the same. There was no girl stuff or boy stuff; there was just 'us' stuff. Kids' stuff. We rarely had dolls in our house – I wasn't a dolly-type child –we had army soldiers, footballs, bikes and cars, loads of little cars. Social Services would drop off toys for us, and if there were ever dolls in the packages, my brothers would take great pride in burning their eyes and singeing their hair. They would sit them at the end of my bed to try to terrify me. I never cared, though. I loved my brothers. I loved their games and their toys.

I wasn't a 'girl'. I was just a kid. Back then, I had no real idea that girls were meant to do some things and boys were meant to do others. We didn't have gender role models in our house. Mum wasn't wearing an apron while Dad brought in the money. Obviously I watched TV and saw how my neighbours' homes ran, but, growing up with three brothers and not having anyone to really 'gender' me, I didn't realise I was a 'girl'.

I was just me. Katriona.

I took great pride in the fact that I could play football as well as any of the lads on our road. I wouldn't pull out of a tackle –

ever! My body was strong and capable. I wasn't the only girl who could play football on our road. Maggie Doyle was brilliant too. She would take on any player and always win. I thought she was deadly – just one of the lads.

Back then, I was proud to be a girl.

Back then, I was proud of my body and what it could do.

Back then, being a girl didn't matter.

I was a fighter too. If anyone gave me shit, I would stick up for myself. I would punch them or kick them before they got a chance to hit me. My brothers taught me never to get hit first. 'Throw the first punch' was their motto.

But one day, I hit the wrong person …

We are losing three-nil. They are playing us off the pitch. I hate losing. I charge at the ball. Maggie turns me inside out, gliding past me and shooting the ball just over the bar. She walks past me and smiles. I barge into her, shoving my little seven-year-old shoulder into her twelve-year-old chest. I am a full five years younger than her, but I don't care. Red burns behind my eyes, blinding me to any sense of fear.

She grabs my arm playfully. 'Kat, don't be like that. It's a game, kid.' Her red hair glistens in the hot afternoon sun. She is smiling down at me.

I see my fist hit the side of her face before my brain has connected with my actions. Hit first, think later – isn't that our motto?

She grabs me now, anger rising from behind and within her. She slaps me hard across the face, twice, front and back hand. I reach up, try to grip her hair, to pull her head down towards me, but she is too smart – and strong. She pushes me away, more gently than before. 'I'm warning you, Kat. Don't take the piss now.'

I take my kicking. I storm home, plotting my revenge – unsure how I will get her back, but knowing I will.

Michael stops dead when he sees my red cheeks. 'What happened to you, Kat?' His face is soft and open.

'Maggie Doyle hit me for no reason,' I cry. 'She's always hitting me.'

Before my words are out, he's through the door. By the time I follow him out, a gang of kids have formed a circle. Squeezing my way through the excited crowd, my heart drops as Maggie and Michael square up to each other.

'You hit her, Maggie. She's my little sister.'

'She punched me in the face, Michael. I'm not taking that from anyone, especially not a kid. She needs to learn.'

'Yeah, she does, but not from you. She's my fucking sister! If anyone is going to teach her, I am.'

'Well, what are you going to do about it now?'

She is offering him out for a fight. We can all see it. Maggie is so brave. Even though Michael is quiet and kind, we all know he is hard, and no one ever wants to fight him. Except for Maggie. Brave Maggie, who would take on anyone, on the pitch or on the street.

'I'm not fighting you, Maggie. Don't hit her again!'

'Or what, Michael? Or what?'

Michael gives me a glare as he storms back towards our house, pushing his way through the kids who had gathered around them, hoping for a fight. His pride was clearly hurt by the fact that a girl had offered him out and he had turned her down. But he was a good boy at heart. Like he is a good man now. And hitting a girl, a girl who wasn't his sister, was something he would never do. But Maggie rose in everyone's estimations that day.

The soundtrack of my life back then was 'She's good ... for a girl!' and I felt that and knew that. And, without question, I accepted that I was not seen as being as good as the boys. All that mattered was that *I* knew I was as good as them. And I was. I was strong and fit and capable. I didn't know that there was anything to be ashamed of. That my hips or my lips, my hair, my face or my innocence could attract men, could make them want to hurt me. I didn't know it was possible to lose control of my body: that the bleeding or the babies or the hormones could take over.

I just knew the wind in my hair while riding on the handlebars of a robbed bike.

I just knew the joy of abandon.

I just knew my feet could do as many keepie-uppies as Matthew and Michael, but not James.

I knew my strength.

Sexual abuse robbed me of this.

His

Teacher

SHE SCRUBS THE TV cupboard with a dirty tea towel, trying to erase the dirt and dust that have filled our house since he got sent to prison two years ago, when I was seven. A sheen of perspiration decorates her brow, and the morning sun splays through the window, highlighting the moustache of sweat formed across her top lip. She hasn't used today. Her angst is felt everywhere, and her twitching eyes, hands and mood reverberate around the house.

'He should be here soon,' she says, to herself more than to us kids. We sit. Side by side on the couch in the front room. Stepping stones: Michael, then James, then me, then Matt and then Emma, the baby, born just before he left; all washed, dressed and warned! A car pulls up outside; she attacks the window, her eyes wide: fear, hurt, anticipation. He hasn't been here since everything went bad.

'He's here! He's here!' she says, smiling.

I love her smile. It spreads across her whole face.

She only smiles like that for him.

She stands tall, straightens her blue denim skirt, smooths her permed hair, raises her chin and opens the door.

The sound of his footsteps hits me before his voice. Fast. Hard. Hopeful.

He is home.

My dad is home!

They have been in the bedroom for too long. I hear their voices rise and fall, rise and fall over and over again. Is she telling him what she has done? Does he know about the men? The prostitution. Will he stay now?

My heart races at the thought of him leaving again.

I will make sure he stays.

I will be the best girl he could ever have. He won't want to leave me if I am good.

And then I hear it – the squeak of the bedstead, the sound of her gasps and his grunts. I know now what that is. I didn't before. He has forgiven her.

'Come sit with me, my Katriona. Come read this with me.'

His tanned face lights up when he speaks to me. His face open. His eyes, green and bright, his pupils disappeared.

'Come practise your words with me.'

He never has to ask me twice. I'm clambering on to his lap, or snuggling up to him, eyes on the pages, heart full. I look for his lesson, longing for the connection these moments bring: to feel special, to learn, for him to tell me I am good.

'Read this to me' is our routine, my dad and me. I was about four when we started, before his first prison sentence. He picks up his book – Wilbur Smith or Stephen King, or some historical fiction – and finds a word for me to try. Each word a sign that he cares, each lesson deepening my love of words and books and him!

'What does this say?' He points to a word I have never seen before. 'Sound out the letters,' he encourages, patient and kind. He is a good teacher. He relaxes me.

'C-c ... omp ... comp ... ass ... COMPASS!'

I get it right.

'Yes, yes ... ... that's it! Compass! Do you know what a compass is, my Katriona? It's something that helps you find your way. It's something that tells you what direction to go in.'

He turns the book over – a picture of a big compass is drawn on the front.

'This is a compass, Katriona.'

Back then, before everything, before the drugs and the lies and the hurt, my dad was my everything. He was my compass. But he was also an addict. Addicted to drugs, to drink, to women, to lies. His focus in life was getting high, and his addiction eventually robbed me and him of everything.

But he wasn't always this way.

My dad was once a good boy; he was a boy who studied hard in school, read books, played tennis, swam. He grew up in a lovely middle-class home in Dublin, Ireland. A home he ran away from at age nineteen to pursue his heroin addiction. He sought solace in a bag or a needle or a bottle. Unsuccessfully. He was trying to escape from the trauma of being placed for adoption, from the loss of his first five years, where he was passed around five foster homes, a commodity for Irish 'baby farmers' – women who fostered children for financial gain. My dad was fostered and returned, fostered and returned, so many times that his centre was permanently unstable. And even though he eventually settled in leafy Clontarf with my lovely grandparents, Jim and May, my dad couldn't find steady ground.

He was fucked up. A broken man who spent most of my childhood seeking solace in drugs. Everyone can get lost to hunger ... lost to an uncontrollable hunger for drugs, abuse, food or harm. My dad was no different.

But my dad tried to do for me what wasn't done for him. In those early years, in the days when my memories are a hazy shadow that casts across my life, he tried to show me that he loved me. He taught me to read, he hugged me, he showed me that I was worth something – that I was valuable.

'You put the loop like this, and the other loop like this, and then you cross them and do this ... and there you go, they're tied!'

The summer sun beats down on us. We have been on the concrete tennis courts at the top of Hillfields for hours, my dad, James and Michael and I. They are playing tennis – my dad teaching them how to swing the racquet and how to compete. He never lets them win. He had been home for a while now, building the trust. The gear hasn't taken hold of him yet.

'Now, try again.'

I have been learning how to tie my laces – trying, for ages. He watches me, taking his time, gently urging me on, not letting me give up.

'Yes ... yes, that's it! Now loop it over ... that's it ... and PULL ... YES! YOU GOT IT! YOU GOT IT!' He swings me around.

I had tied my first lace, and he had taught me, slowly, with heart. Never letting me stop. That was my dad. That's how I want to remember him.

He spoke soft words to me, read me stories. He danced around the labour ward when I arrived. 'It's a girl! It's a girl!' he chanted. He named me, ensuring I had an Irish name, so I would fit in with his family. And, despite his madness and the addiction and his shaky start, he tried, he really tried, to love me. And I felt that.

'All you have to do is control yourself.'

My dad is talking about the pissing. He has been home six months now, clean from heroin. He is trying to be 'a proper dad'. To make up for things.

'If you say to yourself one hundred times before you go to sleep, "I must not wet my bed; I must not wet my bed", it will stop it. There is this thing called the unconscious mind – you can do it, my Katriona. You can do anything you put your mind to.'

That night, like every night, I lie in my small bed counting myself to sleep, his words whirling in my head. *I must not wet my bed; I must not wet my bed.* Willing my body to do as it is told. Wanting so badly for my body to please my dad!

One – *I must not wet my bed.*

Two – I must not wet my bed.
... Ninety-nine – I must not wet my bed.

Every day I repeat my mantra. And every day I wake up wet – and ashamed. The battle between me and my body is lost. I have no control over it. I am failing. I am nothing. I am no good. Every night I try so hard to be a good, clean girl. To please my dad, to control myself. And every day I fail. Even now that we have more 'stuff' in our house, even when I can wash myself clean in the mornings, I never feel clean.

I never feel clean.

When I think about why I made it out, why I am here and some of my siblings are not, I think of him, of him shining his light of love on me in those early days, in the days before his addiction took him and completely twisted him up.

But his love had reached me.

My dad had succeeded.

He had provided me with something he didn't have.

He gave me a steadier start than he had.

I sometimes question how I compare my mum and dad. I think that maybe I am biased, that I blame her more than him, because she was a woman, a mum, and I expected more – the world expects more of women! But the truth is, he was a better parent to me. He took me by the hand and taught me to read, to think, to consider.

He had some control over the darkness that drove him – she didn't. The truth is that when he was home, it felt safer; when he wasn't in prison, when he was providing her with drugs so she didn't need to go elsewhere for them, there was a level of security in our home that made it possible for me to breathe. To smile. To eat. Especially in the early days, when a child forms the sense of themselves as a human being, my dad was there for that. He was with me in a way he wasn't with the others, with the younger ones especially.

His first prison sentence was when I was five or six years old when he disappeared for around twelve months. The baby was born almost a year after he came home. His second sentence happened when I was around seven, until I was nine. Those two prison sentences marked his most significant absences from my life. Each sentence and a couple of later ones represented a downward spiral as he went further and further into addiction. Each sentence marked by a change in his ability to love me.

In his ability to be good.

To share with me his real self.

To be safe!

Chosen One

'WHO WANTS TO come on a drive with me?' His tone is alive, excited. 'Who wants to be their dad's pal for the day?'

We have played this scene out a thousand times. We all know who he will bring with him. But we play along, satisfying his need to feel like he is the centre, wanted.

Matthew and James both shout, 'Me! Me! I'll come, Dad!' But he turns to me, 'Do you want to come, my Katriona?'

I smile up at him. Of course I want to go with him. He is my light, my everything.

'Yes, please, Dad. Can I come?'

I start towards the door, knowing what comes next: my part, his part, their part.

'Next time, boys, I promise, next time ... '

We all know there won't be a time when he will bring them.

I am the chosen one.

I am his favourite.

I am his girl!

*

'You know she was out last night with that guy Simon again? I think she likes him. The way she looks at him ... She might leave.'

The wind blows in his hair; his tanned hand rests on the door of his green Cortina, tapping away to the sound of the Paul Simon tape playing in the car stereo. He doesn't take his eyes off the road.

'She didn't get home until late. He was with her, couldn't look me in the face. I think she likes him.'

This talk fills me with dread and joy.

I like being his special girl. The one he can speak to. But when he talks about my mum, when he says that she might leave, that she likes other men, that she isn't to be trusted – it fills me full of dread.

Questions whirl around my little head. Will she leave us? Does she love me? I watch the street signs whizz by, confused, scared to say anything that will take his affection away. Scared to question him or her or us. I push it all down. Be quiet, and he will love you. Be good, and he will continue to treat you as his special girl.

We are heading to the White Swan. I recognise the streets and the buzz in his voice. This is his pub, a place where he goes to pick up his things, where he leaves me sitting outside for what feels like hours.

'Wait here, my Katriona. Dad has to go and see a man about a dog.'

My dad, my very own Del Boy.

'Don't tell her I said that. This is our secret. You know, you're my special girl, my pretty little Katriona.'

This feels special: to be his confidante, his friend. To be the one he takes places, and he shares with.

But sometimes, when the sun shines and the mood is high, he talks to me about other things. Things that hurt my heart. Things I want to hide from.

'Wow ... look at the legs on her! Fuck, she's a bit of all right! The tits on her ...'

Smile and nod, smile and nod. Confused. Am I supposed to say something? Should I agree? I am accustomed to his type, those who will draw his eye. I watch out for them, anticipating his words, knowing what or who he'll comment on before he does.

Worried.

Sometimes, he stops the car. Gets out to chat. 'Hey, Donna, how are you, my love? Haven't seen you for a while!'

Their eyes light up at him. My handsome dad, with his tanned face, his full hair, his moustache. Even in the height of addiction, he finds a way to hold it together. To deceive. Hurt women are often unable to see past his façade.

'Hi, Tone, lovely to see you. It's been too long.' Her arms wrap around him, familiar, sexual. She smiles at him like they all do, like my mum does.

Women love my dad.

And he loves them too.

And it's their bodies he focuses on. *Nice tits ... great ass ... sexy legs.* His focus only on the sexual. And he shares this with me. Forgetting that I am a child – a girl – ignoring that I am a sponge; that how I feel about myself as a female will be influenced by his lusty looks, by his sexualisation of women, by his focus on women's bodies as their point of value to him as a man.

'Donna ... you're really rocking that skirt!' His hand pats her at the top of her thigh. Her head flies back in a familiar cackle.

Back then, in the eighties, there was a plethora of women with big hair and blue eyeliner wearing short stonewashed denim skirts. Samantha Fox and Linda Lusardi were the Page Three icons. It felt as though every woman we met was modelling themselves on them.

But childhood is strange. Things are magnified when they hurt. And my dad, by including me in his ogling of women, hurt me – a lot. It gave me the same creepy feeling I had when the bad men were in our house. The men who tried to steal moments with me or my mum. The men who paid her for her spirit, who hurt our family.

'Look at the tits on her!' made me feel the same way.

He wasn't safe.

I wasn't safe.

And my body, or women's bodies, were to blame!

It's dark outside. The dark came ages ago. I have the doors locked. The car feels cold, no heat – he didn't leave the keys. The lights in the pub are still on, so it isn't closing time yet. I see the shadows moving through the marbled windows of the White Swan. The lights from the DJ box change from red to green to yellow, the music is louder now.

A man leans against the red-brick wall, his face glinting in the shadows. A cigarette hangs from his mouth. Is he watching me? I check again that the doors are locked. I have done this six times already. Pressing on the little black buttons on the matte-black doors, I slide down in the passenger seat so he can't see me.

A woman emerges from the door of the pub. She stumbles a little. The man calls her – she moves towards him, grabs on to him. Are they kissing? I pop my head up a little higher to get a better look. Do I know her? Her hair flashes green and red and yellow. His hand is on her arse. I look away. Watching the side of the door, hoping he will come out soon. It has been too long.

Is he OK? Did he forget me? As quickly as these thoughts come, I push them away. I am his girl. He wouldn't leave me. I am his special girl. He couldn't leave me. I try replaying this in my head, pushing away the dark thoughts. It feels as though the night sky has got into me somehow.

I get out of the car and run to the pub, push open the big mahogany doors. The whoosh of booze, bodies, smoke and music hits me. The heat feels good. My hands are frozen now.

It takes my eyes a while to adjust, to make out the figures, to move through the bodies. I know where he sits.

I try to navigate my way there through the music and the dancing and the noise. I feel the smallest I have ever felt. I spot crisps and red fizzy pop on a table, and wonder if there is another kid in here. I reach out for the crisps, stuff them under my jumper. I haven't eaten all day.

Before I reach his corner, I notice his hand draped across her shoulder. Donna and my dad are entwined in the corner of the six-man booth, his arm resting over her shoulder, his finger moving back and forward over her exposed cleavage. She is smiling up at him, her hand high up on his thigh. The table hasn't been cleared for hours – empty pint glasses strewn everywhere. The overflowing ashtray disgusts me.

'Dad ... ?' My voice comes out louder than intended.

He looks at me, unsure of who or where he is. The slow realisation of who I am, where I have been and what he has done sweeps across his face.

And then he resets. Hardens. Moving his hand slowly from around Donna's neck.

'My Katriona, you know your mum's friend Donna ... we were just talking about you.' He is asking me to play along, seeing if his lies can become mine.

'Hi, Donna ...' I fake-smile. 'Dad, can we go home now?' My eyes plead with him. Scared of sitting in the car on my own again, scared of the drunken men who are emerging from the pub ... scared of letting him down.

'Yes, yes ... go back out to the car and I'll be there in five minutes, I promise you.' He lifts his pint glass to show me he still has half to go. There is not one ounce of regret in him. Or feeling.

He doesn't really care about you.

'Come sit over here with me, my Katriona.'

He's slurring his words. I prop myself up on the arm of his chair. It's uncomfortable. I don't want to let him down, though. Or miss this special time.

I love being his special girl.

'Look at this picture here. She's a beauty, isn't she?'

The newspaper is open on the table, page three looking out at us both. A pretty face and huge boobs fill the page. I don't know what to say. A creeping feeling crawls across my shoulders, arms and up into my face.

'She's beautiful to me; your mum was like that when I met her.'

I look at the picture. Pretending to be interested. His cigarette ash is about to fall off. I reach for the ashtray and put it under the fag. He doesn't notice me moving.

Why is he showing me these pictures?

'She doesn't care about any of you.'

He sits on his chair, can in hand, his eyes half-closed. It's 3am. The fake carriage clock that sits atop the gas fire reminds me it's late. I'm ten years old and it's a school night. This is the third night this week that he's called me down to sit with him while everyone else is in bed. He whispers into my room. 'Katriona, my Katriona ... want to come down and keep me company?'

And I run. I always run to him. He's my dad.

'She's left us for him.'

He's talking about my mum again. She left the family home, our new family home on Stoney Stanton Road in Coventry, three weeks ago. He hit her. He forced her to the ground and hit her in the face. He calls it a fight. I call it a fight. He said she started it. I say she started it.

The truth is, he hit her. His stronger hands grabbed her weaker body and hit it. His stronger hands grabbed her weaker face and punched it.

I can't think of him like that. I am not allowed to see the truth of him.

He won't let me.

I won't let me.

It hurts too much.

Because, without him, I am nothing.

Some love is better than no love.

To a ten-year-old girl, who walks around every day hungry for food, for nourishment, for care, this is what love is – being his confidante, sharing twisted stories about my mum, ignoring his abuse of her. The way he talks down to her; the drugs, the drink, the women – the lies ... Playing along with him so that I can feel like his special one. Feeling resentment from my brothers – they hate me for supporting him. This is what love is.

I can't do anything else. I am so hungry for someone – anyone – that I will adapt and listen and lie and hate just so I can feel something other than the dark hole that is growing bigger and bigger with each day.

Some love is better than no love!

Hers

My Mum

The pub is jam-packed, music coming from everywhere. She is laughing. My mum, Tilly, is at her best when she is like this: surrounded by friends, drinks and spliffs flowing, and the music filling her. Every ounce of her moves to the noise. Even her eyes feel the rhythm. I perch on the high stool at the bar. The ripped ruby leather cuts into my bony thighs as I watch her in her element. I love her like this.

Her eyes catch mine and shine. She loves me too.

'Kat, Kat, come over here. Come over here and sit with us.' Her hand is outstretched, promising me her warmth. 'Come over here and show these lot what you did for us last night ...'

She grabs the hand of the blonde lady in the brown corduroy dungarees sitting next to her. She is young and pretty. The blonde's other hand rests in the lap of my mum's oldest friend, Emily. 'Jane, this is my daughter, Katriona. She's seven now. Isn't she just beautiful? She can sing like a bird, and she can dance ...'

Jane is a new face, one who hasn't been through this routine. The booth in the corner of the Queen's pub is overflowing with Tilly's friends. Pints and half-pints and ashtrays and Rizlas line the table; tobacco from the spliff-rolling lace the plastic table top. Yellow flowers weave through the faded, red-velvet chairs. Tilly stands up, grabs my hand.

'This is my little girl,' she says, words slurring, her eyes smaller, less focused. 'She is the most beautiful girl you will ever see, and she can sing.'

The table turns to face me now. I hang on to the edge of the table, smiling at them, hoping I will get my chance to perform for them.

This is when I feel alive.

This is when I know.

I am special.

'Dave ... DAVE!' she shouts over my head towards the bar. 'Turn the jukebox down for us, just for a minute.'

Dave knows not to argue with this group of drinkers. I watch as he reaches high above the counter, turning down the reggae music playing in the background. She shoves me a little harder than intended into the centre of the room now. All eyes on me.

'Go on, Kat, sing the song for us. Sing the song you did for us last night ... do the dance too. Wait until you see my Katriona perform for you – she's so good!'

Her pride spurs me on. When she shines her light on me, it is impossible to resist.

I kneel in my start position. Now is my chance to show them

how good I am. I lift one hand above my head, then another. Slowly, I imagine the music starting, the four counts of eight before I sing. I look up, catch her eyes, their brightness blinds me, pure love shining out.

She loves this.

She loves me when I do this.

My voice comes out strong. In tune. I hear myself over the noise of the pub. Watching them watch me. I know I can sing. I hear it sometimes in the tone and texture of my voice. I feel it in her response to it. I have been practising this song for weeks. *Flashdance*, the movie, came out last year and, since then, I have learned the song and dance. I know every move, my body capable. Like her, I feel each sound, each move. I raise my hands above my head. I do the body rock, singing. They all watch, drunkenly mesmerised by this seven-year-old girl giving it socks in the middle of their afternoon drinking session.

She watches every move, every second of my dance, not changing her focus, proud of me, proud of her. She made me. She loves me. She loves the dancer in me, the performer in me. She loves what she is not.

'Come on, Kat, dance with me.'

She sways to the sound of Bob Marley and the Wailers' 'Three Little Birds'.

'Come on, Kat, show me your moves.'

I don't need to be asked twice. We hold hands. The song fills me, in all places, moving my body and my heart.

We sing as one, words about not worrying, words that say everything will be all right.

'Michael, come on ... get up here too.'

She pulls Michael up. He laughs and does his best reggae dance, pulling at an imaginary string between his legs as he raises his left leg, then his right leg to the music.

We are all singing it now. Music brings us together. It always has. She turns me around under her arm. The old jive moves don't suit this song, but she doesn't care. She is happy. She is the best when she is like this. Dancing, smiling, singing, half-stoned on dope and drink, she can get us all on side.

Don't worry ... about a thing ...

We try singing with the same accent as Bob Marley. It sounds weird, out of key, but no one cares.

I was born into this freedom. Music and life filled my home. Even when I was hungry, even without food, the music filled me. Her enigmatic ability to wake me to the beauty of life filled every hole. We were all loud and bright, and we could all sing and dance. And even though the songs would often turn to shouting and the dancing would often turn to fights, we were alive through all of it. There was freedom in it all.

My earliest memories of my body are attached to this. My memories are full of dancing in our living room; of watching my mum and dad sway back and forth to Dr Hook songs, reaching out to me to join them when 'Sylvia's Mother' came on the record player.

I see her naked, wandering down the hall laughing, her soft belly, decorated with purple and white slashes from carrying five children, softly slapping against her hipbone. A cigarette hangs from her lips. She smells of sweets and fags and hurt. I watch her from the shadows of the hallway.

She stops in front of her bedroom mirror. She pulls at her loose tummy, turning sideways, then frontways, then sideways again. She pulls her boobs up so they face the sky, then drops them. She shimmies a little and laughs and slopes back into bed.

Sometimes, though, she cries. I watch her pulling at the pockets of fat that come from having had five babies, screaming about her big, sagging boobs, her wonky nose, that she thinks she isn't pretty enough for my dad.

I watch how she loves and hates her body all in the same moment.

I climb into her bed some mornings, dodging the metal springs that stick out of their frayed mattress. I love when she stays in the foetal position, letting me tuck in behind her as I snatch the heat from her skin and bones. But, sometimes, she hides herself from me. Hands across her chest and private parts. Even though I come from her, from within her, even though she made me, she tries to hide herself from me.

She teaches me the balance of womanhood – that we are meant to love and hate ourselves.

But she knows she is sexy and appealing to men. Tilly is small in height, with skinny little legs and massive boobs. Top-heavy. Insecure and confident in equal measure. She swings her hips to the music, shakes her shoulders to the beat, sways sexily to the soundtrack of the Eagles, Fleetwood Mac and Dr Hook. Mesmerising my dad with her rhythm. She can move. She laughs with abandon. Her head flips back and she cackles.

Hours are spent watching her in the mirror 'prepare' herself for them: the blue eyeliner, the short denim skirts, the see-through lace tops, the cleavage, the laughter, the dancing – all meant to catch and keep a man's eye. She teaches me about the male gaze, to desire it, how to get it – and how it hurts you. Her relationships with her body and men are the blueprint for me.

Her relationship with her body is clear to most. She knows her body is good, while she believes her body is bad.

I want you to know that my mum wasn't all bad. She was the person who taught me how to love. How to be free. How to dance, and cry and say, 'Fuck you!' I want you to know there was an exhilarating sense of freedom that followed her, alongside a terrifying madness.

She was a wonderful mix of hurt and heart, torment and tenderness. She loved and loathed herself and her body in equal measure.

And she shared all of this with me.

She always wears turquoise jewellery; her earrings too heavy for her small ears, dragging the pierced holes down so far that they look like straight lines. I worry they will completely split; that she will be left with only the line.

'Do they hurt you?'

'No, not any more. I'm used to them now. Do you want to get your ears pierced?'

'Dad said I'm not allowed.'

'Pfft – fuck your dad! Will we go and get them done?'

'YEAH!'

She takes me by the hand, and we head towards Coventry town centre.

'Eileen Boyle, my old friend, pierced my ears for me when we were kids. Back then, you had to do it yourself. She got a needle and heated it, put some ice on my ear and put the needle through to make the hole. Boy, did it hurt!'

'Will this hurt me?'

'I don't think it's like that now. They use a gun thing now. Don't worry! And don't tell your dad. He'll kill me.'

My happiest memories of her come from these moments and those early mornings, snuggling in next to her with her wispy hair all over the place, her milky white boobs and her big earrings shining in the morning sun. She is herself in these moments. She doesn't really have a body. She is just her. I watch her relationship with her body deteriorate.

I watch her lose her rhythm.

I watch her forget that she is beautiful.

Her sweet mixture of love and hate erodes over time.

It becomes a shadow of our past.

I remember when she loses it completely.

It's when she sells it for sex.

He sits at the glass table in the back room all day, every day. His face fixed, frozen, unreadable. He is her little guard. The men, they travel up and down the back stairs, following her tiny, blistered legs up to her damp bedroom. Paying for her shame, and any future she had hoped for. Using her body for pleasure. Ignoring the cry for help that her needle-pinned arms shout at them.

'Stay out all day ... DO NOT COME BACK,' he warns us all. His heart hardened by his new role. Her confidant while our dad is away. They whisper at night, calculating the number of men she will need to fuck to earn enough to feed her habit, my dad's habit in prison and to afford to buy chips for the kids.

'Stay out all day ... DO NOT COME BACK.'

She never came back to us after that.

'You think you're so pretty, don't you? With your perfect hair and your perfect face and your perfect waist!'

She slurs her words at me. Staring through me, her eyes dark and wide.

She hates me now.

'You think you can have it all, don't you? You'll see! You'll see!'

Her anger grows by the day, all of it directed at me and my body – and I don't know what I've done. It's a Sunday afternoon and we are all sitting in the living room of our new house in Blakenhale Road in Birmingham. We moved here from Coventry for a 'fresh start' after my dad got out after a short stint on remand for credit-card fraud.

A new start for us all.

I am eleven years old. Blossoming into womanhood. My body growing upwards and outwards, uncontrollable curves catching the eyes of strange men. Triggering the vitriol my mum is spitting at me. She is different here, in this new house. The heroin is gone, replaced by drink. There is less history here, the creaks and cracks of the house are unfamiliar. The street is calmer, more rich-poor than poor-poor. My parents haven't found a network yet. No one to party with. No pubs or places to hide.

'You think you're so perfect, don't you? So fucking perfect.'

I don't understand the shift; the move from me being the girl she loved to the girl she hates. Why does she focus on my face, my hair, my hips? *How is this my fault? How can I change any of it?* I want to cry out so badly. Tell her I hate myself too. Show her the voice that lives in my head – the voice that never stops critiquing. That wakes up before I do; that screams about the size of my hips, the smell of me, the way I move. It says I will never be loved or liked, never succeed. She sees perfection in a place filled with hurt and self-hate.

I can't tell her, though. She isn't reachable any more. She left a while ago and has never come back.

I sit next to my dad on our new three-seater sofa. It's green velvet;

it was bought for us by the community service. Michael is on my left and James is on the other side of my dad. We are squashed but happily squashed.

Matthew and the baby – who is now four – sit on the two-seater, while Tilly perches at the edge of the armchair closest to the TV. Her can of Breaker wobbles in her hand every time she turns to glare at me, dangerously close to spilling it on to the newly fitted grey carpet. Dad's can of Special Brew sits securely between his knees. He won't risk spilling one drop. She doesn't care about what she loses now, me or her precious drink. When she gets onto her fourth can, nothing matters any more. The real Tilly comes out.

'Come on, England ... come on, England!' my brothers are chanting, trying their best to distract her, and rile me up. It is the 1988 Euro finals. The match between Ireland and England has been the centre of our chats for weeks now. The tensions are high. Dad and I are shouting for Ireland while the St George's Cross marks everyone else in the room as England fans through and through.

'You think you're so pretty, don't you? With your thick hair and your lovely face ... I never had any of that when I was younger. You just take it all for granted.'

She is spitting out so much hate now that it doesn't even make sense. No one is doing anything to help me. Why isn't anyone saying anything?

'Dad, will you tell her to leave me alone, please?'

My dad gives her a look.

'Oh yeah, Daddy's little girl now. You think he will protect you ... he couldn't protect a fly. He's just another waste of time.'

'Tilly, I'm warning you ... leave it alone.'

'What are you going to do about it, Tony? You and your precious daughter. You and her are welcome to each other. She won't stay pretty. She won't stay slim. She won't always love you ...'

'TILLY, I AM WARNING YOU!' He starts to stand.

'Yeah, Mum, come on, now. Let's watch the match.' Matthew interrupts. He knows where this ends up. We all do: his hands around her throat or her hands on his face. Alcohol has brought a new level of violence to the house, one that has shaken all of us. Matthew often comes to the rescue.

She looks at Matthew, refocusing. The venom recedes. She smiles her watery smile. She loves Matthew. He never questions her, is always there for her – for her hugs, he never criticises. He is her favourite.

'I'm sorry, my darling. Did I disturb the match?' She slips back into the armchair, swivelling to face the TV. The anger gone as quickly as it came.

'Come on, England ... COME ON, ENGLAND!'

I don't know when she started to hate me. I can't remember the exact date or time. I just remember a general shift, a change in her.

I think it may have been when the gear was gone or when the men had taken everything from her or when the drink took over. Gear was better. It made her silent. It took her inwards. She would hide when she was stoned. Silently wasting away. Waking up only as it was wearing off, and then the chase for more would begin.

But alcohol sent her the other way. It was like venom in her, a poison that needed to escape. And me, my body, my beauty, my freedom were her target. They triggered her. Maybe they reminded her of the innocence that she no longer had – or maybe she just knew what was coming for me.

Or perhaps, in her maddened mind, she saw me as her competition. Her world had been so fractured from hurt and harm, that she did not – could not – mother me as I deserved. She could not see me as her child. Instead, she saw me as a threat to her relationship; she saw me as someone who stole her man's gaze, someone my dad loved and wanted to be with. My beauty, my girlhood, my body were no longer an extension of her, a trophy for her to hold up for her friends. I was now someone to compete with, someone to battle with for the attention of my dad.

She treated me as a woman, even though I was a girl.

Them

You Are Bad!

'MATTHEW, GO TO the shop for us and get an ice cream for us three.'

Matthew's eyes are bigger than his belly. He is up out of his seat before he – our 'uncle' Bob – can get the fifty-pence piece out of his jacket pocket.

'I'll go with you, Matthew.'

I don't want to be sitting on this chair with Bob. He smells of drink, sweat-beads rolling down his forehead, his fat belly flopping over the top of his trousers. I am seven years old. I don't know where my mum is that day, but my dad is in prison. I feel uneasy, as if something bad is going to happen.

'Don't be silly, Katriona. You stay here with your uncle Bob. Be a good girl. Matthew will get us a lovely ice cream.'

I look at Matthew, sending him a silent signal to take me with him, to insist I go too. He doesn't notice. His mouth is already salivating at the thought of the ice cream.

As the front door closes, Bob pats the sofa beside him. 'Come, sit by me for a minute.'

I sit by him, doing as I am told. Being a good girl.

'Let me look at you there.'

His words slur. His head reminds me of the troll that hides under the bridge, waiting to pounce on the 'Billy Goats Gruff'. I jump slightly as he stands up, takes off his belt and pulls down his trousers. I feel as though I'm in a dream. What is he doing? Why is he doing this?

He turns to face me. My heart and my stomach know something bad is coming – they know it way before my mind does. I don't understand sex or bodies or men. I am innocent.

I was innocent.

Lying underneath him, I am convinced I am going to die. I cannot breathe. All of me hurts, inside and out. My head hurts the most, fracturing, separating from itself to cope with the adult act that is being inflicted on my body. I watch the hazy sun splay through the slight gap in the dirty curtains. The dust in the skylight seems to be moving more slowly than it ever has before. I listen for my Matthew. *Please don't let him come now ... please protect him from this ... please don't let him see this ... please don't let Bob do this to him.*

As darkness engulfs me, lying under the weight of this disgusting man, I hope that I will never wake up.

I have never woken up.

Pulling back the sheets of our piss-filled bed, Matthew doesn't stir. His breath is deep and sure, safe in sleep.

The joyful late-night journeys to the kitchen cupboard with Matthew holding my hand have been replaced by a sinister drive to feel nothing. Matthew is robbed from me, his love sitting sadly outside of the glass case I hide in.

I dodge the creaks on the stairs, hoping no one is lodging on our sofa tonight. Fear is constant now. The back room is dark, the silence empty – no drunken sleepers tonight. I flit towards the kitchen, mount the countertop and open the cupboard. Barren and bare, like me. Bread and beans, an old tin of corned beef, mouldy green crumbs stare back at me. I heap three spoonfuls of sugar on to the bread. Sweet crystals spill across the grey-and-white-flecked sideboard. They glisten in the dawn light. I lick the tip of my finger and sweep up my spill, tasting sweet and dust. I feel nothing. Sugar stolen, with my sweetness.

Wrapping the sandwich in an old bread bag, I start towards the door.

Then I hear her crashing in through the front door. Frozen to the spot, holding my breath, I wait. She stumbles through the front room, angry mumbles coming from her. She must have been on the drink tonight: heroin the silencer, drink the aggressor. I listen as she snakes her way up the stairs. Dodging the creak on step thirteen, she drops hard on to her bed. The squeak of her old bedframe tells me she is gone for the day. She didn't even notice me. No one notices me.

I sneak up the stairs, finding my way to the top in complete silence. When I open the door of the airing cupboard, the smell of wood and heat slaps me in the face. I burrow my way into the tight space at the bottom, fitting my tiny bones underneath the red-jacketed boiler. I lie silent. Still. My heart slows. I pull the door to –

only a slice of light seeps through. My breathing slows. The warmth of the boiler and the security of my hiding spot draw sleep closer.

Reaching behind the boiler, I take out the bread bag I left three nights ago and replace it with the new one I just prepared. I open the older one and the smell of warm bread and sugar fills me. No time to think: I shove one sugared slice into my mouth, my breath taken by the hunger, by the drive to forget. Without stopping, I swallow, pushing the second slice into me as quickly as the first.

This ritual started after Bob. The little girl who existed in the 'after' sought solace in hurt. Food, gorging, being filled, feeling empty became her life. My life.

Hiding.

Hoarding.

Controlling.

Knowing that I have food, that I can feed myself, that I can escape my thoughts, the feeling of my body, is my survival mechanism. When the food is gone, shame emerges. Dark shame. The worst sort. The rocking between hurt and harm and hopelessness. Destabilising. I have no centre, no stable ground to grow from. There is a crack in my foundation, driving erratic and irrational behaviours. Storing and hoarding food. Shoving it in. Shaming. And then there is the voice, the critical voice, the voice he placed in me.

You did this.

You made this happen.

You did something wrong.

It's your eyes – they're too bright.

It's your hips – they're too rhythmic.
It's your face – it's too pretty.
It's you – you're wrong.
You're bad. You're no good – and everybody knows this!

The food, the privacy of this space, the sugar, the gorging – they silence it for a short minute, then it gets louder. And louder. AND LOUDER!

As I sleep, still aged seven, in my tiny bedroom, a tingle of pleasure wakes me. My eyes closed tight, sleep still in them, I can't figure out what is happening.

Then I can.

My body responds to his fingers touching me between my legs. My body awakens before me. I smell vodka and I feel sick; I hear his heavy breath – it fills my room. I freeze and open my eyes fully. This has happened before.

Don, my dad's friend and our lodger, is kneeling beside my bed. His bald head is tilted to one side, his eyes focused on mine. I stare directly at him, afraid to move or breathe.

'Sorry,' he whispers. His Scottish accent, the one that I loved a few hours ago, seems sinister now.

'I'm sorry,' he says again while he continues to push his fingers further into me.

I hear a voice come from far away. 'FUCK OFF!' it says.

I can't hear my own voice over the loud beating of my heart. Did I just say that? I think I did, but I can't be sure. I don't recognise my own voice; I'm afraid that I will get into trouble for using a bad word. I must have said it though because his face changes. A tear rolls down his cheek as he yanks his hand from underneath my blanket and tumbles backwards. He backs up towards the bedroom door.

'I am so sorry, so, so sorry,' he says as he stumbles back down the stairs to the couch he has been sleeping on, on and off, for the past few months.

He leaves behind shame and a hatred of the smell of vodka.

'Morning, Katriona.'

Don is still here. I hear his Scottish accent in my nerve-endings.

'I'm making some toast and tea for your mum. She's in bed – do you want some too?'

'No ... thank you.'

Stay away from me!

Matthew is sitting on the floor; the bin of cars is spilled around him. He smiles as he makes his imaginary ramps and roads. I look at his face closely. Is this happening to him too? Did Don get to him before me?

Maybe this only happens to girls. *To pretty little girls.*

'Come, sit down here with us and we'll eat this together before we try to get Tilly out of bed.'

His breath and the stale smell of vodka from the sofa fill me with dread.

'I have something for you both.'

Matthew jumps up, excitedly. Don takes out two twenty-pence pieces from his stained jacket pocket.

'I've been saving this for you guys for a special treat, and you were so good last night, I decided today is the day.'

Matthew snatches the money out of his hand. 'Come on, Kat! Let's go the shop!'

He is smiling. I take the money. I put it in my pocket and walk out the door after Matthew. He is paying me for my silence. That's how it feels, anyway. He has paid twenty pence for me to carry the shame of having a body that responded with pleasure to his abuse. To carry the confusion about how good it felt to be touched in my private place.

I know now that the brain, the pleasure centre, does not know what age you are. It has no concept of consent either. A woman's body, her vagina, the clitoris, are ready for pleasure from the start. Touch it, at any stage, and the pleasure centre fires. Dopamine surges and the rest of the brain acknowledges the joy of touch. As a child, my body reacted in the way it was programmed. My young mind, however, was not prepared for the confusion of feeling intense fear and pleasure.

You must have wanted this to happen!

There was no space in my small brain to integrate this experience. It didn't match what I knew. Being scared and feeling pleasure did not go together.

You must have wanted this!

The music is blaring 'Take it Easy' by the Eagles, the lyrics bursting with women. The front room is full of smoke. Clouds of marijuana fill every crevice. It's hard to see who is here.

Tilly sways in the middle of the room. The ashtray, made from a block of salt that my dad stole from a farmer's field, is filled to the brim. Tilly's hair and hips float from side to side to the beat, her eyes closed, hair over her face, spliff hanging from her lips – freedom. It's dark outside. The curtains are open. Moonlight splays through the smoke-screen, casting weird shapes and shadows across her face and hands.

Enya and Chrissy, the prostitutes she hangs out with now, slouch across the brown, bloodstained armchair. White Coke and Black Coke, her dealer friends, and Eli, our so-called 'Rastafarian uncle', are strewn around the room. Laughing, smoking, singing, dancing and fighting, they switch positions like scenes being played out in a graphic novel.

She stays in the centre, abandoned, filled with the music. Matthew and I squeeze up tight in the corner of the sofa. Hoping for a bag of chips with the generosity of a few coins that often come when the Special Brew and the spliffs are overflowing. The front door is on the latch, open to all who have cans or a bag.

'Anyone home?' His Scottish accent sends my nerve-ends alight.

'Don … Don … come in, come in.' White Coke assumes the role of man of the house. Tilly raises her spliff in the air to him as a way of welcome. His eyes flit between her, Chrissy, Enya and me. He pulls a can out of a blue plastic bag, its handles strained. It's filled with cheap, strong lager. He sups, smiles and pulls a friend in behind him.

'Is it OK if Paddy comes in for a quick one? We just finished last orders in the Queen's. Got a carryout – figured Tilly might have afters happening.'

She ignores him. His friend plops himself down next to us on the sofa. Matthew's head rests on my shoulder, his eyes falling back into his head, sleep beckoning.

'Matt ... *Matt*!' I nudge him awake. 'Don't leave me here on my own!'

He ignores my plea, tiredness too tempting to resist.

'MATT!' I pinch the soft skin of his tummy hanging from under his nylon school jumper. His eyes jump open. The shock of my pinch sends him up on to his feet. He pushes me. I fall on to Don's lap and freeze, catching the smell of old drink and piss and the pub off his clothes. I retch.

'You OK, hen?' He grabs my arm, really gently. 'Let me help you.'

He stands me up, and I yank my arm away. Matthew slinks out of the room, sleep calling him. I follow, not wanting to look at Don or Tilly, hoping that no one is coming up behind me. I gallop up the stairs behind Matthew, up the steps, two by two.

'Matt, MATT! Please stop!'

He stands still at the top of the stairs and glares at me. 'Why did you pinch me?' He rubs the red marks on his tummy, my fingers imprinted on his little bulbous belly. 'You hurt me, Kat.' His face is a ball of innocence and pain.

'I'm sorry, kid. I'm sorry. I didn't want to be on my own down there. They were getting a bit rowdy,' I lie. 'When Don came in, I thought for sure we would get a few quid. Didn't want you to miss it.'

My explanation is incoherent. Matthew is confused. I want to tell him the truth. I want to tell him that I was scared, that Don is a bad man, that his voice sends me over the edge. I want to tell Matt – my Matt – that all the men are bad, that I can't stand to be alone, that I need him to stay with me.

'I'm going to bed, Kat. See you tomorrow.' He trudges off down the landing towards the boys' bedroom. Three beds fill the boys' room. Matt and James and Michael are forced to share a room because my dad insisted that a girl cannot sleep in the same room as boys. The irony of this decision. Separating me from my brothers to protect my vulnerability made me more vulnerable. It wasn't my brothers that I needed protecting from!

'Please, Matt, come into mine tonight. We can play cowboys ... or kings.' He walks on.

'MATT!' My voice comes from my belly now. The deepest, darkest base of my soul cries out for him. *Please don't leave me alone.*

He hears it. Even if he doesn't understand it, he hears my cry for him.

'Get into bed, and I'll come in in an hour. Let me get a sleep first. I promise I will come back in to you.' He opens the door to the boys' room and closes it behind him.

Panic rises. A night of watching the door awaits me. Waiting for someone or something bad to enter. Holding my breath so I can hear everything. Counting myself to sleep, gripping tightly onto my piss-stained blankets. Focusing on the familiar sounds of our house, hoping no one remembers I am in my bed alone.

My heart slows. I hear its beat in my ears. The familiar sense that I am shrinking overtakes me. With every beat, I get smaller and smaller. Everything else gets bigger and bigger. Each beat louder and louder.

I have had this before.

After Bob.

The shame shrinking: I'm afraid I will completely disappear.

I reach out to the walls to ground myself. *I am here. I am important. I am someone.* I tap my fingers – the only way to come back to myself. 'One, two, three, four … one, two, three, four …'

The handle of the airing cupboard door glints at me from across the hall – a place to go! I don't need Matt to guard me.

The familiar heat and wood smell fills me as I squeeze into my safe space. Pulling the door to, I hear 'Sylvia's Mother' begin to play downstairs. I see Tilly in my mind's eye in the centre of the room, swaying to the keyboard introduction, telling all and anyone who will listen, 'That's my name, you know – my name is Sylvia, not Tilly. My dad christened me Tilly – but I'm actually Sylvia!'

I like this game, the imagination game. In this story, I am her audience and, when the song plays, she grabs my hand and insists that I get up to dance with her. She wraps her arms around me, tells me she loves me, and that I am safe. As the song echoes up the stairs and reverberates around the landing, volume on full blast now, I fall asleep, dreaming of a time when we can all dance again, a time when I can feel safe again.

This scene was played out over and over again. When the music got loud and the drink was flowing, when the living room was filled with strange men, I'd squeeze my little body beside the red-wrapped water tank. Finding comfort in the smell of old wood and heat, the cupboard became a secret place to feel safe, or a place to shove sugar sandwiches down my throat and enjoy the escape that food provided.

I would feel nothing in those moments. Protected from the darkness that drank beer downstairs and the looming shadow within. When sleep eventually found me, I would dream of a time when my dad would come home, when he would chase away the strangers and make it safe for me to breathe again.

'Who wants to play war?'

Michael is leading the crew today.

'I'll lead a team and, James, you lead the other.'

Although Michael and James are close, there is always an underlying competition between them. Michael is physically stronger, but James is smarter by far! Michael loves to remind James that he is the strongest and the eldest. Beating him at war is one of the ways he does this.

'I'll play!' says James.

'I'll play!' everyone shouted.

Michael has this magical way of gathering us all together for group games. And, even though I am good and strong, I am always picked last. I'm only small, and no one wants an eight-year-old on their team. James' friend Joe and I will be picked last. I don't care, though. I know the game will be fun. Running around with imaginary machine guns, trying to track the other team, is one of my favourites.

Michael's team ends up with both me and Joe on it. Joe is thirteen, the same age as Michael. He's from an Irish family too – the O'Connors, who live at the top of our road.

'Right, we should all go hide down by the hexagon, in the bushes.'

I love it when Michael is in military mode like a real-life army sergeant. We will do anything for him.

'Kat, you come hide with me in the bushes over here.' Joe is pulling me over towards the small bushes at the furthest end of the school.

'OK, Joe!'

Joe is Michael's friend; he is really protective of him. It's well known in the area that no one picks on Joe or Michael will get involved.

'I love your dress, Katriona. What do you have on underneath it?'

'My pants, of course.' I feel the creeping feeling but ignore it. It's Joe!

'Show me – I don't believe you.'

Show him. He's Michael's friend. You don't want to let him down.

The creeping feeling.

I show him my knickers.

'Look what I have on under my trousers.'

He pulls down his grey bottoms and his pants. His thing is right there in front of me. Having three brothers and living in a madhouse, I have seen a boy's willy before. I bathe with Matthew still.

But this is different. He is not my brother.

I am not safe.

'Want to show me what's under your pants?'

I slowly pull down my pants and show him.

I don't want to. But I don't want to say no.

'You can touch me if you want to, then I could touch you …'

I stay still. As he touches me, I look out for anyone coming from the other team. Will James catch us? Will they see us?

He takes my hand and puts it on him.

I like this feeling.

I hate this feeling.

When he is finished, he says, 'Come on, let's go and find the others. It's been ages – they've probably been caught.'

We come out of the bush and run straight into James and Paul.

'*It!* You're dead!' James screams as he points his imaginary gun at me. He is delighted with himself. 'We got you!'

James is laughing. I smile at him and Paul. Glad we have been caught. Wondering if I look different.

The next day, we are all out again. The sun is high in the air, and we're all waiting for someone to make a plan for us.

'Let's play tracking,' James says.

'Yeah, great idea.'

Michael is in, so everyone is in. I am on James' team this day with Joe and Matthew.

'Can I hide with you again?' I say to Joe. 'We could go into the bushes again.'

By the age of eight, I had experienced sexual abuse at the hands of three different men and boys. The first, the worst, involved being raped by my mum and dad's friend, 'Uncle' Bob.

The first took everything from me.

He cracked me.

There was my body before him and my body after him.

In the 'before', my body was safe. It belonged to me. It did cartwheels, knickers flashing as it went head over heels. It laughed fully. In the 'before', my body was trusted. It was connected to my brothers. It was the same as theirs.

In the 'after', my body was a place of terror. It shook uncontrollably. It felt dirty. It was responsible. It was the thing that made the bad things happen. In the 'after', there was a ball of fire in its pit that made it hard to breathe, to eat food, to go to the toilet, to smile.

And there was a loud voice. A new voice.

A voice that had never been there before.

A voice that said bad things about me and my body.

You did something.

You liked it.

You made this happen.

You are bad.
You are bad.
You are bad!

Two little boys had two little toys; each had a wooden horse ...
He is singing. The sound comes from the back of the house. His sweet voice echoes around the bathroom; the acoustics of the bath, the lino and the tiles add to the alto tone of his voice.

My dad used to sing in a choir as a boy. I have a picture of him dressed as an altar boy, with a big group of altar boys, singing hymns in St Gabriel's Church in Clontarf, Dublin. His favourite hymn was 'Amazing Grace'.

Like the Pied Piper, I follow the song, enchanted by its tone; I love the 'Two Little Boys' song, the way they find each other throughout their lives. It reminds me of Matthew.

Dad has taken to singing this to me in the evening when he tucks me in, stroking my hair, telling me stories of how he has changed, how prison was good for him. Through the crack in the bathroom door, I spy his tanned hand hanging over the side of the bath. Is he bathing the baby? I glimpse my little sister's bare backside through the door and, before I can catch my breath or my thoughts, I hear my voice coming from outside of my body, loud and strong.

'GET AWAY FROM HER! GET AWAY FROM HER!'

The baby and my dad turn in fright.

'GET AWAY FROM HER! YOU SHOULDN'T BE IN HERE ... GET AWAY FROM HER!'

He turns towards me now, understanding what is wrong,

understanding my response. He holds his hand out to me. 'It's OK. It's OK. It's me ... It's your dad. I'm not hurting her.'

I can't see. I can't hear. I cannot feel. I shake. Uncontrollably.

'You shouldn't be in here. You shouldn't be in here.'

He wraps a soft white towel around her, one of the new purchases that have turned up in the house since he has 'got out'. He pulls her close to his chest. She is crying now. She is only two years old. She has no idea why I'm shouting, has no real idea who he is. He was gone just after she was born.

'It's OK, my Katriona. It's your dad. I'm your dad. She's fine. Look at her. Come sit over here with us while I dry her off.'

He perches on the edge of the bath, wrapping her up tight. He dries her through the towel, patting her head, her arms, her feet.

I don't trust him.

I can't trust him.

I don't trust any man.

Any connection I had to him, to them, to the boys, to myself is questioned. Frayed. Detached. He isn't to be trusted. None of them is. I look at her face. My beautiful baby sister, her chubby legs and arms freed now from the swaddling. I search her face for a sign of hands on her. In her. Did he touch her? *Will* he touch her? All these things I think while edging towards them, wanting so badly to reach back to the girl I was before he went away, the girl I was before they took my trust and hope and faith. But she is gone, replaced by the doubter, the hoarder, the gorger, the frightened one. Substituted for a girl who cannot control her heart rate, her fear, her mind, her hunger or her bodily functions.

Theirs

You Made This Happen

'Has anyone ever told you you look like Kelly LeBrock? Do you know who she is?'

His words slur, a faint smell of vodka on his breath. A shadow of my lost childhood rises behind him.

'She has blowjobs lips too.'

The words drool out of the side of his mouth. His gaze fixed on the third button of my blouse, he watches my burgeoning bra press against the cream silk, the gap between the third and the fourth button an invitation.

'Barry, stop! She's just a kid, for fuck's sake!' A good man sees this. The prying eyes of a forty-year-old man, preying on my twelve-year-old body. I pull self-consciously at the gap in my blouse.

'If she's old enough to bleed ... and she's definitely old enough.' He slaps the good man's shoulder. They laugh. Conspiratorially.

We are in the garden of my friend's house for his little brother's christening. His mum and stepdad said he could bring some friends. We're in the first year of secondary school together –

Mark, Leigh, Carl and I, all on the cusp of puberty. We are running around the party, sipping on the adults' drinks, playing football in the garden, eating sausages and cake, laughing.

This man – their neighbour from across the way – is here with his wife and their kids. He is drunk. The more he drinks, the more he says. His eyes burn through my blouse. Hot. Dogged. Hoping to grab a glance at my chest. The hot tip of my nipple his target, no care for maturity or legality, his arrow focused on the jackpot. The creeping feeling follows me for the day.

You made this happen.

'Come on, Kat, let's dance.' Leigh is half-cut now. Her multicoloured leggings and matching hairband sway to the music: 'Love Shack', 'Ride on Time', 'Push It!' She drags me on to the makeshift dance floor in their back garden. I love to dance – every step of every routine, memorised by Leigh and me. As I sway to Marvin Gaye, I feel someone swaying behind me. The creeping feeling rises. Barry stands behind me, rubbing himself against me. Smiling. His face as red as his hair, eyes glazed, full of intent. 'Hey, Kelly,' he laughs. 'Me and you, *Weird Science*.' He doesn't make any sense. Leigh grabs my hands and pulls me away.

Looking in the full-length mirror in Leigh's mum's bedroom, I scan my body for failings. Pulling at my stomach, my legs, pinching the skin that sits taut around my waistline – the internal monologue playing loudly on repeat.

There is something wrong with you.

There is something wrong with you – that's why he doesn't want you.

Leigh's house is full of food and fun. I stay here most nights, five hundred metres from my own house; eating, laughing and crying. Leigh is a chubby kid – beautiful and chubby. Our chats revolve around our bodies and boys. She cries about the lack of boys she has. She blames her body, while I criticise every ounce of my body despite having plenty of boy interest. Our bodies are central to our friendship. They still are.

'Let's play cafés.'

I am out of the chair before she can finish the sentence. I love Leigh's house. Her mum does a weekly shop. They even have a treat cupboard full of snacks! 'Cafés' is our favourite game. We cook everything in the cupboards and serve the meal up on the table, as if we are in a café – and then we eat as much as we can. Chips, eggs, bacon, sausages, pickled onions, mushy peas, beans, Daddies Brown Sauce, red sauce, fizzy pop. We cook and eat, and we laugh, and we cry over boys and our bodies.

Leigh's house is where I eat, and where I get my clothes. She lends me her stuff and her mum's stuff, so the shame of having little is lesssened. And she never judges me. She's just glad she has a friend, and so am I. Peas in a pod. Both insecure, both fun, both hating our bodies. In the era of waifish Kate Moss and lean and leggy Naomi Campbell, we are both failing. The 'heroin chic' standard being inflicted on girls in the early nineties is hurting everyone, especially those of us who aren't 'skinny-skinny'. Everywhere I look, there is a girl with anorexia and bulimia, trying her best to match the impossible standard set by the genetics of a few famous supermodels.

Leigh and I don't have the dedication it takes to starve ourselves; instead, we criticise ourselves, feeling disgusting in our bodies. When it comes to being with boys, we take drugs or drink alcohol to reduce the body noise that accompanies being kissed or touched by someone.

'Look at the tits on her!'

My stomach turns.

'Hey, hey! Get your tits out for the lads!'

The men on the scaffolding all laugh; a wolf whistle comes from another.

I catch the eye of an older guy. He isn't leering. He looks embarrassed. I make a silent plea for him to help me. For him to protect me from the wolves he works with.

He looks away.

Pulling my school bag closer to my shoulder, I feel my whole body. The disgust rises from my toes, slowly filling every crevice.

You made it happen.

You are bad.

I hunch over, trying to hide my burgeoning chest, walking as fast as I can to escape the building site. My grey school skirt and my white school shirt feel tight around my growing body. The shirt belongs to James (who has no boobs). The outline of my 32D bra is clear for all to see – my well-developed tits a trophy for the male eye.

I am thirteen years old.

And I feel ashamed.

Jace

'Let me have a little feel, Kat, please. I won't tell anyone.'

'No!'

I am laughing at how desperate he is to touch me.

'Just let me have a look, then. Please.'

I undo one of my shirt buttons. He is mesmerised. I love the way he looks at me. I slowly undo the second button. His mouth opens slightly, his tongue waiting for its opportunity to pounce.

'I'm not letting you touch me. Not yet, anyway.'

I laugh now. He doesn't even hear me, his eyes transfixed by my hands moving over the third button.

Don't do this, Katriona. He won't respect you if you let him have you too soon.

I undo the third button of my shirt, and he can see my bra now; it's off-white – my mum washed it with my brothers' trousers. For a moment, I feel ashamed – then I look at him again. He doesn't care about the colour of my bra.

He just wants me.

Or he wants my body.

His desire shocks me. I don't deserve it. I am no Kate Moss or Helena Christensen. My hips are wide, shoulders strong. Heroin chic will never fit me. I am slim because we have no food, and I play sports: netball, hockey, football and athletics – running and shot-put. I love sports, but my growing body doesn't match the standards set by the skinny pop stars on the cover of *Smash Hits*. Still, being good at sport fills a lot of angst. Also, I have great hair: permed auburn locks that roll down my back. It's not all bad. And he is so into me. That is what matters: how he feels about me.

I lean into him to give him a soft kiss on his mouth. His eyes stay on my boobs until I'm close enough for him only to be able to see my face. He kisses me with more passion than he has ever done before.

My breath is taken away.

He reaches up to try to put his hand inside my shirt. I gently pull him away, but he resists. I pull harder. He still resists.

'No, Jace, I don't want you to.'

I can feel my heart in my ears. Is he going to listen to me? His eyes are red almost, full of passion. And, is that anger?

'You're a prick tease!'

He stops kissing me, and passion is replaced by anger. He pushes me back from him. My heart beats even faster. *You've lost him now!*

'No, I'm not. I'm not ready yet, Jace. I want to. Just not yet.'

He is staring through me now. I button up my shirt. I feel rotten. Did I tease him there? Am I doing something wrong?

I started going out with Jace on Hallowe'en night 1991, when I was fourteen. Frank's mum and dad were away for the weekend, so the whole gang from the Poolway Shopping Centre and the Meadway Estate were heading to Frank's for a party.

I had been going out with Frank for two weeks but decided I didn't like him. I told him I wanted to end things as we were walking to his house for the party. He didn't seem to care. I was fourteen and he was fifteen. Plenty more girls were going to be at his house, and, as the king of the party, he probably knew he could pull someone else easily that night. Leigh and I had robbed a fiver from her mum's bedside table and bought four bottles of Diamond White to have between us.

'Kat ... Kat? Are you OK? You look wrecked.'

Leigh's face looms into mine at the party. I am swaying back and forth, can't focus properly. I'm hammered. Two bottles of Diamond White have blown my head off. Despite being terminally cool and having a family full of addicts, I don't drink a lot. I don't like being so out of control. Two bottles and I'm steaming.

The music is blaring, and the house is a wreck. I see someone in a red hat run past me, stop and slowly turn back to face me. The lads from the Poolway have trashed the house – throwing talc and toilet paper everywhere. Red Hat approaches me and throws some talc over me. I recognise him: Jace from the Poolway crew, one of the quieter lads from the gang. Never says much. He's the best at robbing cars, though. He comes flying around the bend on the Meadway Estate in stolen cars and is well known in the area for robbing a Subaru Impreza.

He is standing in front of me now.

Staring at me.

'What, have I got something on my face?' I yell.

He laughs and throws some talc over me again. 'You have now!' he shouts as he runs off.

I chase after him, following him into the little downstairs bathroom. I try to reach the taps to splash water on him in revenge and end up falling to the ground, pulling him on top of me. 'Sorry, sorry,' I say, but he stares into my eyes intently.

'I've fancied you for a while, Kat,' he says.

I'm speechless. I have never noticed him before now. As I look at his face, I realise he's really handsome. His eyes are a lovely cool grey. He has a sharp nose and a lovely jawline.

'Will you fuck off!' I say, laughing.

'No, I mean it. I thought you were out of my league, though.'

My heart flutters to hear him say that. I am not out of anyone's league. He leans down and kisses me softly. I kiss him back. Much more passionately than I planned to. The Diamond White, the soft words and his shyness all blend to make this moment feel special. We spend the rest of the night lying on the ground in Frank's bathroom snogging, him stopping occasionally to stare into my eyes as if he cannot believe his luck.

'Play 'Wind of Change' again.'

I lean over the side of my mum's bed and rewind the cassette. He holds me so I don't fall out of bed – my heart races. I am so glad I recorded the Top 40 this week. 'Wind of Change' by Scorpions is number two. I play it again.

'Wind of Change' and 'More than Words' by Extreme become

the soundtrack of our first night together. I'm not even sure I like the songs. It's OK though if he's happy.

After leaving Frank's at about 2am, we came back to mine. My mum and dad are in Ireland for the week, so we got into their bed, and spent the night talking and kissing.

He doesn't try to do anything else, which makes him even more attractive to me. Every boy I've ever kissed up until now has tried to get their hands under my bra to get a good feel of my tits. Jace seems content to just kiss and talk. Well, he lets me talk and he listens.

He does say a few things. He tells me he has fancied me for ages, that he couldn't believe I was with Frank, that he knows my brothers, and he lives at home with his mum, stepdad and little brother. He isn't in school and doesn't have a job. He is fifteen. He gets money from his mum and from going robbing. Car stereos mainly. Sheds. Tools. He has had one serious girlfriend ('before you,' he says, which makes my heart lift). He says she was small; she looked a bit like Kylie Minogue (this makes me feel sick). I think he is a virgin, like me, as he isn't pushing anything sexual. And we are on our own, in a bed in my house. I like that. In fact, I LOVE that about him.

I am obsessed.

From the very start.

He is the answer I have been looking for.

'I'm going in now, lads – it's freezing!'

Mark waves goodbye as he heads down towards his house, leaving us standing at the top of the Meadway. It's just me and Jace.

He has been ignoring me for two weeks and I don't know what I've done wrong.

I never know what I've done wrong.

I look at him and wait for him to speak.

'I'm going to go in now, then. You want me to walk you halfway home?'

He has a little glint in his eye. This means I am forgiven. This means, that whatever he was angry about has passed.

Relief fills my chest. I can't stand being frozen out. His silence is so loud. I lie awake at night listening to Phil Collins and Bette Midler, crying, forlorn, not knowing what I've been rejected for, knowing that I'm not good enough for him. Knowing, hoping, that he will come around and pick me up again when he's resolved whatever imagined slight he thinks I've committed against him.

He never, ever tells me what's going on. He just ignores me. And it always comes out of the blue.

The first time was about three weeks after we got together at the party. He just turned cold. No chat. No kisses. He was cruel. Slagging me with the lads. Laughing at my clothes. Pure mean to me.

Shocked, I broke down every time I left the group. *What have I done?*

I moped around the house. Crying at the drop of a hat.

Carl, my friend, begged me not to care. 'He isn't good enough for you, mate,' he said. 'Come on, Kat, there are loads of lads who want you. Why cry over him?'

I cried harder, turning up 'Separate Lives' by Phil Collins.

And then it was over. Seven days of tears – over and forgotten. 'I'll walk you home, Kat,' he said after a week of silence.

And I jumped to attention. Thrilled to be back in his limelight.

'I thought you wanted Mark. I saw you laughing when he made a joke.' The only explanation for the hurt.

It happens every couple of weeks now, the same cycle but, apart from that, we are going great. We hang out in the gang. 'Want me to walk you home?' he says most nights.

I follow along behind him. We walk down the Poolway Park, me chatting, him smiling, until we stop at the end of the park and head to the long grass. We kiss. He has his hands up my tracksuit top now. We are way past second base, but I refuse to have sex with him. You can't sleep with someone unless you know he's 'the one'. Otherwise, you're a slag.

Nothing worse than being a slag.

There's a girl we know who has fucked loads of lads. She's older than me and has the biggest tits I've ever seen in my life. She has fucked and sucked every lad from the Manor – and other manors.

Back then, being a slag was worse than being fat, ugly, smelly and poor. In my case, the added layer of being sexually abused by multiple men, and the fear of letting someone touch me, letting someone take me, added to the need to keep my virginity safe.

But I loved Jace.

He was not like the other lads.

A boy who wasn't driven by sex was easier for me. I didn't feel threatened.

But he was getting edgy now. It had been over a year since we started getting off with each other and I wasn't putting out.

'Will I walk you home or what?'

He is smirking at me. It's New Year's and I am feeling brave tonight.

I want to give him it. I want him to stop finishing with me all the time. Maybe if we have sex, it will bring us to the next level.

'I want you to do more than walk me home!' I say in the sexiest voice I can conjure, my heart beating in my ears.

'Yeah, yeah, you're all mouth. You won't let me do anything.'

'I am *not* all mouth, you are. I'm ready and willing whenever you are.' I reach over and touch him between his legs. 'Maybe you're scared.' I look him in the eye.

'Me, scared? No way! Come on, then, let's head to the garage and see!'

'Yeah, yeah, yeah ...' I say.

He takes my hand and walks me over towards the garages at the back of the houses on the Meadway. There is an abandoned garage that we sometimes use to make out. It has an old mattress in it, and it's warmer than hanging around in the Poolway Park. I follow behind him, worried that I'm making a mistake. I don't want to lose my virginity in an old garage.

But I want him. I want to keep him with me. To please him. I look at his eyes and they are smiling. I love him so much, I will do anything for him.

'Kat, I love you, you know.'

He looks down at me between passionate kisses. I smile up at him. Wanting so much to believe him.

If he loved you, he wouldn't blank you and hurt you and slag you in front of the lads.

'I love you too, Jace. You won't tell anyone?'

I don't want people to think I am a slut.

He kisses me harder now, his finger pinching my left nipple. He has his hand under my Nike T-shirt and inside my bra. I shiver. It feels nice to be touched. I worry that he can feel the fat rolls on my stomach.

You made this happen. Your body is bad.

I look up at him and see how happy he is. I close my eyes, and I blank out for the rest of it.

I know he pulled his jeans down to his knees. I know I pulled my burnt-orange shell tracksuit down, and I stepped my left leg out of the trousers, leaving my right leg still in. I know he pulled my leg around his waist and put his dick inside me.

I know it lasted less than two minutes.

I know he came.

I know I didn't.

Just for the Sex

After that first time, everything became about sex. Everything became about finding somewhere to go to ride – or for him to ride and for me to pretend I enjoyed it. I never, ever liked the sex with Jace. Not because he did anything wrong. It was me: my shame, my inability to be present, my age, the lack of knowledge I had about my body and its capacity for pleasure. It was the abuse, my past, the hurt, and all the lessons I learned from my life – girls are objects for pleasure, not recipients of it!

We hung around the shops, a gang of us, the girls in one group, the lads in another – smoking, stealing cars, taking drugs, the usual delinquency that goes on with poor kids from poor communities. At 11pm, Jace would say to me, 'You right?' and I would walk a step behind him towards my house.

I loved the walk towards the house. The moments before and after the sex were what I wanted. The act itself I could take or leave.

His eyes would glisten with anticipation as we walked through the park. Me chattering about things, knowing he was listening, knowing he wanted me.

'When I leave school, I'm going to do something with my life, honestly. I think I will do law or something, or even English.'

'I hated school.'

He is sixteen now and has already left school – suspended or expelled, I'm not sure what for. He spends his nights out robbing with the lads, and he sleeps all day. His life is a Groundhog Day of delinquency.

I am good in school. Well, I'm good and bad. I have a brain in my head. If I could just control my temper and attend more, I could do something. Some of the teachers tell me this: Mr Poulter says I am great. Mrs Buckley thinks I can be a professional sportswoman. My science teacher likes me. If I go to school more and calm down a bit, I could do well. But I am terminally cool. Can't afford to let anyone see that I am not one of the lads; that I am not cool or hip or crazy. I can't let Jace know that I love books; that I understand Shakespeare; that I feel moved by the inequalities in the themes of books by John Steinbeck and Harper Lee.

He holds my hand in the darkness of the park where no one can see his softness. He walks close to me, hand in hand. It feels like heart to heart.

'What time have you got to be in at?'

'Twelve tonight as it's Friday.'

'Great, let's go into the garage.'

One of the houses at the corner of Blakenhale and Outmore Road has been left empty, and the garage has an old mattress and some other stuff strewn around. Jace has figured out how to break into it with a screwdriver. Only a few of us know about it – a place the lads take their birds.

My heart drops at the thought of what is to come. I love being close to him. I love being wanted by him. But having sex in a disused garage at the bottom of the Poolway Park is uncomfortable.

'OK.'

As he flips the door open, I notice that the mattress has been moved, some candles have appeared, and someone has had a fire burning in there. My stomach churns. Has he been here with someone else? Am I his only girl? I want to say something but know better – boys don't like needy girls. *Act cool. Make sure he knows you love him.*

'Come lie down with me. We don't have long.' His eyes are alight with desire.

I lie over him. Kissing him hard and fast. His breath taken away by my passion.

'I want you!' I hear myself say.

Isn't this what boys want? Girls who want them, girls who act like this?

He is pulling at my clothes, trying to touch my tits and kiss me and undress me all at the same time. He pulls his trousers down. He is hard.

'Kiss it ...' He speaks quietly, eyes alight.

He will leave you if you don't give him what he wants.

'Where do you want me to kiss you?' I say in my best grown-up, teasing voice.

He pushes his groin up towards my face, pressing slightly on the back of my neck. I have seen this in the porn films that Carl makes us watch when we wag school in his house. Blonde, busty women sucking men's cocks until they come. Looking up at them while they're doing it.

He will leave you if you don't please him.

I do as he wants. I pretend I'm one of the girls from the films we watched. Making eyes at him in the dark, tasting sweat and piss while he moans with pleasure. I am good at this. This thought gives me some joy. Giving him what he wants will surely make him love me. I am a good girl. His girl.

Just before he is about to finish, I stop and lie on my back so he can enter me. He lasts a minute longer and grunts and then rolls over.

His eyes bright with love.

He thinks you are a slut now for doing that.

I roll into him, squeezing into the hook of his arm, looking up at his face. 'Did you enjoy that?'

'Yeah, did you do that before?' He looks slightly pissed off, as if I've done something wrong.

'No ... no ... never! You're the first boy I have been with, Jace. I love you. I would never do that with anyone else.'

'You know that I would know if you were with someone else, like I would be able to tell now from the feel of you when I'm inside you. If you are ever with anyone else, I will know.'

He must really love me to be so worried that I might be with someone else.

'I will never be with anyone else, Jace – I love you!'

He is standing, dressing now, back to me. It is over. The connection – it's gone. The emptiness is all-engulfing.

You are not lovable.

'Get the fuck away from me, you dirty tramp.'

His face is red, his eyes on fire.

'You disgust me. I don't know how I was even with you, you slag.'

I stand in front of him, tears rolling down my face. Worried that it's my face, my body, my imperfections making him hate me. I place my hand over my stomach, worrying that it's too big, too pudgy for him. I know I am bad; I just don't understand which bit of me is bad.

'What did I do? Why are you being like this? I don't know what I did!'

'Don't fucking talk to me. I don't exist to you – you make me sick!'

He walks away from me, back towards the lads standing outside the Kwik Save at the Broadstone shops. They are all looking at me, laughing.

I don't know what I've done.

It started three nights ago. I'd gone up to the shops to hang out, and had walked up to him to say hi before chatting with the girls, and he'd completely blanked me. The twins, Darren and Dean, had laughed at me standing there like a twat.

He ignored me as if I didn't exist.

My stomach is permanently twisted from this coldness.

See, I told you – you are not lovable.

I spent the night racking my brains for something I had done to upset him. The day before, we had been in his mum's house, a Sunday afternoon, lying in his single bed watching the Villa get beaten on his small portable TV. We'd had sex after the match, and he had walked me out and said goodbye like usual. Now he is angry with me, and I have no clue why.

This was a normal pattern for us now. We would be going great guns, laughing, chatting, riding (most nights), and then he would turn. Some imagined slight would get into his head, and he would start to abuse me.

First came the silence.

The blanking me.

The cold stone walls too high for me to jump.

My heart would ache.

Stomach turning.

I was already a nobody, but without him I was nothing. Some love was better than no love.

Then, he would start the abuse. Calling me names. Getting the lads to join in. I became the butt of their jokes: *state of you; your clothes are stinking; your mum was pissed on the bench again*. The usual stuff.

But coming from him, the person I had let in, the person I had let into me, was worse.

I would wait around for him to cool down.

For the thawing.

Heart thumping, head racing.

What did I do? What did I do? What did I do?

It never occurred to me that he was wrong. That he had something wrong with him.

It had to be me.

It was always me.

I would lie around my house. Crying myself to sleep. Longing for him to want me again. I had nothing inside of me. No worth. No idea of how special I was. How beautiful I was. How I deserved so much more. I was like his lackey. Willing to be dragged from pillar to post if he threw me some scraps of light.

Leigh convinces me to demand answers. She is much braver than me. She has a confidence about her, even though she's chubby and doesn't have the boys after her like I do. She is stronger in herself. Having food and a nice home can do that for you.

'Don't take this shit from him, Kat,' she says. 'He can't just blank you all the time. It's not right! Call him over and ask him what's going on.'

'Do you think I should?'

I know he won't like it, and that he's nowhere near forgiving me, but I hate this feeling so much that I call out to him.

'Jace ... Jace!'

He is standing with his mates on the corner. He looks over really slowly. 'What?'

'Can I talk to you for a minute?'

My voice sounds quieter than I intended. My heart is too loud in my ears. As he walks towards me, I know this is pointless. His eyes are on fire.

'What did I do wrong? What happened?'

'Don't call me. Don't talk to me. We are done. Over. You make me sick.'

The vitriol. The anger. The hate. All his hurt dumped on to me, and I don't know why. I feel myself hanging in the balance. I don't know if I can live if he doesn't want me any more. He is everything and nothing to me. The proof I need that I am nothing, I am unlovable.

The drive I have for connection, to be wanted, to feel the light of his love on me one more time is intoxicating. I can't escape it. The more he rejects me, the stronger the drive gets. I am caught in a trap. A trap made for me by my history – by the loss and lack of love I felt when I was age two and age four and age six and age everything. His rejection reignites the old flames; his acceptance extinguishes them. I can't stop myself from falling for this hurt.

See, I told you – you are unlovable!

John's Birth

The phone rings out. This is the third time I have tried calling his house. The third time there has been no answer. My stomach contracts again. The pain is unbelievable.

He has to be there.

He has to be with me.

I can't do this on my own.

'Katriona, my love, are you having more pain?'

Sheila is the nurse from the homeless hostel I have been living in for the past five months. She looks at me with concern. It's Friday evening and the place is quiet. All the other girls, all the other teenage mums, are out visiting their boyfriends, families or friends. We can stay out at the weekend if we have somewhere safe to go. I don't have that luxury. I have no family home to stay in; they kicked me out when I told them about the baby. No boyfriend waiting to welcome me and his growing baby into his house at the weekends.

I am alone. No one wants me and my baby.

I pick up the phone and ring the number again. It rings out.

I know he's there because he told me he was going in three hours ago. I know he went home because I watched him walk towards his house.

'Jace, you know I'm three days overdue now. Do you think it might be a good idea for us to stay together tonight, just in case I go into labour? I don't want to be on my own when it happens.'

The last part comes out in a whisper.

'Nah, Kat, you know my mum doesn't like people staying over in the house and, besides, the size of you now – we wouldn't fit in my bed!'

He laughs to himself.

I push the hurt aside. He has a point. His mum isn't over the moon about the baby. She makes sly comments about ruining his life, her life, my life and the baby's life. He only has a single bed in his bedroom, and I am huge now – belly and boobs and body everywhere. Every part of me is stretched.

I hate my pregnant body. I have no control over it. The stretching and the strains of child-growing are everywhere: stretch marks on my arms, my belly. My weight is out of control. I eat chips every day. I have never had the means to feed myself before. Being in the hostel, getting my welfare, means I can eat what I want, when I want. And I have an insatiable drive for food. I am not eating for two; I am eating for my stolen childhood – and all the meals I never had. The widening of my hips, in a world of waifs, is making me feel shame and anger. I am sixteen, pregnant, alone and fat! I have left school without any qualifications. The shame of my pregnancy is too much to share with the teachers who hated me. Living here in the hostel, with no family connection, the shame is all-consuming.

'Do you want to try your mum instead? She's agreed to go to the hospital with you, hasn't she?'

I can't look at Sheila as she speaks to me, her kind eyes, her soft words. The gentle touch of her hand on my arm as she reaches for me makes me want to scream. Or cry.

She doesn't know that Tilly has only been out of the hospital a few days herself. That she nearly died four months ago from bleeding varices, that my dad has gone back to Ireland, that they love drink more than me and their impending grandchild. I can't share that I feel alone and scared.

That I never had a mum – ever.

I can't tell her any of this because it is her job to assess me as a parent. If I tell her how bad it all is, she might not let me keep my baby.

'OK, yeah, good idea.'

Another pain washes through me, tightening around my belly, grabbing my insides and reminding me this is going to be hard.

I call the number. I know it off by heart. It's a phone box. It is our phone box, on the corner of Blakenhale and Outmore Road, beside the little cul-de-sac where my family home is. It's our house phone. Anyone local knows that when the phone box rings, it's usually a call for one of the O'Sullivans.

Tonight is no different.

Tonight I am calling for my mum, praying she will be able to answer me.

Ring-ring, ring-ring. It is 11pm. I see the dark road. I imagine that the steel double-glazed windows of our three-bed council house are open, a party going on inside.

Maybe it's different since Mum got out of hospital. Maybe they are all cosy in their beds. I push that thought aside.

'Hello?' A breathless voice answers.

It's Matthew! My Matthew.

'Matt, it's me, Kat. Thank God you answered.'

'Kat, why are you ringing this late? I was just going to bed and heard it. Where are you? You OK?'

'I'm in the hostel, of course.' I try to keep the anger out of my voice. Where else would I be? No point fighting about it now. 'The baby is coming, Matt!'

'The baby? What baby? YOUR BABY! What, now? Shit, hold on, Kat. Let me get Mum.'

I hear him run away before I can stop him. My money is going to run out. I look at Sheila sitting at her desk, half-reading her notes, half-listening to me. Her black hair reminds me of Ms Atkins, her accent the same, but different. She's Irish, but from Mayo, not Meath. She is beautiful, in an older lady way. I have no more change. Shit.

Sheila looks up, feeling my eyes burning into her.

'Sheila, sorry, he's gone to get my mum, but I'm worried the money will go.'

'Of course – I have lots of change here.'

She jumps up and brings me change. The public telephone is situated in the long entrance hallway of Trentham House. The bold circles and squares in the eighties-style brown carpet help hide the fact that it's threadbare and old. The payphone sits on a cream table at the foot of the stairs, next to the main office door – the office where the nurses stay 24/7 to make sure we're behaving. The wall separating the hall and the office features an Apex glass window across the top, enabling them to watch our movements while maintaining their privacy.

'Here you go, my love.'

Her soft Irish tone reminds me of my grandma, who died ten months ago. She was saved from the shame of her granddaughter being a 'gymslip' mum, fifteen and pregnant. This news would have shaken her to the roots of her Catholic faith.

'Thank you.'

I put twenty pence into the phone before the pips start. I hear footsteps down the line.

'Kat, are you OK, love?'

She's here. Someone is here.

Another pain sweeps through me, and this time I can't stop the tears. 'Mum, Mum. Is that you? It hurts, Mum.'

The tears flow. The need for her never leaves.

'OK, it's OK. That's normal, my love. Do you know how far apart the pains are? Have you been timing them? Is the nurse there with you?'

'About eight minutes, I think. I tried timing, but I was trying to call Jace and he wasn't answering, and I lost track. It hurts, Mum. It hurts a lot.'

I hear her chuckle softly and, for a moment, I forget who we are and where we have been.

'I'm scared, Mum.'

'I know, I know. It's going to be OK. Don't worry, I'm here. Can you get yourself to East Birmingham Hospital? I'll get Michael up and get him to bring me to you. Is that OK, my Katriona?'

She never calls me that.

'Yes, they'll get an ambulance for me. Mum, can you go and knock Jace up on your way, please? He won't want to miss this.'

She pauses for a second longer than needed, and I know what she's thinking.

'Please, Mum! I need him to be there.'

'OK, OK, of course. I'll ask Michael to stop in on the way. Get your bag now, and we will meet you there. Don't worry, we'll have a lovely baby after all of this – a new life!'

'Does she want the pethidine to help with this?'

This is the third midwife I have had since I was moved to the labour ward at four o'clock this morning. It's now 7am on Saturday, and the pains I had last night have paled in comparison to what I am experiencing now. My body feels as though there is a hot vice inside it, and every five minutes it tries to squeeze my insides out.

It is the most predictable experience of pain I have ever had in my life. Knowing it's coming again makes it difficult to enjoy the reprieve between contractions. I spend the four minutes and fifty-eight seconds between the racking pains begging for someone to make it stop.

'Mum, please help me. I can't do this ... I can't do this!'

'Yeah, yeah, give her the pethidine. The gas and air is making her sick.'

My mum speaks for me now. No one in the room acknowledges me. The midwives talk to my mum or to each other. I am a child, having a child; I don't deserve their care.

I lie with my legs open, rotating between screaming and begging to be let free.

'Where is he, Mum? Where's Jace?'

'Don't worry, love. He's here, outside in the waiting room. They didn't want the room to be too full.'

She's lying. Her eyes and her tone tell me the truth.

As soon as the midwife leaves, Tilly takes the gas and air mask from around my neck and puts it over her face. She looks at me and laughs as she takes a few deep breaths.

Nothing has changed.

3.45pm. 18 September 1993.

'KATRIONA! KATRIONA! Look at me now, look at me now.'

The midwife looks directly into my eyes, and I can tell she's scared. His heart rate fills the room. It sounds like a horse galloping through a barren field. He slows down and speeds up and slows down.

Every time he slows down, she scrunches her face and gets louder.

'KATRIONA, YOU MUST PUSH. YOU NEED TO PUSH HARDER NOW!'

The air in the room has changed. They all look scared. Tilly is standing close to me, her face contorting into a fake smile.

'Come on, love, you're nearly there now.'

Nearly where? I am so lost in the pain that I have no idea where I start and where I end. They all see me now.

For the past thirty hours, I have felt invisible. The people passing through my room directed everything through my mum. Tilly. The one who did this for me. The one who did nothing for me. And now they see me. The air has changed and he is stuck.

He is stuck.

HE IS STUCK.

I open my eyes fully and bear down on my backbone. Pushing with every ounce of hurt and love I have.

He will be OK.

He must be OK.

'OK, OK. Well done, well done, that was brilliant, Katriona. Wait now, breathe a little.'

I can't see her face. She is between my legs, staring into me – staring into him.

'When you hear him speeding up, the horse, you need to push as hard as you can. Give it everything.'

I don't know if she said 'the horse', or if I imagined it, but I know what I have to do.

I finally know what I am made for.

Clip-clop, clip-clop, clip-clop. He is running towards me.

'OK, NOW, PUSH! PUSH!'

CLIP-CLOP, CLIP-CLOP, CLIP-CLOP, CLIP-CLOP!

I bear down on myself; every ounce of me is focusing on every ounce of him. *Come on, baby, you have to help me here.*

Clip-clop ... clip-clop ... clip-clop ...

He is running away from me again, slowing down to a canter.

They whisper between them. I look down at my mum's feet. They are swollen to the size of balloons. I look into the yellow-stained whites of her eyes. 'Are you OK, Mum?'

She looks at me with the tenderness of my lifetime. 'You worry about our little light. We have to get him out now.'

She is tired. I am tired. They are whispering, the strangers between my legs. Their faces tell me everything. *Clip-clop ... clip-clop ... clip-clop.* He is advancing again.

'PUUUUSSSSSSHHHH, HARDER HARDER HARDER. KEEP GOING.'

Clip-clop ... clip-clop ... clip-clop. He canters away.

'What's happening?' My words echo around the room. They speak to each other in hushed tones. A white jacket appears with two big silver spoons.

'What is happening to my baby?'

'Katriona, your baby is what we call 'angel-faced'. It means he is facing upwards, towards the heavens.' *(Clip-clop, clip-clop, clip-clop.)* 'We are going to have to help him out. These are forceps.' (*CLIP-CLOP! CLIP-CLOP! CLIP-CLOP!* He's galloping towards us all.) 'They will help him. When I say push, you must push, and when I say stop, you must stop, OK?'

I can't speak. Every part of me knows this is my entire job, my life's work. He must be OK!

'AAAAAAAHHHHHHHHHHHHHHHHH ...'

I hear myself screaming from somewhere far away, somewhere

in the history of my being and her being and his being. I hear my call to the world while this man in a white coat, who didn't bother to tell me his name, pulls my beautiful boy into the world.

'He's definitely a little Villan, arriving dead on 3.45pm! He knew it was half-time and his dad was taking a break from the match!'

I smile, never taking my eyes off John. Jace bought him a Villa babygro, and we struggle to get his little limbs into it. John's toes look so long compared to the rest of his body.

'And he's a good luck charm too. We were drawing until he arrived, and we won two-one in the end, my little Villa mascot.'

I can't work out who he looks like, this little bundle of love lying next to me in a see-through plastic cot. His face moves towards the sound of his dad's voice. I wonder if he can hear him. Does he recognise us?

'I bought you some Monster Munch in the shop, pickled-onion flavour, your favourite.'

Jace is smiling down at me. My heart could explode, all the angst of last night forgotten. The disappointment that he didn't want to 'watch' the birth is gone, washed away by the oxytocin and the remnants of pethidine and epidural.

He leans over and kisses me softly on my lips and I know it's all going to be OK.

Weight Watching!

'Well done, you got your silver star – seven pounds in three weeks – amazing work! Are you staying for group? I hope you are. We need some good news!'

I look up at her as I put my shoes and socks back on. Smiling, I take the little silver sticker and paste it to the week three line in my WeightWatchers book.

Weight: 13 stone 2 pounds
BMI: 29
Measurements: Waist Up 32, Waist Down 34, Bust 42.

My stomach gurgles loudly. I look at her face ... she didn't notice, thank God.

I am starving. I didn't eat a morsel of food today: three coffees, a water retention tablet and two poos mean I'm ravenous, but

I'm down two pounds. I pay for two packs of WeightWatchers bars: a five-pack of toffee fudge bars (only two points each) and a pack of chocolate Rice Krispie bars (one and a half points each).

'They're lovely if you put them in the freezer.' The chubby lady on the desk points at the toffee bars and smiles at me. 'They last for ages if you freeze them first.'

I smile at her. Fuck the freezer – I plan on eating two of them now.

It isn't even my idea to be here. Leigh was always the fat one, the 'bigger' girl, while I was the smaller friend. The skinnier one. When we did our French and Saunders impressions for my parents during their drunken parties, she was always French; I was Saunders.

But that has all changed now. When I was kicked out on the street, I got a hostel place and then a council flat after having John. Having my own money and the ability to eat what I want, when I want has meant that I have ballooned. I got fat and have stayed fat.

My body didn't 'bounce back' after I had John. It got looser and lesser. I didn't even really appreciate what I had before the baby; my critical head was always telling me my body wasn't enough. But now, after the baby, with the loose skin, the stretch marks, the spare tyre that hangs down over my crotch, I *know* it is not enough.

And I am still only sixteen.

Everyone is going to raves. Belly tops are in. Cycling shorts and vest tops are standard for girls my age. But I am wearing fat clothes: shell suits, oversized jumpers, jackets, even in the heat – anything that will cover up the shame of my failing fat body.

Jace says he doesn't care, but I know he must. If he could have me slim or me fat, I bet he would choose me slim any day. And I say it to him – constantly bemoaning my baby body, hating the vessel that produced my beautiful baby.

I thought I would just shrink after having John. That's what all the women in the magazines do. I thought that I would pop back into my skinny self. But that's not how this works. The bingeing, the chips and the lack of food education and understanding have resulted in my bigger body, my failing body. And this feels familiar. The disgust is real, and old. The failure magnified by the purple stretch marks and the stomach overhang that will never bounce back because it has been stretched way too far.

'So Katriona got her silver seven this week: seven pounds lost in total, seven pounds lost in three weeks – well done, you! Can you give any hints or tips to anyone in the rest of the room?'

'Yes, yeah, of course.' I'm beaming now, a good girl! 'Well, I drank a glass of water every time I felt hungry. I made the no-point veg soup. And I definitely moved a lot more this week. Leigh and I did an aerobics class up in Stechford Leisure Centre.'

I look over at Leigh, who is chewing on one of the toffee bars. She didn't lose this week. She blushes as I say her name.

'I write everything down, too.'

'There are some great tips there – well done, Katriona. Keep focused and you will have your first stone in no time.'

My first stone? How many fucking stone does she think I need to lose?

'Hurry up, Leigh I'm fucking starving. I can't believe she made me stay to get my silver badge thing. I'd prefer weighing and leaving. The way she talks gets on my nerves. She dresses like she's going to a wedding, too.'

'Oh, Kat, stop moaning. At least you lost something. I feel like I was so good this week and I didn't lose a pound.'

'Well, at least you didn't gain, Leigh. To be honest, I think starving myself on weigh day is what is helping the scales move. And I got some of those waterfall tablets that Leslie recommended. I don't feel as bloated, even though I'm pissing all the time.'

'What can I get you?'

'Oh, yeah, sorry, can I get a mini fish and chips and mushy peas please, loads of salt and vinegar and a pickled onion on top? Leigh, what do you want?'

'I'll have a chicken kebab, chips, curry sauce and a pickled onion.'

Every Monday evening was the same for the year 1994. At 7pm, Leigh and I would face the dreaded scales in Silvermere Youth Club. Our feeling of success or failure – of worth – correlated to the amount of weight we had lost or gained that week. Both of us starved all day to increase our weight loss that night, then it was off to the chippie for a splurge. If you had to graph my weekly eating patterns that year, you would have seen vast amounts of food eaten on Monday evening, a bit less on Tuesday, less on Wednesday into Thursday – and then next to nothing on Friday, Saturday and Sunday.

It helped that, on the weekends, I was out raving with Jace. With his mum or my mum on babysitting duty, we would go out from Friday to Sunday. The odd dab of speed here or there or an ecstasy tab was great for restricting the appetite.

The first month or so after joining WeightWatchers that first time, Leigh and I stayed for the entire class, eagerly waiting for the leader's motivational talks that reminded us throughout that she was like us, that she was once fat too – but was maintaining her newfound skinniness through the points system.

If it wasn't bad enough that she told us her story every week, she also had a life-size cutout of her older, fatter self standing tall next to the weighing scales, perfectly positioned to remind us that she was once like us – a fat failure. A faded WeightWatchers magazine from 1991 lay on the snack table, featuring her before-and-after pictures on the cover. She had been featured in the 'loser of the year' competition and was very proud to have been runner-up to Sally, who lost over twelve stone. The leader's credentials were proven by her four-stone weight loss and her ability to maintain it for nearly three years.

That first year in WeightWatchers was the only time I have ever 'succeeded' in reaching my goal in a slimming club, even though

I have joined many since then. On the first day, the leader set my target weight or goal based on my Body Mass Index (BMI) or weight divided by height. According to my height, which is 5'5" or 5'6" or 5'7", I should weigh eleven stone or less. This is the upper end of the healthy range for a woman of my height. The lower range for me is eight stone, three pounds. I don't think I weighed eight stone three when I was born! I've always been a big girl. Not fat but stocky, strong, big-boned. I've got tits and hips. I have big strong thighs. I remember being called 'strapping' by my nanny. 'You're a big strapping girl,' she said. I was nine years old and felt proud. The idea that I would be deemed healthy at eight stone, three pounds seems scary to me now.

I learned many rules for losing weight during that first year of WeightWatchers. The most important ones for most slimming clubs involve counting. Recording every morsel of food that goes into your mouth is essential for weight loss. Knowing how much you're eating and tracking food as 'points' is key. You get points to spend every day and we are taught how to translate food into points. All foods have a point score based on their calorific content. We don't need to worry our chubby little heads about the calories and the fats and the carbs. We don't need to know that level of detail. We just need to understand that we have an 'allowance' of points to eat every day based on our current weight. If we eat that allowance every day for weeks and months on end, we will eventually become like the leader – a success, a winner, an example of good discipline. Thin. Beautiful.

A good girl.

In that first year in WeightWatchers, I also learnt the concept of 'earning' points. Not only do we have our daily points allowance, but we can also earn extra points by exercising. The leader gave us a plastic folder of WeightWatchers books and the tools to help us learn which foods and exercises are low and high in points.

The folder contained a cardboard wheel device to calculate the points of foods not listed in their books. We looked at the back of the box or packet to get the calorie content per hundred grams and then tried to estimate our portion size. I would always underestimate. I still have no idea what thirty grams of oats actually look like. Some of the WeightWatchers leaders would have pre-weighed portions of food on the table so we could see what a 'good' portion was. The thirty grams of porridge oats always shocked me. It was a tiny amount – gone was the idea of a breakfast of kings.

To be good at WeightWatchers, you needed to weigh and measure everything.

Only eat potatoes that are the same size as your fist.

'What's for dinner, Kat?'

He's home from work. He finally got a job, working in the petrol station on the Bromford Road. He looks pissed off, ready for a fight. I moaned at him for months about getting a job, trying to earn legally for his family and now that he *is* working, I moan at him about how I'm stuck at home all day with John. Nothing makes me happy. The darkness is overtaking me.

'I've made baked potato with beans.'

It's 7pm and I haven't eaten all day. I've had three cans of Diet

Coke. They keep me going, keep my appetite at bay. It's weigh day tomorrow. I can't afford to let anything pass my lips. My WeightWatchers diary reads like a good school report, points left over every day.

I am a good girl.

'Jackets again? For fuck's sake, Kat. We eat that every night. I'm fucking sick of this dieting shit. I'm not the fat one. I shouldn't have to eat that crap all the time!'

His words sting. I AM FAT. Baked spuds are the lowest in calories, beans a point per teaspoon. This is my go-to meal – low calories, high content – that tides me over until tomorrow, until weigh day and the splurge. My mouth waters at the thought of tomorrow night – the chips and the crisps and the sweets.

'I'm going to my mum's for something decent to eat, then down the club to the lads. I'm not sitting here eating this shit with you again.'

He is up and at the door before I can speak. The wave of shame and loneliness rides over me. I have no say here whatsoever. He can stay or leave any time he wants. I am trapped. The sleeping baby in the next room has me trapped here.

'Jace, if you walk out that door, I swear to God, don't you fucking come back!'

The 'hangry' rage has been waiting for someone to scream at all day. The door shuts behind him. I have no power. No say. I am his captive. The flat. The baby. Jace. I have no say.

I flip the oven off, tea towel in hand. I grab the tray with the spuds on and empty them into the bin, my appetite gone, sick with the anger. I won't eat a dinner today. This thought makes me feel better.

In 1994, there was no real discussion of health in WeightWatchers. No introduction to healthy eating or the importance of balance. I told my group that I had eaten four bags of crisps in one day and nothing else. I told them all that I was so happy that I had been able to 'stay on track' and 'stay within my points' while eating what I liked. I was applauded for my self-restraint.

No one said, *That isn't healthy. Maybe you should try to eat balanced meals.* I was a teenage girl who clearly had issues with her body and her self-esteem. I needed care and guidance, not a clap on the back for my disordered eating.

*

Teacher: Mrs Buckley
Class name: 2M2
Year: 1991
Grades: A+
Katriona has made great progress this year. She has exceptional ability in hockey, netball and athletics. With her competitive spirit and physical capabilities, she has the potential to make it at the highest level in sport.

I read it again. Every time it has the same impact. 'Exceptional ability' ... 'highest level of sport'. The words reverberate, hitting me somewhere deep in my chest. Pride. Physical and emotional. I have kept the report.

I like to read it and remember when I was enough. Mrs Buckley said so. My performance in sport said so. I was enough. Every school team I played for – netball, hockey, football, athletics.

I not only played for my own year, but I also played for the years above me. Mrs Buckley stalked the school at lunchtimes, looking for me to fill in on the third-year netball game or for the fourth-year hockey team. I was only in second year then. But my body was strong, and my hunger to win insatiable. You can't teach a kid that. They either want to win or they don't. And I wanted to win from the deepest parts of me. Those days are among my best memories of school.

'Katriona, you and Natasha have been selected for trials for the Birmingham Netball Squad. We've never had a girl from Sheldon Heath selected for trials, so we're extremely proud of you.'

I beam down at her. She is four foot nothing, as wide as she is high, but strong and supportive. Mrs Buckley never lets me get away with anything.

'It is over in Edgbaston on Saturday and Sunday this weekend. Will you be OK to get there?' She hands me the letter. There it is, my name, selected for trials. Edgbaston, the posh area. I don't know the place, but I'll get there. I know without a doubt that I will get there.

*

'Pass me. I'm here!'

It has been a long two days of training and matches. Emlyn Hughes was here, the Liverpool player. He presented us with a certificate and gave us a talk. He was smaller than he looked on TV.

She passes to the wing attack. They are dressed in the same colour outfit, racing green with yellow stripes. Five girls from their school are here – Edgbaston girls – and they only pass to each other. I have nearly hit three of them already. Swearing and shoving are part of my thing. It doesn't feel so bad when I'm with my own school, my own people, the comprehensive kids. Here, I stand out. I wear my PE kit: off-white T-shirt and grey sports skirt. Big black pants underneath. I stand out – not only for my clothes, but for how I play. I am rough. Hard. I will fight you to win. It's hard to take a childhood on the streets of Hillfields out of a girl.

These girls are polite; they are also talented and winners, but they are polite. I don't have that in me. And they have support. Their parents are watching from the sidelines, calling out their names. 'Great pass, Amanda!', 'Great score, Sarah!' I'm here on my own. I hitched a lift from Michael this morning – I've no idea how I'll get home.

I feel self-conscious.

Every time I open my mouth, I feel ashamed of it.

Natasha doesn't seem to care. She sits on her own, plays the best she can, but doesn't care about the others. Me, I boil over. As the days pass, the fear and self-rejection affect my ability to do what I love, which is playing netball. My body was made for this. For running and shooting and tackling and strategy, but the fear and the difference block my ability to shine.

I don't make the team.

From as far back as I can remember, the most joy I have ever got out of my body was when I was playing sports, running around at school or after school with my brothers. In secondary school, in the midst of all the madness at home, I shone at sports. Sports were the place where I could feel joy and freedom; where I could win. The hunger that existed in me for food, love and recognition was satiated by sports. WINNING!

And my body was good. It was strong and tall and fast. I could make a difference on the pitch. Every school term, we did cross-country. Every school term, my time improved. Every school term, I finished just behind Julia While, a small runner who could have given Sonia O'Sullivan a run for her money.

Every term, we did a bleep test; every term, I improved. The first three years of secondary school saw my sporting abilities grow and grow. And even though I was terminally cool, I would not let that stop me from being the best on the team – or at least trying to be the best. I won medals for swimming and running, and still hold the record for the furthest shot put thrown by a third year at Sheldon Heath School!

I keep that report to remind me of those days.

The WeightWatchers cardboard wheel-thing had the facility to calculate how many points you could earn for exercising. You put in the type of exercise and how sweaty you got, and it calculated the points your workout was worth.

You got the most points from cardio – WeightWatchers encouraged cardio above all else for earning points. Strength training or lifting weights gave you next to nothing, even though we now know that these are great for women. The thought that I could commodify movement, that I could place a value on going to the gym or aerobics or attach a good or bad feeling to movement, seems insane to me now. But, back then, it was great. I counted everything. Every step, every morsel of food, every dance move – every thing became a means of succeeding or failing.

For someone with little or no self-worth, who craved more than anything in life to belong, to feel accepted, to feel love, this was ideal. I could succeed through starvation. If my belly stayed empty and my body moved more than I ate, I was good enough.

The problem was – the problem is – that no one can restrict food forever. I definitely could not. The problem was that once I began to equate success and failure with food and movement, they became pathological. Eating became something to be good at or bad at. Moving became something to succeed at or fail at. The love of sport ended. The appreciation for my body and what it could do came to an end. Exercise became a commodity.

'Could you step off the scales for me for a moment?'

Her face says it all: shocked, confused. I know why. The scale reads a gain of seven pounds in one week.

'There must be something wrong with the plate.'

I step off slowly, heat rising in my cheeks, my stomach growling from no food today. I've starved myself since last night at 7pm, trying to pull back a week of bingeing. I was determined not to fail at the weight-loss game.

'I can come back to tomorrow's class if that's better?' I try to buy myself more time. If I starve for two full days, maybe I will win.

'No, no, no.' She raises a skinny arm. 'There is obviously something wrong with this machine.'

She presses reset. The queue of women sways with hunger and agitation behind me.

'OK, now pop back on there.'

She takes my card, wipes it on her skirt and puts it into the weighing machine. I am heavier than I was five minutes ago before the scale reset.

'It's reading seven and a half pounds up this week. Can I ask if it's your star week?'

I nod my head, faking a smile, lying. 'Yes, yes, I got it this morning.'

My smile feels like a grimace; a tear prickles the corner of my eye. *No, I'm just a fat failing cunt who has no control over myself.*

'I saw the way you were fucking looking at him! You won't make an idiot out of me. You're a fucking slut.'

'I don't know who you're talking about. Who? Where? I don't know what you mean.'

We are lying in bed. John is asleep in his cot. It's 3am and we've only been home for an hour. The two of us are still awake from the whizz (speed); the beat from the music rings in my ears. I thought we'd had a great night. I thought he was in a good mood. We've just had sex. He seemed to enjoy it.

Lying here, with him berating me for looking at someone else, has been happening a lot lately.

He loves me so much that he is afraid of losing me.

'Jace, honestly, I don't want anyone else but you. We're happy. Look at John there – he's ours.'

I put my hand on his arm, and he slaps me away. A red mark appears immediately.

'Don't lie to me. From now on, you are not going to the Institute. You can stay here with John.'

'OK, OK. If that makes you trust me. I just want us to be OK.'

I absently stroke the mark on my arm as he turns away.

'You just lay there tonight like a sack of potatoes under me. Were you thinking about him? Do you want him here?'

I stand up and walk towards the bedroom door. 'I'm going for a shower.'

In the bathroom, I stare at my face in the mirror, my pupils huge, my head whirling. Why doesn't he trust me? I feel sad for him. He must have so much love for me that fear takes over. I know that feeling. I get jealous too. But he doesn't believe me. I get under the hot shower. His comment about being like a sack of potatoes hurts.

I don't want to have sex with him. Sometimes, when I lie underneath him, when I can't muster up the pretence, I feel like I'm dying. Like I'm suffocating. I thought I was hiding it from him.

I am eighteen years old, and we have been together for four years now. He is the only boy I have slept with. He is the only boy I have let touch me, have let in. And I've never enjoyed sex with him. I love the connection, I love being wanted and pleasing him; but, sometimes – most of the time – I hate it. Sometimes, I lie next to him and want to put a pillow over his face and squeeze the life out of him for making me do it. The only time it's easy is when I'm on drugs or drunk, which I'm relying on more and more lately. I need substances to help me ignore her. The voice – me. Little me. Screaming out under his weight. Drugs help calm her. And me.

Everyone talks about sex as though it is something to enjoy. The Spice Girls are number one, telling us what they really, really want. I have no idea about my body, about orgasms, about how to ask for my pleasure.

I have been shrinking myself. Yet, how or what my body is supposed to be and do becomes more distant to me. I spend hours staring at my fat stomach, the overhang from the baby, the silvery-purple stretch marks that remind me of my mum. My body is fat and failing, even though I'm losing weight – even that doesn't affect how I think or feel about my body. The connection is becoming less, not more. And everything I do sexually is based on him and his needs. Occasionally, I get the odd tingle, the odd desire to fuck, to let go, but it never becomes anything.

He is still in the room next door. I take the shower head down and spray my whole body. If I stay here long enough, he'll be asleep by the time I go back to bed. I spray my hair and my chest and I point the shower head at my vagina. I feel the biggest sexual thrill I have ever felt in my life. I move the shower a bit closer and feel my head starting to spin. The pleasure. Every nerve-ending is alive. I look at the bathroom door, step out of the bath, and quietly pull the lock across. I listen. He isn't moving. Back into the shower, leg up on the side of the tub, I place the shower head on to my vulva, and, after a minute, I have my first orgasm.

Wow.

This is what they mean.

This is what my body is made for.

This is what I am missing.

I turn off the shower, wipe the water, which has sprayed across the room, with the towel, and head back into bed. As he snores, my head spins. How will I have sex again, knowing that this is what I'm missing out on?

All of the Men

'Hey, do you want a drink?'

He is shouting over the music; his eyes are an ice-cold blue and he has windswept mousy hair.

'Kat, isn't it? You fancy a drink?'

I wave my hand in his face and smile, shaking my ass to the dance tunes. The ecstasy I took two hours ago has kicked in, and I feel the oozing of confidence. I know I have power here. His eyes tell me he wants me.

'No, I'm fine.' I hold up my bottle of water to show him I'm sorted for a drink.

He smiles and moves to stand behind me. He has rhythm. I love a fella who can dance. He stands up close behind me and sways to the beat, to my beat. We have been playing eye tennis for a few nights now.

Bakers nightclub on Broad Street has been my regular haunt since Jace left me. It's only been six months, but I am moving on, slowly. The music and the ecstasy help me forget. This is my third night in Bakers this week. It's the week before Christmas week and the party season is in full swing.

'My name is Wayne.'

'I know who you are.' I laugh now.

He looks at me shyly.

'You know one of my brothers.' I point to Matthew, selling E, standing in his usual spot in the darkest corner of the room.

'Oh, yeah, Matthew. He's a mad bastard.'

His face is beautiful when he laughs.

'Want to come to the chillout room with me?'

'After this tune. I love this one.'

We dance closely. I am a great dancer – all the O'Sullivans are – born with madness and lots of rhythm. When the song ends, he takes my hand and we head to the chillout area, plop ourselves down on beanbags and stare at each other.

'Have you got a boyfriend?'

'No, but I have a kid! And an ex who is an arsehole.' I laugh. He laughs too. I'm trying to act cool. It's working, I think.

'I notice you here a lot, but you're never with anyone – any lads, I mean.'

'I just split up with someone and I'm taking things easy.'

He is intense and very cute. I am delighted he has been watching me.

'Where are you from?' I ask.

He starts telling me about himself. He's from Nuneaton. He works on cars. He has a BMW. He's single. He likes the way I look.

'Thanks, I think.' I laugh again.

'Do you want to meet up tomorrow night? Not here – it's loud here. We could go for a spin or something.'

'Yeah, yeah, OK!'

I give him my address, tell him to pick me up at six, worrying that I won't be able to get a babysitter for John. He leans in and gives me a little peck on the lips. My first kiss since Jace – feels nice.

'Are you going to come with me to Bakers tomorrow night – officially with me?'

We're sitting in his car outside my brother James' house. It has been a whirlwind of a week. I've seen him every day since last Sunday. It's Friday now, four days until Christmas. I want to say yes, but I'm not sure who will babysit. I've asked everyone this week, and everyone has agreed because I've bored them all with stories about the lovely Wayne. They all want me to settle down.

The past six months have been a roller-coaster for me and my family and friends. I spent three weeks mourning Jace and then three months chasing oblivion: drugs, drink, parties. The heartbreak diet has meant I am the skinniest I have ever been. This is the first time I can see a different type of future. Wayne is so sweet and patient. He isn't pushing the sex issue either. I want to, badly, but I know I won't get respect if I fuck every man who shows an interest. You have to hold back your flower till you're sure they like you for you! Isn't that the rule?

'Yeah, I suppose I could come, if you really want me to.'

He smiles, my heart racing as he kisses me. He is so sweet.

'I'll pick you up at eight! Can't wait!'

I float into James' house. My heart and head are in the clouds.

The music is louder than usual tonight. He is stuck to my hip. Dancing beside me, smiling, holding my hand. He has got us two Es and I can feel mine kicking in. He kisses me. My heart feels like it's going to explode. We dance as one. Could he be the one?

It's 1am and I'm cooler now. He is still beside me. His friends are all around us. I know them all now by first name. They seem lovely, nice lads. He is cute, telling them he's mad about me. Telling them what a stunner I am. I look over at him and he whispers in my ear.

'Shall we go outside for some air?'

I follow him, his hand in mine. His car is parked on the path outside Bakers, gleaming in the shadows. I sit in the passenger seat. He leans over me and lowers my seat. He does the same to his own. I let him. He is so kind and nice. He has shown me how much he likes me this week. What would be the harm in sleeping with him? He starts kissing me and I kiss him back passionately. He slides his hands up my skirt and for the first time I let him. Why not? He's a good one. I can trust him.

We take things slow at first and then, when we are both near the edge, he climbs over to me on the passenger seat and enters me. It's over pretty quickly; he smiles and kisses me. 'Tomorrow we'll find a bed to finish this off properly!' he whispers into my mouth.

We head back into the club – me to the ladies' to freshen up, and him back to his pals. When I walk back in, I sense something has changed. Are his friends looking at me differently? Is he holding my hand less? The insecurity of giving him my body takes over. Will he still want me now?

He must sense this as he comes behind me and hugs me, whispers into my ear, 'You're beautiful.'

On the way home in the car, he holds my hand and talks about all the plans he has for us. He talks about meeting John some day, saying he doesn't care that I have a kid. My heart feels so full. Finally, I've met a good one. As I kiss him goodnight, he says he will see me tomorrow at noon. He will collect me from James' house. I smile as I head into the house. Finally, I've met a good one!

'What time is it by your watch, James?'

I am anxious. It's way past twelve o'clock now and no sign of Wayne yet. He's been on time every day. Why is he late today of all days?

'Kat, stop asking me the time. What's wrong with you today? You're very jumpy.'

John is sitting next to me on the settee, watching *Power Rangers*. We have a VHS tape of twenty episodes recorded, and he loves this one the most, the one with the mirror-headed monster. I look at him and my heart aches. Could Wayne have used me? Is it possible that all he wanted from me was sex?

I push the thoughts to one side and focus on the things he said to me all week – the plans he's made for us. There's no way he would spend a whole week with me just so he could have sex with me. No one is that dedicated to the cause.

You are not lovable. No one is ever going to love you.

I jump out of the seat as I hear a car pull up outside, convinced it's him. It isn't – it's Michael pulling up with Leigh. They've been going strong as a couple for three years now, deeply and madly in love. Who would have thought that my Leigh would end up marrying my brother Michael? But there's no denying the love they have for each other. My heart drops when I see them stop for a quick kiss before they come into the house.

No one will ever love you like that.

By 4pm, I convince myself Wayne has been in a car crash or that something else bad has happened to him. My stomach knows different, though. I have never felt so empty and so used. Every ounce of my past, every man who has ever hurt me, every second of the sexual abuse I endured is sitting on top of my chest, reminding me of how worthless I am, of how I am only good for one thing. The rejection, the shame, the loss, the little girl who was always hoping for different, overwhelm me. I feel sick.

He has used me.

They used me.

They all use me.

'What time is he coming for you, Kat?'

Leigh knows something is wrong; I am hardly speaking now. John is still watching *Power Rangers*.

'I must have got the time wrong, Leigh. I thought he said twelve.'

I can't tell her what has happened. I can't tell anyone. Even though we've been best friends since we were eleven, there are things you can't share with your friends. Having sex with different lads is a no-no. A taboo. Being a slag is the worst sin, and now that she's with Michael things have changed. She's more respectable. Settled. Now that I am not in a couple anymore, I am on the outside. Now that I am partying hard, I am on the outside.

I want so badly to reach for the old Leigh, my Leigh. I want to tell her I have been used, hurt, fucked and left. That this boy made me feel like a queen, only to blank me after he got what he wanted. I want to hug her. Or for her to hug me, to tell me I am good and true and worth more, that I am lovable. But I can't risk being called a slag. Or being the centre of gossip in our friend group. Instead, I suck it all up. Every ounce of shame gets stuffed down deep.

'Fuck him anyway, Leigh. It's his loss if he doesn't turn up – plenty more fish in the sea!'

I lie to her and to myself. The space between me and I is becoming bigger.

'Kat, Kat, come sit by your big brother Shag!'

Michael is half-cut. It's 6am on Sunday and the house is full of friends and strangers. The tunes are blasting in the kitchen. Robin S. has been played at least six hundred times. Michael's record player is pumping out Black Box, 'Ride on Time' now. I can see Leigh and Carl arguing in the kitchen. And James is dancing with his eyes closed. He is probably wrecked.

Our house is always the after-party gaff. Everyone knows that the O'Sullivan house is always open for business or a party. Or a sesh. My mum and dad have left for Ireland, trying to change their ways, running away from his last prison sentence. Their old house on Blakenhale Road is now my house. I swapped my fifth-floor flat in Bromford for their house through the council before they left for a new start in Ireland, taking my little sister, the baby.

I am my mum now.

'Kat, come sit here.'

Michael is smiling at me. My eldest and then-closest brother is still tripping. His pupils are massive. His jaw moves from side to side as he smiles over to me.

I snuggle in next to him on my mum and dad's old velvet three-seater sofa. There are bomb holes in every cushion and armrest. Rocks from the ends of my mum and dad's spliffs or their friends' spliffs or their kids' spliffs. All have created a pattern of their own in the sofa given to us by the community service in 1988. There is a faded piss stain on the two-seater. Fat Pat left her mark when she came to visit us just after we moved here from Coventry.

'Kat, you know what, I need to tell you something. You and Leigh – I know you're going to WeightWatchers or wherever, and you're trying to lose weight after having the babbie. But I need to tell you something. You're beautiful. I mean, so beautiful. Out of all of us O'Sullivans, you got the looks. We all have big eyes, big teeth, you know it – look at me, Kat, look at my face.'

I am trying to turn away from his love. I don't – I can't – hear it.

'Kat, you don't need to change. You are my beautiful little sister. You have always been beautiful. And if I'm really honest, I prefer you with a bit of weight on you! You look better. Fuller. Stronger.'

I look into his face and see that he means every word. As he speaks to me and tells me I am beautiful, something inside me heats up. My heart opens and catches the words and closes again.

He means it – you are beautiful.

The music is so loud, the ecstasy flowing. How many did I take … one, two, three? Who knows. I'm off my head. Dancing. Hiding from myself.

He looks over at me again and I smile. I've never seen him before. I'm wearing a sheer blue dress, a white thong and matching bra underneath. The lack of food and the drugs have me at my smallest. I look fit, fuckable. The drugs have silenced all my body hate.

The high heals the hurt – for a short minute.

I like myself like this. Having no thoughts or feelings suits me.

He comes over and starts talking to me. His voice sounds far away. I can't make out what he's saying. I smile and point to my ears and keep dancing. He leans in and kisses me. Hard. I kiss him back. Fuck it.

It's 4am and we have been having sex for hours now. His name has escaped me – Paul, Paddy, I can't remember. The E and the coke are driving a never-ending ride. He is behind me, up on his knees. He can't come, and I never come. It's the drugs stopping him; for me, it's all of it. I look at the head of the bed, the wall, the door.

This was my parents' bedroom. I am in the bedroom where they made love. As he pushes harder and harder into me, I can't help but wonder if my mum looked at the same spot on the ceiling while my dad was on top of her. Was she with other men in this bed? Was this where they fought, laughed and cried together? My head is fried now. Why am I thinking about them while I'm here with this stranger?

Why are they always here?

I flip him over and climb on top of him. I want this to end now. Every nerve-ending fills with shame. My heart is completely empty.

He doesn't even know my name.

I am what I was made for.

Fucking and using.

I roll off him and lie on my back. He stares up at the ceiling. I light a smoke.

'When I was small, I wanted to play football. That's all I ever dreamed of, being a footballer, playing for Wolves. I don't know what happened to that. I'm thirty-three and selling drugs in a fucking nightclub – three kids and a lovely missus at home – and I'm never there.' He takes my smoke and takes a long hard drag.

'I wanted to be an actress or a teacher. I'm stuck. So stuck. Every day I say I'm going to change things, then it ends up the same.'

He looks at me.

'You are really beautiful, you know that?' He strokes my face with his free hand.

For a moment, I believe him. For a moment, I feel it – loved.

He kisses me softly. I lie there, not moving. I can't even respond to it. His kiss, the kindness – I can't take it. I am not even worth the hope.

He rolls over and gets dressed. I lie there looking up at the ceiling, the E and coke comedown starting to hit me now. Knowing that tomorrow will feel worse than this.

'Leave me a line there, will you? I don't think I'll be able to take the comedown tomorrow.'

He throws a bag of coke on to the bedside table, pecks me on the lips and says, 'Laters – see you on the other side.'

He laughs at his own joke and walks out of the door, down the stairs. I hear the front door close behind him.

The silence is so loud.

Did he just pay me with the coke?

Am I like her now?

I live in this cycle now. Tilly is reborn.

Drugs.

Men.

And hunger.

The low hum that underpins all of it. The lack of food, the starvation, the drug-induced malnourishment brings me joy. Control. They are intertwined. I fuck, I drug, I starve – I fail.

All stop me feeling. All stop me seeing. Tilly lives here now in Katriona's body. She is me and I am her. With added value –

with more misery. A further hurt. I have food issues too, a hunger – a drive to shrink myself so small that no one will ever see how bad I am.

How dirty I am.

I reach for the bedside drawer. Eyes shut, I feel around for the small plastic bag. I know it's here; it's here every morning. I find it, pull myself up in the bed. The morning light plays through the dusty room, the floor covered in my dirty clothes, the ashtray overflowing with old spliffs and cigarette butts. Half-empty cans of Diet Coke and tea-stained mugs fill the bedside table.

I lick the tip of my little finger and dab it into the white powder. Without thought, I dab it on to my tongue, repeating the routine three times. Just enough speed to ensure I won't eat for the next few hours.

My body aches.

Nights and days mash into one.

Drugs, drink, men, drugs, drink, men – at least I am shrinking. The constant flow of amphetamines has removed any appetite for food. I am surviving on packets of crisps, cans of Diet Coke and speed. Being empty feels good, removes the noise of everything else. John is in Ireland. They took him, Mum and Dad, to give me a break. Dad is sober, clean and serene – trying to help.

I am lost without him. John.

The house is a shooting gallery for anyone and everyone. The speed keeps the food noise at bay. At least I am achieving something. I feel my stomach. With the weight I've lost, the overhang from

John and his pregnancy feels bigger, looser. I remember how much I hate my body still.

I lick the tip of my little finger, dab it back into the bag, hoping it will silence it all.

The music is so loud. The drinks are flowing. How many have I had?

Who knows? Who cares?

I am off my head. Hiding from myself. He looks over at me again and I smile. I like his friend, but he will do for now. I have a sheer top on, a matching bra underneath. The lack of food and the drugs have me at my smallest ever.

I look fit. Fuckable.

He comes over and starts talking to me. His voice sounds far away. I can't make out what he's saying. I smile and point to my ears and keep dancing. He offers to walk me home. I say, yes, why not?

We are kissing at the front door, and then we are inside. He asks if I want to go to bed; if he can stay over.

I can't get it together.

I can't shake the feeling.

His breath smells of vodka, his eyes small and serious. The creeping begins.

'Come on, Kat, I know you want to.'

He is trying to push me to the floor now, in my own living room, with the old velvet sofa and the old chairs and the old memories.

'Slow down, slow down …' I push him back a little, we fall on to the floor. The smell of the old carpet and our beloved dogs, Bonzo and Libby, fills me with memories of happier times.

He kisses me harder.

I kiss him back.

Trying to give in to him.

Trying to give in to me.

He kisses me harder, pressing his cock into me. It's hard and threatening. I push my hand against his chest, trying to get more comfortable, trying to see if he means it. He pushes me down, pressing me into the floor. His arm lies across my neck while his other hand frees his angry cock and grabs at my trousers.

I freeze. I don't move, I don't shout, I don't say stop. I freeze. The ghosts of Bob and Don and Joe O'Connor stand over me – reminding me that this is what I am made for. That this is my fault.

He rapes me.

After he stands up, his small eyes nervously watch me. Looking for any fight that might be left in me. I watch as he fastens his jeans, how they sag around his arse as he walks away.

This is what I am made for.

PART TWO

What Am I Made For?

The Rutland Centre

'KATRIONA, CAN YOU talk to me a little bit about your relationship with food? Have you ever had any issues with binge-eating or vomiting? Would you say you have a good relationship with food?'

He sees how fat you are.

I pause before answering. Taking a swift, sideways glance at my dad, who is sitting up straight in the sumptuous Georgian chair next to me.

He hasn't moved. Maybe he won't mention anything.

We are in the Rutland Centre. They are assessing me for 'treatment' for rehab. I am eighty-four days clean and sober: eighty-four days in my body, eighty-four days running to Narcotics Anonymous meetings, eighty-four days living with my mum and dad, eighty-four days ignoring it all, eighty-four days wanting to die.

'No ... no food issues really. I like the odd cake or two, as you can see from the size of my arse ...'

Why do I always try to make jokes?

'But no real issues?'

My dad coughs.

This nice, modest man, sitting behind his large mahogany desk, waits for my dad to talk.

He knows you are a liar.

The silence gets louder.

'Katriona, I'm not trying to hurt you here, you know that.'

My dad is looking at me. I face forward. Frozen. Willing him not to speak.

'Gerry, she has had issues with food over the years. Even in the past few weeks I've noticed her hiding or gorging on food. We thought it was just an early recovery thing, switching one thing for another. But there was stuff years ago – with food, I mean. She's been on a diet since she had her son. Before that, well, we had addiction issues, me and my wife ...'

Why is he using his posh voice?

'When she was small, there were some issues with food too, hiding in cupboards and eating.'

How does he know about that?

Nobody knows about that.

'Is this true, Katriona?'

Gerry looks me in the eye, his eyes gentle, his accent soft, and his care chips away at it. The secret.

'I wouldn't say it's a problem though. I'm not anorexic. Look at me! I just feel so hideous sometimes and so hungry for something that I have to fill myself. I'm not bulimic or anything. I just want to be the perfect size. I starve myself, then I eat loads because I'm starving, then I starve again. It isn't an "issue", though. All of my friends are the same – we all want to be skinny.'

I laugh.

I lie.

'That's totally OK. With your history and your experiences, it's totally OK. However, for you to come into the Rutland Centre, you must be ready to admit you have a problem. Ready to work on all your problems – whatever they are. In your case, you seem a little resistant to working on this problem ... maybe you don't realise it's an issue yet.'

The silence gets louder.

Is he waiting for me to fill it?

I can't tell him about this.

The food.

The hunger.

I don't even know what 'this' is.

I can't.

Trust.

The issues with drugs and drink are easier to admit: the using every day, the neglect of John, the men. It's easier to see that they were hurting me. But the food and the hunger and the obsession to shrink – that's deeper. It's so ingrained in me that to admit the problem could bring my whole life crashing down. If I don't have the dream of the perfect body, that thin destiny and the freedom of skinniness to aim for, then I have nothing.

These thoughts spin. He is speaking but I can't hear his words. I want the world to swallow me up.

'What I suggest is that you come and attend our Friday group meetings, here in the centre. That way we can see how you're progressing with things, with food and drugs. Does that sound OK?'

I nod along.

I can't talk.

I can't tell them this.

The decision to go into recovery was made for me. My mum and dad saw it, the cycle I was stuck in – men, drugs, parties, food, lies and pain. My parents wanted to help. To be forgiven.

They were clean, sober, doing better. They took John to Ireland and gave him security. Hugs. Food. Love. He started to shine. When I arrived for a rest and for some of his hugs, I saw him, his security. I wanted to be part of that.

I moved to Ireland on a whim; left behind the debts, the council house, the men, the parties. I thought that geography would heal me, but Ireland became the same Groundhog Day – men, drugs, parties, food, lies and pain.

My body hate increased with each day. Unable to shrink, to control, to stop myself from eating, I felt a deeper, darker shame than ever before. Sitting in piss-smelling pubs in Summerhill, Dublin 1, waiting for a line or a man to find me. Hating every part of me, constantly hungry. I dived into the darkest waters.

The cycle had come with me.

The cycle *was* me.

The only change was the accents and the locations. My radar

for unavailable men had travelled with me on the Stena Line from Holyhead to Dublin.

The hurt came too.

'It is late. Will we pack up for the night?'

He stood up out of my grandad's huge electric support chair. It sat in the corner of the tiny back room of their Clontarf house, a room swathed in books and newspapers and religious relics. On the small glass coffee table stood several AA books: *Daily Reflections, Just for Today, As Bill Sees It*. My dad's new paraphernalia – AA books and prayers.

An AA slogan stood beside them: 'One is too many, one thousand never enough.'

That still applied.

He had swapped the drink for AA meetings, AA books, a sponsor and sponsees. And even though I was glad he was sober, I resented it. Why then, when the hurt was so deep that he couldn't help me heal?

Something cracked.

'I can't do this any more, Dad,' I called out to him. 'Every day, I want to die.'

The hurt swam across his face; a tear, just one, escaped before he righted himself. Composed, he sat back in the chair. 'Do you want to talk about it, my Katriona?'

He hadn't called me that in so long.

Too long.

The floodgates opened. I started with Bob and the hurt. He flinched.

'You left me, Dad, you left me,' I cried. 'And then there was the drink, and when I had John – you made me leave.'

His hand reached for me, inviting my words, hearing me for the first and maybe the only time.

'And then there was Jace, his hands on me, his hate. I couldn't please him or you or me.'

His tears flowed then: no righting himself through that, no hiding. I couldn't watch him cry. If I saw his tears, I might've stopped. I couldn't stop. I needed to say it all.

'And then there were the men, all of the men, and the drugs and John, my beautiful John, who I tried so hard to be good for and to love and to stay home for – but there is this darkness in here.' I pointed to my heart, to where it all came from. 'I can't stop it now, and Ireland and you and the sober you and this house and Grandad and how good he is – I thought that would help me, but the darkness is here still, in here.'

He was sat beside me then. I didn't know how he moved seats or how he had his arms around me or how I hadn't flinched.

'I just want it all to stop, Dad ... please, Dad, help me to make it stop!'

That cold December night in 1999, I cried out for help. It felt as though recovery was an easier choice. It was that or death. Waking up every day hoping to die was no way to live.

It was the first, and the only, time that I ever told my dad the whole truth. I told him what I had done to myself, how the hunger had taken me towards the darkness.

How he had hurt me.

How I needed him.
How I needed her.
And he held me.
Softly.

He shared his sorrow with me. His regret. He said sorry, over and over again. And we cried, together. And then he shared how he had stopped drinking, how he had done it.

He spoke of AA and God and the programme and the meetings. His sponsor, a kind little man, who sold second-hand cups and saucers at Killester sales of work.

He said I could do it, that I could change too.

And here I am, three months later, being assessed for rehab when I'm not even sure what I am yet. Eighty-four days clean. Having thrown myself into recovery. Being a good girl. But am I an addict or am I just a child of two addicts or am I just hurt?

The decision to get clean, to stop partying, to stop drugging is easy. The meetings and a day recovery programme are helping with that. *One is too many*. I just need to stay away from the first one. That's easy. It's the other stuff that I can't cope with. It's the things that drugs have helped me with that I can't handle. The deep emptiness that I was escaping, the shame of the things I'd had done to me and, then, as my addiction progressed, the shame of the things I had done.

The drugs helped me to hide from myself. Who I really was. They masked the deeper hurt; they made it easier, and harder. I missed the obsession. The single-mindedness of drug use is intoxicating. One mission every day: get high, get more, get high.

This masks all other thoughts and feelings. Behind this drive lies a complex well of unresolved pain, some mine, some theirs, some his, some the world's. *One is too many.* Staying away from one means living in the world. The fear. The darkness that wakes up before me. That tells me everyone hates me; that they want to hurt me. The shake inside my heart. The constant feeling as though I need to go to the toilet.

I can't cope with being awake.

The recovery people see this. I have been in a day recovery programme run by Soilse. The good-doers and the do-gooders who work there suggest that I go to treatment. I have a medical card because I have been social welfare-dependent my whole life, so I can go there for free.

I say yes to everything.

I will try anything that helps.

Apart from giving up the food and the men.

I need those. For now.

'Katriona, we've decided that you're ready to come in to the Rutland Centre now. You've been doing great work.'

Gerry is smiling at me like I'm a good girl. I love being a good girl. It hasn't been hard to fool them. Talk to them about my obsession with drugs, intersperse it with some reference to my food obsession, my desire to binge, my body hate. Tell them some half-truths, while keeping the full truth to myself.

I am rotating between starving and bingeing nearly every other day. I don't tell them that. I tell them I *want* to starve myself. I *want* to binge. I don't say 'I *am* starving myself', 'I *am* bingeing'. I'm not ready for that.

'OK, OK, Monday ... this Monday ... I'll need to get sorted. Wow, Monday ... I'm scared.'

I say too much.

Gerry smiles at me, with care and heart. He says, 'It's normal to be scared.' My face burns with embarrassment. I didn't mean to say I was scared.

'Katriona, this is your last day of group, your last day in the Rutland Centre, and we wanted to go around and get the group to give you some feedback before you leave. Would that be OK with you?'

Paul pushes his long salt-and-pepper hair behind his ears as he talks; his gentle voice and his blue gaze still make me nervous.

I nod. No words can hide the tears about to spill over. I don't know how I'm going to cope on the outside.

The past six weeks have been a roller-coaster. I've learned new rules, new food rules, new words: denial, repression, trauma-response, regression-hurt, so much hurt. I've cried for everyone I have ever been.

And I have no idea who I am now.

Every idea I had of myself has been challenged in group. I've been taken apart by Paul and Tammy, my therapists in the Rutland Centre, then built back up by them. I've been told off. Told I'm good. Told I'm bad. Hurt. Hammered. Hugged. Treatment has made me question everything I ever knew about me, my life, my choices and my hopes.

And I've learned new food rules. The therapists say I'm a food addict. I am diagnosed. Officially. Food addict Katriona. Food Addicts Anonymous says no sugar, flour or wheat for us food addicts. They say these foods are triggers for us addicts. We must avoid them. Stay clean from them. Treat them like drugs. *One drug is too many, one thousand never enough.* I have new food things to avoid. New diet rules. I like the control of this regime. I like the ribs I can see in the mirror, the way I fit into my size twelve jeans comfortably.

I don't tell them this.

I pretend I'm recovering; I know the words now. Shape-shifting is easy when you have no foundation. I can be whatever they want, say whatever they need – I have a lifetime's experience of this. Sometimes, I even believe the words myself.

I'm happy to give up drugs, to stop the parties, to talk about them in meetings, to get a sponsor, to share this part of me and my issues.

But the food ... and the men? I'm going to keep them for myself. These go deeper than drugs and parties and drink. They fill a hunger in me that existed way before I could speak or think or dream. The physical hunger from my childhood, the emotional hunger from being neglected as a child, will not be healed in a six-week treatment slot. They are me, I am them; and, without the search for both, I fear I will be nothing.

The idea that I will be healed through the perfect diet, the ideal shape and a man who loves me, is stronger than anything else – and is the hardest thing to share. There is no way I'm letting them go – not yet!

Jean points to the little door on the right-hand side of the darkly lit hallway. We are in the After Care Recovery Group (ACRG), a restored tenement building at the Five Lamps in Dublin's north inner city. The ACRG holds a drug-free structured day programme supporting people recovering from drug and alcohol addiction. I've been in the day programme for three months. I started straight after I finished the Rutland Centre and Soilse. It's part of the Community Employment Scheme, so I get to keep my benefits and rent supports, and I get an extra few bob in my pocket to live. We do group work, therapy, art and singing, and we have the craic. There are eight of us on the programme.

I have been seeing their therapist, Jean, for the past few months, talking about my 'issues' with men, telling him about my childhood, my parents. Now that I'm clean and recovering, all the past is bubbling underneath the surface.

He suggested a few weeks ago that we have a family session. That my mum and dad, who are both still in recovery themselves, come in for a session with me.

They want to. They know how hurt I am. They see their mess staring them in the face every day that they look at me and my siblings.

My dad is more enthusiastic than my mum. She knows the

hurt. My dad thinks he is great; he thinks he's untouchable; that he has been a great dad and nothing is wrong.

'Hi ...'

My voice doesn't even sound familiar to me. I am sitting on the comfy chair. It's a red, therapy-style chair with a tall back. There are two wooden chairs from the kitchen on the left of me and then Jean's chair – a swivelling office chair. He has added a flowery cushion for extra padding underneath him. The dark-grey and pink flowers sit in juxtaposition, offering hardness and softness in equal measure.

'Please sit.'

Jean's voice sounds a bit posher now that he's talking to my parents. *Why is he acting differently?*

'OK, OK, thank you for agreeing to come here today. I know from Katriona that you have both been really supportive of her recovery, looking after John for her while she was in treatment and stepping in to support her with her bills and her life.'

My dad's shoulders straighten a little. He loves to be told how great he is.

'It's nothing we wouldn't do for any of the kids. We want Katriona to have a good life.'

My dad is using his posh voice too. What is going on with these two?

My mum is shrinking into the chair. I can see her disappearing into herself.

'Mum, are you OK?'

She smiles at me, tears brimming in her eyes. She knows what's coming.

'Is it OK if we use first names, Tilly and Tony? Is that OK?'

My dad nods, shoulders fixed now. He knows what's coming.

'So Katriona has been doing so much great work on herself this last while, and she is really, really coming on. We've been doing some inner child work these last few weeks ...' *(Cringe.)*

'... and while I know you all have done great work towards healing, and, Tony, you participated in her rehab programme, there are some things that I thought would be helpful for Katriona to be able to say to you both. Especially since Tilly ...'

She looks up.

'... Tilly, you were not able to participate in the Rutland Centre's concerned-person programme because of your own addiction issues at the time.'

'That's right,' my dad interjects. 'Tilly was in a relapse then and they felt it better she wasn't there, so I attended all of the sessions.'

She slides further into herself.

I don't think I should do this.

I don't think she should do this.

'How are you both feeling about being here?'

My dad nods enthusiastically. He is confident in every situation. His middle-class upbringing and his deep delusion of grandeur convince him he can con his way out of anything. My mum doesn't look up from her hands.

'I just want Katriona to know I love her.' She whispers this. My heart jumps. She looks at me. I see her.

All of her.

All of me.

Small me and small her are the same person.

I am trying my best to get off that roundabout.

She is stuck on it.

'That's a lovely way to start this session: with love. I know from the work we've done here that there is a deep love in your family. Katriona talks of the love she has for you and the support you've given her to get to where she is now. But there are some things unsaid for her and we were wondering – Katriona and I, that is – would it be OK if she read out a letter she has written to you both?'

I look at Jean. He is about thirty-five or maybe forty. He's wearing a grey Aran-knit cardigan over his blue corduroy shirt. The cardigan is fitted, almost too small. Square black glasses frame his face. A salt-and-pepper beard. Small, tight frame, blue jeans and Adidas runners. His socks are pink. The only part of him that stands out.

I am so happy he's speaking for me now. My mouth is dry. My hands sweat; I hold them tightly underneath my thighs.

I don't think I should do this.

We practised this last week, Jean and I. We walked through the session: what he would say to them, where they would sit, how he would introduce the letter. He has followed the script exactly.

I DON'T THINK I SHOULD DO THIS.

They both nod. I open the A4 pages I have been grasping under my thighs. I've read the letter four times to Jean in recent weeks and have not got to the end without crying. I hope I can hold it together now, especially with them here.

'OK, Katriona, whenever you're ready, we're ready.'

He gives me a soft, encouraging smile. Since I started with Jean, I have had a recurring conversation about wanting an apology. I can't move on without it. The hurt. The lies. The neglect. All of it, I want it acknowledged.

This is it.

This is my time.

Dear Mum and Dad,

I want to start by saying thank you. This last year, I have needed you, and you have stepped up. You have loved me and John. You have given me somewhere to start again from. I am so grateful to you both. I look at the way you love our John, and I am so grateful. My life wouldn't be here without your support. I know it is hard work, and I know I can be hard work. I appreciate you for the support and patience. Even though we have a lot of peace now, there is still a lot of hurt in me that I find it hard to talk to you about. When I try to, it comes out wrong, and we end up fighting. I thought writing it down might help. Reading it might help.

Since going into treatment and coming into therapy, I have been haunted by some of the things we went through as kids. Some of the things that I went through. The more I try to forget, the more I think about things. It's like I'm stuck. I can't get away from the sadness of it all. I'm haunted. Watching you both dying in front of me. Having no food, having no love, feeling scared all the time – it has left me marked. Hungry for something, hungry for something that doesn't exist: to feel connected, loved, safe, like my body is OK, whole. I think the real problem, the thing that lies beneath it all, is that I don't know if you ever really loved me. If I was ever enough for you both.

I keep thinking about the little girl I was. The beautiful little girl who fought for herself, who tried so hard to tell you to be better. I see her when I close my eyes. Being brave enough to shout, to tell you that I was scared. That I was being hurt.

I think about her not being heard. Lying awake at night, scared that she wouldn't survive, or, worse still, scared that YOU wouldn't survive. That worry, that girl, she is here; she is behind me, ahead of me, beside me and inside me – hiding. Searching for something. I know you see it too, all the men I choose, the crazy diets, the drive for something. You try to stop me, to help, but she won't listen to you now. She is too hurt to even hear you now.

She wasn't always like this, though. Mum, you know, you remember. I think you know why! Maybe if we talk about it, it will get easier for me and for you. Maybe we can move on.

Mum, do you ever think about that day in the lift, after we had left Bob's flat in Hillfields? I think about how I had been so brave. How I told you he was hurting me. His body squashing all the hope out of me. And I see you standing there, telling me that he had raped you too, as if your pain was a trade-off for mine. As if we were equal. As if we were in this mess together. Me, a seven-year-old child asking her mum to protect her; you, my mum, ignoring my cries for safety. You made me feel we were comrades in this, like my hurt wasn't valuable. I don't know if you know this, but it took all my strength to ask you to save me, and when you did nothing, it destroyed me.

Did you already know?
Was my body easier to give than yours?
Was I a sacrifice?
My world broke that day, the day you didn't save me. I knew then that no one was ever going to come for me.

I have been stuck in that lift since then. Alone. Waiting for my mum to come and open the doors and tell me it's OK, that I did the right thing; waiting for her to say, 'I'm here for you!'

I know we can't go back, but I want you to know how much that hurt me. How I have no value, how I start from minus in all my relationships, how I trust no one, how it all started there.

And, Dad, when you came home from prison, all clean and fresh, with no drugs in your system, you acted like you were the saviour. You acted like you could rescue us all.

You came home and shouted at Mum for prostituting herself, for doing what she had to do to feed her habit and yours. You got rid of Bob, but you never said anything to me. You didn't tell me that it wasn't my fault. You never tried to help. We moved house, to Stoney Stanton Road, and you told us all you had changed. That life was going to be better.

But you lied. You always lied.

You went and did more crime and hurt Mum over and over again. And when she eventually left you, when she went to try to get herself together, you used me as your ally, telling me she had cheated on you, that she was with some man called Simon. Making me hate her more than I already did. I would ignore her in the street. Pretend she didn't live. Thinking always that she had chosen another man over me again. Only to discover years later that it was all lies. You had lied. That, in fact, you had cheated, you had made her leave. I felt like a pawn in your game. I FEEL like a pawn in your game.

As a girl, I tried so hard to get you to love me, Dad. I changed my hair, my smile, my voice. I danced, played sport, read, followed you, kept quiet, just so you would love me. And you didn't or wouldn't or couldn't and now, as a woman, I am still trying to change myself. Still striving to be different, to be better. I don't know how to stop. And with you, I still do it sometimes.

And you still forget that I am your daughter, your little girl. You drag me into your arguments like I'm a referee, forgetting that I am your daughter, your child. I can't be in the middle any more. I can't take the lies and the hurt. I need to have peace for me. And for little me. And for our John – he deserves better than all of us!

I need to be able to rescue myself, and I want you to respect me and take responsibility for your own mess. I can't carry yours and mine any more – it's too heavy. I want to know if you are sorry. Really sorry. I think saying this and hearing it might help me. I didn't deserve the hurt I felt. I don't deserve it. I know that now. There is still a part of me that still believes I did something wrong. That I wasn't good enough or kind enough or nice enough. That, if I had changed, you would have loved me.

Thank you for being here for me, and please know I say all this with love.

Katriona

Tears roll down my face. I don't want to look up. I can't look up. To see the hurt. Or anger.

My mum leans forward, her face underneath mine. Looking up into my eyes.

'I am so sorry for what I did to you. Never a day goes by when I don't regret all of it. All of you. The kids. The mess. I am sorry.'

She means it. Her eyes wide open and her heart.

I feel nothing.

I look at her face. Waiting for the relief to rush in. For the big shift. For her sorry to mean something. Hadn't this been the thing I had wanted? Needed? Hadn't sorry been the answer to what was wrong with me?

But I feel nothing.

I look at my dad. His face stony. Eyes alert. He glances from Jean to me.

'I don't know how many more times I can say I'm sorry, my Katriona. Recovery has taught me to take responsibility. The eighth step – make a list of all the people you've harmed; ninth step – make amends where possible. I'm trying every day to make amends to you. By being here for you and John, I am *showing* you how sorry I am.'

He's saying the words, but they are shallow. Sorry means nothing without action. Sorry *is* action.

I look at Jean, hoping he will intervene, hoping he sees Dad for what he is. Empty. Hollow. Dad's tone tells me he is annoyed with me for saying this here.

'Katriona, what you have done today is very, very brave.' Jean speaks now. 'That little girl you speak of can be very, very proud of herself.'

My mum reaches for my hand. She tries again to catch my eye, but I can't look at her. I am so disappointed. I thought the words would fix me. I thought hearing her take responsibility for my pain would relieve it, would validate me, would make me feel less ashamed, less hurt, less rubbed out.

I thought the lift door would open, and out would step a new me – vindicated, less hurt, less scared. I have never been more wrong. Whatever is wrong with me is in me, and it's going to take an awful lot of work for me to heal.

The lift door is still shut, and I am still trapped inside.

Dylan

'Did you get the present I sent you?'

I look over at him, confused. Dylan has been my friend for four months. He is the kindest, sweetest guy I know. He is thirty-one; I am twenty-three. He has his shit together. He works snagging on building sites. He has a car. He has a job. He has a life.

'No – what present?'

I have no idea what he's talking about. We're sitting in my flat in the heart of north inner-city Dublin. I moved in a month ago, only next door from where John and I had lived in a one-room bedsit. Every night, I would pull out a springy little silver fold-out bed to let him fall asleep, moving him on to the big green three-seater when I was ready to settle down on the fold-out bed myself.

I loved the bedsit. I had painted the walls yellow myself and stencilled music notes in lilac around the top. That was the first home I had decorated myself. Rehab a year before and recovery set in motion a desire to build our home. To grow roots. The music notes reflected my mindset. New hummings.

'I have no idea what you're talking about, Dylan ... what present?'

'Your phone?' He raises his eyebrow as he says it, and then it clicks.

'Did you top me up again? I knew my credit was lasting for ages ... Jesus, Dylan, you don't have to do that. I'm managing better. It's just hard, being on my own, on my book. I struggle, but you didn't have to!' (The 'book' is my social-welfare benefits book.)

'I want to help. Sure, I have it to give, don't I? And if you have no credit, how will I call you?'

He is smiling with his heart and his eyes. Helping me helps him. I can see it there in his face. His feelings.

I look away.

He is too nice for me. Too good. I don't know how to handle this.

'Do you want tea?'

I stand and break his stare. I don't want him to say it to me. To tell me. I'm not ready for this to end. The kindness, the care. It feels like I am something.

'Yes, go on, then. It's getting late for me. I have work early, so just a quick one.'

John is asleep in the bedroom, curled up in our double bed. He is getting bigger and brighter by the day, he's seven now. He's settling into the new flat. Nothing much has changed for him. His school, O'Connell's, is still only at the end of our road. His friends, Ciaran, Dean and Micka, call for him every day and he heads out with his ball. New me, clean me, has added a brightness to him. He doesn't run in as much now to check I'm still here. He knows I'm here. He is starting to trust it.

Going into treatment and leaving him with my mum and dad for six weeks really affected him. He cried at every visit for me to come home. In the past four years, he has lost me and his dad, but this new flat and my recovery are easing things. He is lighter; brighter. He even said something last week that surprised me. We were sitting watching TV, eating our staple dinner – chicken nuggets and oven chips – and he looked at me, his grey-green eyes concerned.

'Ma?' My heart raced a little at his tone.

Be open, be open. He needs you.

'Yes, son?' I look him in the eye as I turn the TV down. 'How can I help you?' I say in a fake posh accent. I don't know why I feel the need to reduce the tension building in me.

'I wouldn't mind if you got yourself a friend – well, a boyfriend ... if you wanted to ...'

His voice trails off as he notices my eyebrows rising. This is not what I was expecting at all.

Be open, be open. He needs you.

'Wow! Thank you for telling me that ... I'll keep my eyes open for one!' I wink at him as I say it, letting him know it's OK for him to talk to me. 'Would you like us to have a man around the place, son?'

He hesitates. 'I don't know ... but I really like your friend Anthony. Any time he comes to visit, he plays the PlayStation with me, and he's better than me at FIFA.'

I start to laugh. My seven-year-old is trying to set me up with Anthony, one of my many recovery pals.

'Well, I'll definitely keep him in mind when I start my search, son. I'm glad you feel you can say this. I really like you talking to me about how you feel.'

His little face flushes and my heart opens an inch wider.

'You know you're the real love of my life, though!'

I squeeze his leg as I say this. He is the love of my life. I am not lying. He is the most beautiful boy in the world.

Sweat pools at the bottom of my back. The jeans are still too tight. Lying flat on my bed, I pull the button together – one last try. I breathe in, I hold it and the zip closes. I stand. The mirror tells me the truth. The joy of them fitting is fleeting. A roll of fat hangs there, a shadow clear to anyone who looks close enough. Even when I'm wearing a loose Adidas jacket, the trained eye would see the overhang.

But I am nearly there.

I am nearly there.

These are my 'skinny jeans' – my measure, my indicator, my achievement barometer. They didn't fit last year before the Rutland Centre. Those size twelve TopShop jeans stored in the back of the large wooden wardrobe in my little flat are what I use to gauge how I'm doing, how my body is doing. I try them on every week, snaking them around my legs, pulling everything into them, hoping I've been good enough. That I will feel it. Those skinny jeans are my goal.

Fancy going to a meeting with me later?

I press 'send' on WhatsApp before I can even think about it.

I need a distraction.

He replies immediately. *Yes, I'll collect you at seven – Meath Street suit?*

I send *Yes* and call my dad to check what time he's collecting John for the weekend.

It feels as though I'm spending most of my spare time with Dylan now. Amanda, my NA sponsor, questioned me yesterday.

'What's going on with you and that fella in the green car? Is his name Dan?'

'Dylan? Oh, nothing. We're just friends.'

She looked at me, waiting for the next part.

'Honestly, there's nothing going on; we're friends, recovery friends.'

'You know he fancies you; you'd have to be blind not to see it. No man spends that much time with someone without having some kind of intention. And you are gorgeous.'

She smiled her warm smile. Amanda never fails to remind me I am beautiful and worthy and clever. Her mantra for me is 'brains to burn' and 'beautiful'. She is one of the only women I have told it all to. Everything. And she wants to love me until I am better. And protect me. And tell me off when I go wrong. That is what she is doing now.

'Ah, Mandy, stop! I am definitely not gorgeous. My arse is growing bigger by the day. I am a single parent, with no job and no prospects – plus, I don't like him like that.'

She looked at me – hard.

'Katriona, if he is into you and you're not into him, then tell him. He's a nice guy. He gets you credit. He seems to be a good person – don't string him along. We're not supposed to be hurting people while we're in recovery, ourselves included in that.'

'Mandy, stop.' My voice went up a notch. 'We're friends, he knows that ... Besides, if he thinks there's more to it, then that's his fault, not mine. I've never said I want to be with him – or that I would.'

'It's not what you say, it's what you do. Don't use him. It isn't nice.'

She cut me to the core. Was I using this lovely man? I knew I was relying on him more and more for company. And, if I was being completely honest with myself, I knew somewhere deep down that he fancied me. That he was holding out hope that we would be together. But that wasn't my fault. I wasn't giving him any false hope.

The reality of the situation was that I *was* using him. Like Jeff, Darren and Paul before him, Dylan was standing in a long line of nice men, decent men, men who were emotionally available, who I could not, or would not, allow myself to be with. These were men I allowed to hang around my life. Men I let buy me credit or give me lifts or sit in with me when I was lonely and watch films when John was in bed. Men who lent me the odd twenty quid to get me through to pay day. Men who never let me pay them back.

These nice men, good men, were not the men for me. They were my fallbacks. My stopgaps. The men I would lean on after being used or fucked over by one of the many emotionally unavailable men I was attracted to. They were the men in the wings, the ones who liked me for me, who laughed at my jokes, who saw me mother my son with love and grace, who wanted to help me build my life, who wanted to help me grow and see me be better.

But I wouldn't see them.

Or I couldn't see them.

'Katriona, I can't keep doing this. I'm thirty-one years old. I have a daughter, a life, and I want to share it with someone. I'm spending all my time with you, hoping that you'll see me, that you'll be ready for us to start something. I know you know this too. Don't look away. We need to talk about this.'

Dylan has finally said it. My heart hurts for this man. He is everything I should want: kind, good, handsome, responsible, ambitious. More than all of that, he loves me for who I am. I cried to him. Told him my fears, about my dad, the fear of my dad leaving me. He has seen John and knows we come together, a twosome, forever.

'You need to decide what you want.' His eyes are angry now, my silence frustrating.

'Dylan, I do want you, like you. I'm so scared, that's all. I've been so hurt ...'

His hand reaches for my hand. The heat from it burns me.

There is sweat in his palms.

It disgusts me.

'I know you have. I understand. But I want someone to be with me. I want you.'

I lean towards him. Maybe if I kiss him, it will stop him asking.

Maybe if I kiss him, he will stop talking about this.

He almost pounces at me. His mouth opens on mine, saliva everywhere. I feel as if I've put my face into the washing machine. His desire for me explodes so hard on my face that I am left aghast. And soaking wet from his spit.

He pulls back from me, breathless.

'I'm so glad you're into this too ... Let's go on a date, tomorrow night – the theatre, you love the theatre.'

As he looks away, I wipe the back of my hand across my mouth. How can he think that that much spit on someone's face is normal? I feel sick to my stomach.

'Yes, that would be lovely. I'll ask my dad to babysit John.'

I stand up from the chair to let him know that it's time for him to go. He looks confused but stands too. 'I thought he was at your dad's for the weekend.'

It's Friday evening now and he's planning for us to go on our 'date' tomorrow, assuming John is gone for the weekend, as he is most weekends.

'Oh, did I not mention it? He has a match Sunday in Fairview, so I said I would bring him home tomorrow night – make it easier to get him there from here, rather than him coming from Donabate. I am sure my dad won't mind, though. I'll text him first thing tomorrow.'

'OK, great.'

I walk him to the door. He looks different now. Lighter. He is smiling from the inside out.

I feel myself sinking.

He leans in for another kiss. This time I peck him on the lips. I'm not getting soaked again!

'I'll see you tomorrow. I'll text you the details of the play – do you mind where we go?'

'No ... no, you pick. I'm sure I will love it.'

I can tell from the back of his head that he is smiling as he walks away. I close the door and lean on the back of it.

You can't even let a nice man love you!

I force my legs into the holes, tugging the waistband up. It feels easier. No sweat this week. I pull the button and its hole together. No need to lie down this time. I've been so good all week, keeping on my 'plan' – no sugar, flour or wheat – and low calories. Even though I'm not supposed to be thinking about calories, I am. I can't stop it. It's ingrained.

The button closes. Easily.

But the mirror tells the truth.

The joy of fitting into my 'skinny jeans' fills me, fleetingly. It leaves as quickly as it arrives. The side-on angle reveals that overhang again, the loose skin from my baby body. It sickens me. My body is constantly failing me.

Why are you not answering me? It's been a week now. Are you OK?

It's a WhatsApp from Dylan.

Me: *Sorry ... I haven't been well.* (This is a lie.) *I'll be in touch when I'm feeling better.*

Dylan: *OK.*

I am ghosting him. This is my way with good men. Hang out. Get them to like me. Know they like me. Try to keep them in the friend zone. They tell me they like me, want me, can help me, will save me. I ghost them. I don't know what is worse, being used or using men.

It's a pendulum.

I am swinging on it.

Tick-tock.

Tick-tock.

Used – use.

Used – use.

Tick-tock.

None of this is happening consciously. Afterwards is always where I see what has happened. After I have been fucked.

Or after I have fucked someone over.

Tick-tock.

Tick-tock.

Used – use.

Used – use.

I Am Normal After All

'STAY RIGHT THERE.' He is looking at me closely. His Scottish accent is gorgeous. It melts me. We are in his little flat in Glasgow. I have flown over for the weekend. I lie naked in his bed. Covering my face.

'Take your hand away from your face.'

I slowly move my hand. Notice my huge tits falling to the left and right of my chest. My stretch marks from John: faded silver lines, the marks of love and life.

'Look at yourself!' He is strong now in his voice.

'Will you stop!' I laugh.

'Look at yourself, I mean it! You're fucking beautiful.'

I feel sick.

I look down at myself. Thank God for fake tan. It works wonders. I look at my toes, my toned legs, my hairy fanny (I'm not shaving for anyone)! I take it all in – my belly, boobs, arms. Sick to my stomach. Disgusted by the sight of me. The hang of my skin, the fat on my thighs – hurt by the truth of my body.

He kneels over me and touches my feet, real slow. He moves his hand up my leg. Softy touching and kissing me. I close my eyes. I have never been with a man like him before. I am twenty-four years old; I am sober nearly two years. I am healing but this ... this is too much.

He is in recovery too. I met him at a convention in Ireland; he's a friend of a friend. We met, talked for hours, then went back to mine and had great, passionate sex. That was three months ago, and we've been texting ever since.

Passionate, sexual texts.

I don't know a lot about him, other than that he is very sexual. We text on his terms. I've tried talking to him about his life, his interests, his hopes, but mostly he turns the conversation to sex. My dad has John, and I flew into Glasgow to see him this morning. I was terrified and excited in equal measure. Could he be the one?

He met me at the airport with a kiss and a hug.

Then, there was nothing but silence on the drive to his flat. I didn't know how to be without the screen to hide behind. Being sober and being with men is still new. And hard. Amanda told me not to come. She says I need a break from men. She says I am not good at choosing them. She says I need to work on me. That's OK for her to say when she has a fella.

I need to find someone to love me. This hunger runs deep.

I booked the trip without telling her. I'm a grown-ass woman, for fuck's sake, why can't I do what I want?

As we pulled up outside the little brown block of flats, my heart skipped. He reached over to me, grabbed my hand and stared at me. 'Don't worry, I'm not going to hurt you!' He laughed, and my heart raced.

His hand slides slowly between my legs and I flinch again; he leans forward and kisses me. I respond, kissing him gently. His hand finds my soft spot and begins to slowly move in circular motions. I have never had someone touch me like this, so slowly, so softly. He is watching my face, my responses. I breathe. Raggedly.

'I'm not going to hurt you,' he whispers. A tear escapes my eye. He smiles. My breathing speeds up as he rubs me a little harder, a little faster. I put my arm across my face; he tries to move it, but I pull back and keep strong. If this is going to happen, I cannot watch him watching me. He moves between my legs, his face by my knees, kissing me one leg at a time. My breath comes faster. He reaches where I meet and touches his tongue against me.

And I let out a long sigh.

The sigh of a lifetime. He knows what he's doing. He cares. He doesn't rush. He's watching my face as he moves his tongue, exploring me. My toes feel the fire of my climax; it moves up my heels, my calves, my thighs. I am going to come. I try to stop it; to move him, I buck my hips – he pushes me down, gently. He continues to focus on my softest spot. I lie back and let it unfold. All of me unravels on the bed. The explosion at every nerve-ending sends a guttural sound through my throat and out of my mouth. I orgasm, for the first time at the hands of someone else. I open my eyes and tears roll down my cheeks. I can't stop the outpour. The gratitude. The relief. I have never orgasmed at the hand of a man before. I've never been able to 'let go', to be present in my body long enough to come. I thought I was broken, that my body had been stolen from me. That I would never be able to let someone touch me until I reached pleasure. But I am not completely broken.

They didn't take everything from me.

When the tears have stopped, I lie there, ashamed of having revealed everything to him. He strokes my face. My eyes. My neck. He kisses me softly. It's then that I notice his erection. Conscious that I have not 'done' anything for him, to him, I try to get up, to move over to him, to take my turn in pleasing him.

'Stay there, rest ... there's plenty of time for me.'

I can't believe this is real. Is he the man I have always dreamed of?

The tears start to roll again; this time I roll over and hide them from him. I'm here for a weekend of 'fun'. He's not going to want to hear my deepest, darkest fears. He won't want me if I start telling him about my history of abuse, about my parents who never loved me, about the many men I let fuck me without ever even trying to enjoy myself. Instead, I turn away from him, curl into the foetal position and let the silent tears flow.

I am not broken.

I am not broken.

'So, are you going to let me touch you too or what?'

I've been here for two nights, and I have had three orgasms and several near-misses. He loves making me come. It's his thing. I've gone from being a woman who could never come for a man, to his orgasm machine.

'I'm fine like this – are you not enjoying yourself?'

'Yes, I'm having a great time, but it feels pretty one-sided – me getting all the action and then you not letting me touch you or get you off.'

He laughs and kisses me. 'I get off watching you get off!'

It's Sunday morning, and I am due to fly home at 4pm. We've spent most of the weekend in bed, some of it in his living room eating and watching TV. I had hoped we might take some romantic trips around Glasgow, might go out for a nice meal, visit some friends of his. Instead, we've been holed up in his maisonette, eating or coming – me coming, that is.

'Don't you like being touched?' I say this using my best sexy voice, putting my hand on his thigh, gently stroking it with my nails. He lets me move my hand up to his cock. It's hard. 'I could help you out with this, you know.'

I'm trying to be as sexy and playful as I can. I have never been with a man who didn't put his own erection first. I've never been with a man who wasn't driven by his own desire to come.

He looks at me and kisses me.

'Mmmmmmm,' I reply to his kiss.

He flips me on to my stomach and pulls me on to my knees. He enters me slowly from behind, pushing my head down into the pillow. He doesn't hurt me, but the shock of him entering me and the position change make it hard for me to get focused on what is happening. He has gone from wanting to control me and my body to now controlling how we fuck and how he comes. I feel like I'm not even there with him. Like he is in charge, and I am just an instrument.

Tick-tock.

Tick-tock.

Used – use.

Used – use.

He comes, and we flop down on the bed. I lie next to him. The tears flow again, silently. I weep for myself. And for him. He may know how to make me come, he may have taught me that my body isn't broken, but he is as far away from me as any of the other men who have used me or hurt me. He is incapable of letting go. He is closed. He needs to be in control, always.

I turn to look at him. He is smoking a rollie, one of the things I really don't like about him. I watch him. Really look at him. I don't even think he's good-looking; don't even like the way he acts. I don't even respect him or his life. He lives in a grotty old council flat, with no real job or ambition. I lie there thinking about all the unavailable men I've given myself to, and how every time I think this one is different ... how even this time, with him, flying to Glasgow for something or someone different, it feels the same.

A thought enters my mind. A new thought. One I have hidden from. One I heard in rehab, one my sponsor says to me after every broken romance.

Maybe you need to take a break from men.

Whack-a-Mole

IT'S RAINING AGAIN. Every single day feels dull. Empty.

'Come on, John! Let's go, let's go! It's time for school – if we don't go now, we'll be late.'

O'Connell Primary School is only at the bottom of the road, but I am still late every day. I can't even get organised enough to complete a five-minute walk to school.

I have no time to put a face on or do my hair. A hun bun on the top of the head will have to do. Who's looking anyway?

'Ma, Ma, look, look, I got the David Beckham card ... Ma, Ma, look!'

Every morning, I let him run down to Bennie's, the local newsagents, to pick up a pack of football cards for his collection. He is so happy, our John. My being in recovery suits him more than it suits me. Without the drugs, the drink, the madness, I feel out of control.

The dark clouds swirl most days. The noise in my head about my body and food is dampening everything. I can't look in the mirror. I hate what I see. My weight fluctuates by stones, not pounds.

Binge then starve. Binge then starve. Constantly searching for the new solution to what is wrong with my body. All my friends are the same: we talk about our bodies as if they are vessels of shame.

The darkness it brings is overpowering. It threatens to completely engulf us both – John and me. My only light is him. And sometimes the noise is so loud, I can't even concentrate on that.

John is waving the David Beckham card. 'Ma, ma, look!'

'Great, son ... you know I was asked out on a date by him once?'

He eyes me suspiciously. No flies on him.

'What? No way ... when?' He hesitates, and I start to laugh hard.

'No, son, I wish. I wish, ha-ha. We'd be living in a big mansion if that was the case.'

We wouldn't be living in a one-bedroom flat in the middle of Summerhill if I were married to David Beckham, I think.

'I don't care, Ma. I love our little flat – it's cosy, and we get to snuggle every night.' His love for me never wavers, even though I have let him down so many times; he still sees the light in me. That guilt comes in waves.

He's right. We do have to snuggle in every night – not by choice. Our flat on North Great Charles Street is small; having only one bedroom means we share a bed. He loves these nights. Feeling me close. No worrying that I won't be there in the morning.

'Come on, son. Let's try to get there on time today.'

He grabs my hand as we walk out into the rain. If it weren't for him, I don't know where I would be.

After dropping him off at school, I have to make a decision: What to do with my day? Where to go? Will I call in to Amanda, my friend and sponsor, who lives in Liberty House? Will I pop in to Darragh, a recovery pal who lives on Buckingham Street? Or head back to the house for some daytime TV?

I am clean, yet every decision, every movement, feels as though it's being made on unstable ground. My body isn't my own. I shake, for no reason; have a constant feeling like I need the toilet. I have accidents. I can't manage my emotional responses. Swaying between angry and sad all day, every day.

The only space I get is when I am in a man obsession. When some unavailable man has become the centre of my focus, I am stuck. In a loop. I'm either hurting, aching for something long lost, or I'm chasing something or someone who is unavailable. My stint in rehab a year or so ago taught me not to trust myself in any situation. To question everything. To doubt my natural responses. It showed me again and again that I am a failure. I hurt people. My family, friends, son, myself. The instability that I had going in there is ten times worse now. I don't trust myself, my instincts or my body; my body is not my own. It belongs to WeightWatchers and Slimming World, and the women I compare myself to constantly. Every morsel of food comes with pounds of shame. Nothing is safe, nothing is nutritious, everything threatens my body – its shape, my size. The food noise is so loud, and the loneliness so deafening, that I feel on the edge – constantly. I am about to crack open. Die.

Being in recovery is like playing a game of whack-a-mole. When you get one thing under control, another thing pops up. The hunger that drives my addiction starts attaching itself to anything that feels good, or bad.

Giving up drugs and drink means that the other issues, other drives, the hunger for connection and achievement, have got bigger. The desire to achieve something, to be something, to escape the here and now, to feel good about myself – it beats away in the background of everything. A hum. The soundtrack of my life. Yearning, discontent, loneliness, hunger – it underpins all things. I swing from one thing to another, always followed by the noise. *You are not enough, your body is not enough.*

Going to recovery meetings has heightened this; it has given me new knowledge; being in 'the rooms' with other addicts, listening to them share their issues, listening to them talk about their own versions of whack-a-mole, has educated me.

Their experience of recovery begins to seep into me. Every person who shares their struggle with food, sex or gambling gives me insight into myself. Their learning becomes my learning. It makes me question everything. Am I overeating? Am I being honest? I hear people talk about their obsessions to escape pain; their drive to eat, to drink, to have sex, to hurt. I start to learn from their experiences, as well as my own.

I start to learn about what is wrong with me. What my problems are.

With every step I take towards the light, I become more aware of the darkness within me. I start to have good thoughts and good feelings.

Small reflections about my choices.

Maybe you shouldn't have sex with people who don't respect you.

Maybe you should ask your sponsor for help.

Maybe you can be happy.

These glimmers grow with every day that I stay clean and sober. Every meeting I go to provides words of wisdom. And, even though I am still hurting myself, I am becoming aware. My spirit is awakening. For so many years, I had just acted. Reacted. I have never decided what I'm doing or where I'm going. It's been decided for me by the dark clouds, by the people in my life, by the hurt. In recovery, this begins to change.

And every day of being clean, the pain of knowing that I have to change gets worse. Recovery isn't about giving up the drugs or drink. In some ways, stopping drugs and drink is the easy part. Staying stopped is the hard part.

Doing the work and staying away from the first drug or drink requires a complete transformation. The longer I'm clean, the more I understand how much I need to transform. I recognise more parts of my life that need healing. Sobriety is only the tip of the iceberg; underneath is where the real work has to happen.

Learning to be honest – ruthlessly honest – with myself, saying no to the hurt, staying positive, stopping the lies, living honestly, being a good mam – these are the remedies. Drugs, drink, men, food, sex – they are only the symptoms of my deeper issues.

The good people in recovery, the ones who shine brightest, tell me what I need to do. They say: 'Stop shagging, stop fooding, stop stealing, stop shopping – feel everything, find love, find peace.'

They make it sound so easy. As if I can just choose to be better, to be good to myself, to be healed. And I do try. I go to the meetings. I get a sponsor. I meditate. I pray (to a God I don't yet believe in). I try so hard.

And with everything I overcome, everything I fix or heal, something new pops up; some new whack-a-mole that I had to find the strength to hit – and hit so hard that it disappears forever.

May the Maypole

After dropping John to school one morning, I find myself standing outside the little community support office at the Five Lamps. This is the place people to go for help. All types of help – legal, social, housing. The little office, with its beige walls, big desk and community worker Jim, is a haven in Dublin for everyone who needs it.

Last year, my recovery pal Kate was facing a long prison sentence for possession of heroin. She came here for help and letters and legal support. One of the workers made a case for her in court, said she was clean, brought proof of her character with them and explained what she couldn't to the court. She got probation –and went back to using. It didn't matter, though. The support here isn't dependent on you being good or clean. They understand what it's like to be hurt. What it's like to be us.

'Hey, Jim, any space in here for a sad single lady?'

Jim looks up from his paper and smiles, a fag hanging from his lip.

'Aww, if it isn't my favourite English townie!' he says,

laughing, as he gets up to make me tea. 'No sugar, isn't that right, Katriona?'

I nod my head, afraid to speak, emotional at the sight of a friendly face.

What is wrong with me?

'What can I do for you?' He smiles as he hands me the cup and offers me a smoke. I shake my head at the fag. I only smoke Benson & Hedges, a carry-over from my British childhood; can't stand a John Player Blue – or a Major!

I pause.

Look him in the eye.

Open my heart.

'Is this it for me, Jim?'

Tears stream silently as he walks towards me.

'Is this it for me?'

'Monica, hi, hi, it's Jim ... Yeah, yeah, I'm good, love. Yeah, they're good too ... Kylie is in college ... I have a favour to ask from you. I have a client here, great girl, local – her and her boy are up in P.J. Bootman's flats. Yeah, yeah. Well, she needs to see someone – urgently, yeah. She needs help. Can you fit her in for me? Great, great.'

He takes note of what she is saying.

'Thank you, thank you. Yes, she will be there. Her name is Katriona O'Sullivan. Yes, chat soon.'

He turns to face me. Smiling. Softly.

'Katriona, you need help, love, with all the stuff, with the men, the way you do things to yourself. You need some support. I know it's hard. I've been there. I'm twenty-odd years in the rooms. But you need more than that. It has to stop for it to get better.'

I don't know how he knows, or what he means, but I know he cares. I know he sees me. Finally, someone sees me. I am listening. The pain of staying the same feels worse than the pain of changing.

'You deserve the world, my dear. It doesn't have to be like this. You deserve the world.'

I cry silently. I hate it when people are nice to me. My heart can't take kindness. Or hope. Better to know what bad is coming. It's predictable.

'I've made you an appointment with a counsellor down in Sheriff Street, Oasis Counselling. It's down there at the back of the church.'

I pull away. Counselling, like the Rutland Centre? No way. I can't take that again. The confrontation. The directness. It hurts. Too much.

'It's not like treatment, Katriona.' He reads me. 'This is caring, and kind – the therapists down there are great people. You'll feel great. I promise you.'

I watch his face. Looking for the lie. I have an instinct for the lie. It isn't there.

He means it.

Even though every ounce of my being is screaming 'no!'. Even though my nervous system is on high alert all day, every day, and it feels impossible to change. Even though I doubt my capability to feel or be different, I believe Jim. I know he is like me. Like us.

I know he cares. Not in a do-gooder way. Not in a charity way. I know that Jim knows me, my history, my hurts, my values, my ideas of the world, my fears – I know he wants the best for me.

'OK, Jim. OK. I'll go. Where is it, when and how much will it cost me?'

'I'm here for an appointment with someone. I don't know their name. Jim arranged it. Jim Dowling.'

The small, square glass window reminds me of visiting my dad in prison, the glass fortified to protect those inside from harm from those outside, and vice versa. The woman stays seated behind the large brown desk, her face weathered, her short dark hair sloping on the top of her head. She is modest. Flat shoes, flat clothes, flat affect.

'Can I take your name, please?'

Shit, I should have said my name.

'Katriona O'Sullivan ... With a K. Katriona with a K.'

She checks her book. Her face is hollow, blank. I hope I have the right day, the right time. Maybe this isn't for me.

'If I have the wrong day, I can come back ...'

I blurt it out before I can think. She shakes her head and points to the seat behind the large brown wooden door. 'You can wait there. May will be with you soon.'

Relief and fear hit me in equal measure.

You shouldn't be here. You shouldn't be here.

The floral cream seat is situated in a bright, square space. I walk from the dark hole of the entrance into a light room surrounded by glass; the waiting area is roasting hot from the glass panels. As I sink into the armchair, I notice a pile of books on the coffee table: *The Road Less Travelled* by M Scott Peck; *The Prophet* by Kahlil Gibran; *Codependent No More!* by Melody Beattie.

You shouldn't be here. You shouldn't be here.

My pulse fills the room. I wonder if Mrs Modest back in the reception area can hear it too. The books grow with every beat, filling my vision. As everything grows bigger, I feel myself getting smaller and smaller. With every heartbeat, I shrink further and further into the chair. I have this experience at least once a week now, since I got clean. The shrinking engulfs me. I used to feel this when I was a kid. When I was scared or alone, I would imagine myself getting smaller and smaller until I completely disappeared. The terror was tangible. I would tap and count my fingers repeatedly to try to stop it engulfing me fully.

I still count my fingers.

One, two, three, four ...

One, two, three, four ...

They call it 'stimming' in psychology. I wasn't stimming, I was saving myself. It gave me control, something to focus on. Rather than shrinking. Disappearing forever.

The books grow and grow and grow until I can't fully breathe.

'Katriona? Katriona ... ?'

I look up into her face. Trying to grab my breath and not let her see.

'Katriona, I'm May. Thank you for coming today. Do you want to follow me?'

She seems kind. Soft.

'Yes, yes, of course ... I was just looking at the books ...' I am always blabbering.

'Yes, they're left here by the trainee counsellors. There are lots of really good books there. You can take some if you like.'

'Thank you,' I say as I follow her down the glass corridor, picking up *The Road Less Travelled* on my way. The heat in this place is unbearable, like a glass oven.

'Which seat would you like to sit in, Katriona?'

She speaks slowly, deliberately. The room feels like the therapy room in the Rutland Centre. Two chairs, comfy enough, IKEA maybe. A clock on the small mahogany coffee table alongside a box of tissues. The tissue box cover is floral, the carpet brown, the walls yellow. Everywhere in the building, the ceilings are high, reminding me religion is never too far away. The Oasis Centre is run by a religious order.

I sit in the chair facing the door. I always face the door. Can't stand not seeing who is coming and who is going.

She sits in front of me and takes a breath. I take one too.

'My name is May. I work here in Oasis. I have been a therapist for several years. Can I ask what has brought you here today, Katriona?'

She is sincere. I feel it. The kindness.

'Well, I don't know really. Jim Dowling – he works in the Five Lamps. He recommended I come and see someone. He said I needed it. I don't know, though. I don't know anything really. He's nice, and I know he wants good for me. But I don't know how to do this. I was in the Rutland Centre a year ago.'

Her eyebrows lift quizzically: she doesn't know what the Rutland is.

'It was a drug treatment centre. I used drugs, drank, partied. I have food issues too ... well, they said I did ... I don't know, though. Doesn't everyone have food issues? Anyway, I've been clean from drugs and drink over a year, and I can't stand how I feel, to be honest.' The tears seep from me. 'Sorry, I didn't mean to cry. I just don't know what I'm doing, or why I'm doing it.'

She leans over to the tissues, shows me the box, before leaning forward and catching my eye. 'That sounds like the perfect reason to be here, Katriona.'

I breathe out. Was holding it in since the shrinking. I breathe in.

'I don't like telling everything at the start. I don't want to have to tell you everything now. Can I tell you some of it but not all of it? My friend was saying the first session is horrible. You want all my family details, all my history, but I don't think I can stand that today.'

I can't believe I'm saying this to her now; that I am brave enough to tell her what I need. Or want. Fuck it: start as I mean to go on.

She waits. Listens. Digests what I'm saying.

'Of course, Katriona, this space is about you. It's all for you. Why don't we start by talking about your morning instead? We have loads of time to get into everything else. I'm here to help.'

I let out the deepest breath.

Over the next six months, I tell her things I thought I would never tell anyone. I tell her about Tilly, about the drugs, the violence of her tongue.

I tell her about John, our John, my struggle to be good enough for him; my heartache, his dad, the way he left us and never came back. The way everyone blames me. How lonely it is, being on my own with John.

Every time I speak, she hears me, focuses on me; she smiles, reaching out with her warmth. Never touching me physically, but emotionally she becomes like a pillar.

When I was small, Ms Atkins had our whole class assemble a maypole; she told us how the maypole symbolised life and community. How the big, strong structure becomes the central focus of villages and towns; how people weave ribbons around it, dancing and celebrating new life. We were all given a ribbon and spent May Day dancing around the maypole in our playground. The strong structure brings people together, representing a celebration of life and culture.

May becomes my stable structure. My maypole. She stands tall in the middle of my village. Giving me something to dance around, giving me the strength to stay, to live, to breathe. She becomes my unconditional, *my* person. Every question I have about myself, every doubt about myself, she queries. She gently reminds me how great I am, how worthy I am, how special I am. She welcomes everything I suggest.

'May, I think I might try to be an actress ...'
'That sounds wonderful, Katriona. You will be amazing at that.'
'May, I think I might do an education course ...'
'That sounds wonderful, Katriona. You will be amazing at that.'

'May, I think I might try to stop having sex with men who hurt me ...'

'That sounds wonderful, Katriona. You deserve that.'

She is always there, every week, standing tall, waiting for me to dance around her. Never shocked, ashamed or scared of the darkness I show her. The real parts of me, the hurt parts, the harmed parts, the parts that I had harmed and hurt too. She forgives and helps me emotionally. Until eventually, really slowly, I begin to look up. I begin to see her. I begin to look at her arms and her face and her feet. As the shame recedes, week by week, I begin to look at her. After eighteen months of being with her, of sharing so much with her, I see her for the first time. Really see her.

'May, can I ask you something, something personal?'

It has been bothering me for a few weeks, and I am dying to know. Every session, I have sat in front of her looking at her feet, until one day I saw them, really saw them, and now I can't get them out of my head. She wears black loafers – I mean proper Clarks-style shoes, no shine, no sexiness, just plain old black slip-ons.

'Of course; you can ask me anything, Katriona.'

I knew she would respond like this. She is always open to me. Available.

'May ... are you ... are you a *NUN*?'

She opens her eyes wide. A smile spreads across her face.

'I'm sorry to ask, and tell me it's none of my business, but I noticed your shoes a few weeks ago and haven't been able to get them out of my head since then. I don't mind, honestly. I'm not Catholic, so I have no problem really with nuns. Sorry, it's not that

I don't believe ... I just didn't get beaten or anything ... oh, God, sorry ...'

'Yes, Katriona, I am a nun. I have been a nun for nearly fifty years now.'

I was stunned into silence. Wow, an actual nun. I could not believe it. May, my May, is a nun.

'Oh, God ... oh, sorry ... Jesus ... sorry ... I was thinking about everything I told you, May. The sex, all the sex ... oh, my God ... the embarrassment. How are you OK with this? Are you OK with this?'

She is now properly laughing at me. She cannot hold it in.

'Katriona, please don't worry about that now. I'm a counsellor too, and it's my job to listen and not judge. And, if I'm totally honest, that's my job as a nun too. I have been taught love and forgiveness from my God. Please don't let it worry you. Do you think you will want to continue now that you know this?'

I stop for a moment to think about this question. My family had nuns and priests in it; my grandad's sister Anna was a nun, and my uncle Bren was a priest in the UK. I have no hang-ups about religion or God. I don't know if I believe, but that's a different thing.

'Honestly, May, I don't care. These sessions have been the most important thing I have ever done for myself in my whole life. I don't know how it's happened, but knowing that you're here for me, that you care, that you think I'm somebody special, has changed my life. I don't care what you are or what I've said to you. I care that we continue down this road together, because for the first time in my life I feel hope; real hope.'

A New Hunger

'May, I think I might do an education course ...'
'That sounds wonderful, Katriona. You will be amazing at that.'

'John, I'm going out to work now, son. I'll be home before you have to go to school ... I love you.'

I kiss his sleeping forehead. It's 5.45am. I am doing what I do every weekday morning – getting up at an ungodly hour to go and clean Connolly train station. A little cash-in-hand gig. Ten punts in the hand for two hours' cleaning a day. John stays home alone. He knows he can call in to Laila, our neighbour, if he needs me.

I have no other choice; I need the extra cash. I have football fees and tracksuits and runners to buy. My lone parent's book doesn't stretch to anything apart from the basics.

I walk the ten minutes to work in silence. I hate cleaning. It makes me sick to have to clean the toilets of the men who operate the trains in the building situated in the heart of Sheriff Street. I am a 'good cleaner', a hard worker. This has meant I have been put in the dirtiest spot. Sometimes working hard doesn't pay off.

Since going to May and building myself up, I've started to question being on welfare, my drive for a council place. Maybe there is more for me. Maybe I can change our life.

'Hi, Jim, any space in here for a little one?'

He smiles at me from behind the desk, stands to make the tea; no need to ask me now. I'm a regular.

'Jim, I was thinking about something.'

'Oh, no, that might be trouble.'

His humour makes asking easier.

'I want to do something. I'm not sure what, but I think I should try to do something other than cleaning. I fucking hate cleaning, Jim.'

He hands me a fresh brew.

'I have the best thing for you: a little course here in the Larkin Centre, for girls on welfare, like you, a few mornings a week. Would be great for you, give you something to aim for – a change.'

And so, I trusted Jim. When he had an idea for me, I accepted it. His last one had helped! When he suggested I try going back to education, do something small, do something that didn't affect my benefits, I said yes. He arranged for me to start a course that I could work around while looking after John. He took me around to Larkin Community Centre, just over the hill on the Five Lamps. The learners sat in circles. There was no hierarchy, no teacher who knew best. The other mums and I, who were looking to learn and wanting to grow, sat in circles and chatted about things. We learned together. I learned about good parenting, about the food pyramid. I learned about the importance of broccoli and carrots and stopped buying all my food in Iceland.

And I got a certificate.

Me.

The failing girl. The girl who left school at age fifteen. The girl who was told by her guidance teacher she wasn't a university girl, like Anne or Sam, the good girls in her class. The girl who was told last month by the lady in FÁS, an Irish state agency for employment and training, that she was only meant for service jobs.

I graduated with my first education certificate – and it felt great. It felt good standing with the other mums, getting our picture taken with the certificates in hand, smiling at each other and the facilitators of the course. It felt good showing May what I had done for myself.

That first achievement shifted something in me. It reminded me of who I used to be. The girl I thought I had lost. The girl I left behind. I remembered her: the girl who loved to talk books with Mr Poulter when she was a chavvy fourteen-year-old. The one who would fight with him about Shakespeare and Steinbeck, who had thoughts and feelings about everything, who wasn't afraid to speak, who loved the words.

I remembered the little girl who would steal books from school or the library, who spent her days reading stories; imagining different worlds, dreaming of the hero who might one day come and rescue her – imagining herself as Sophie in *The BFG* or Margaret in the Enid Blyton classics.

That first achievement shifted something.

Another hunger was awakened.

An old hunger.

A hunger to learn, a hunger to achieve, a hunger to understand.

'May, I think I might try to be an actress ...'
'That sounds wonderful, Katriona. You will be amazing at that.'

*

With May's encouragement, after the parenting course in Larkin, I signed up for a theatre studies course at Ringsend Tech. This course was a full award at Level 5. It was scary. I was so used to starting things and not finishing them that this felt huge. The After Care Recovery Group (ACRG) had felt like a failure, but I had finished the certificate, so hopefully I could do this too. And I loved the theatre – singing, dancing and acting had been an old dream of mine. The dream of a kid who had spent her life unseen – to be centre stage, to be heard. There was so much support for me to do that course. I got a childcare allowance from the state; John went to the afterschool club, School on Stilts, when needed. I got to keep my benefits, my flat, my rent allowance – all safe. I had May too, pushing me through my fears.

I loved it. Learning. Being with new people who didn't want to hurt me. Or fuck me.

The hunger for achievement began to feel like a good thing.

Even though the food noise was still there, and I still hated my body and the way I looked, the achievements gave me something else to focus on. It wasn't like the other things I chased. I was good at assignments. I could analyse the texts and write paragraphs of verse, and I could act. I could play any part. I had been doing this all my life. This was perfect for me!

I got a job, too. I worked on the door, serving and selling tickets, in St Andrew's Lane Theatre, and I helped do the lights for the show, *Alone it Stands*. May was tearing my doubts apart, reminding me at every session that I was good enough, smart enough; she stood tall in my psyche while I explored what I might be one day. I shared everything with her. Well, almost everything. I told her about my mum, my dad, my hurt, the men, the doubts, but I kept some things to myself. Some things I was too scared to say out loud.

I couldn't see or feel the abuse – not with her. I couldn't tell her that I hated my body. That felt like too much. I didn't have the words or the thoughts back then to even identify it as an issue. It felt *normal* to wake up and hate my body and spend my day trying to avoid food or binge on it. It felt normal to compare my body with others. Sure, wasn't every woman doing that too? I didn't consciously hide this from her; I just didn't have the awareness of how deep and how hurt my relationship with my body was. I couldn't connect the hurt and the harm and the hate – I wasn't ready for that.

But I was ready to be educated, to start building up my mind.

May was so delighted the day I graduated from that course. I think she was as happy as I was. The feeling of finishing something felt great. Achievement was slowly drowning out the other voices, especially the ones that shouted at me: *YOU ARE A FAILURE*. Achieving things in education became an elixir. To be good at something felt so good. It became a new drive. A new hunger. A good one.

Having the space to explore the world of theatre, to try out the stage, enabled me to know what I didn't want to do, where I didn't belong. Exploring who you are academically and workwise is a luxury often only afforded to privileged kids. They can start things, stop, start again with support and love and care. And they have networks. They have people to turn to, to give them opportunities. They are told they can.

I was told a lot of things about myself, conflicting but rarely positive. My potential, my teachers, my experiences, my parents' history prescribed my life to me – as it does many others. Having the chance to try things, to talk it out with May, to have support from the state in the form of childcare and grants made it possible for me to say, 'No, that isn't for me ... I think I might try something else.'

I didn't know what else I might try until I met my neighbour on O'Connell Street. She told me she was studying law at Trinity College Dublin. A girl like me studying law ... no way! She said she got in through the Trinity Access Programme (TAP) – a funded course made for people like us, poor and good, strong and resilient. She told me they supported her all the way through the programme. I was alight. The new hunger was activated. I only needed to see her and I knew I could do this too – if she could, I could. May was the added push.

'*That sounds wonderful, Katriona. You will be amazing at that.*'

A Break

'May, I think I might try to stop having sex with men who hurt me ...'

I thought I had cried all the tears I could cry. I thought I had fucked all the bad men I could fuck. But no, it wasn't over. This time, this one was the worst. How was I going to say the words? To May. May the nun!

Sitting in the small yellow room with the big clock and the bigger box of tissues, I blurted it out. I hadn't seen her for eight weeks. Putting off the appointments, not wanting to face her, not wanting to admit my shame.

But I needed her. The work we had done together had created something strong in me: the desire to heal; the desire that had brought me here had a life of its own now. And even though I was still fucking up and crying out, I still had that desire to heal.

'I had an abortion, May!' I said it. I spoke it out loud. I explained that I had gone back to an ex, a horrible, pointless ex who had nothing to offer me but unavailability and familiarity. I had broken my pact with myself for only one night and that had resulted in a trip to Liverpool and a massive amount of shame.

She didn't judge. She didn't turn away. She reached for the tissues as she always did and spoke her soft, kind words, reminding me that healing happens in all directions, and that I am a wonderful person who deserves kindness and grace. Her softness, her acceptance, her ability to remind me of my value sparked something I had never felt before. It woke me up to my worth.

I realised I was too good for this.

I was too good for him; too good for the many like him.

I remembered the words my sponsor Amanda had spoken to me, and all the other people in recovery, the ones who were good and true.

Give yourself a break! they said. Loudly. In unison.

'May, I think I am going to give myself six full months' break from men, a complete six-month break. Just to work on me. To get closer to me. To be here and not be distracted ... what do you think, May?

'*That sounds wonderful, Katriona. You deserve that.*'

A Kind Man

The energy in the car is electric. Every time he moves the gearstick, his hand knocks against my knee and I feel a charge of heat. He puts his hand in my lap and holds my hand. He looks over at me, his blue eyes shining, his dark mop of curly black hair tousled from an evening spent kissing me and pushing his hand through his hair with the sexual tension that exists between us.

'Did you like the show?' I ask him.

I bought us tickets to see *Alone It Stands* – a theatre show that tells the story of when Munster beat the mighty All Blacks. I had worked on the lighting of the show a year earlier in St Andrew's Lane theatre and I wanted to show him theatre, as he had never been before.

'Yes, I can't believe how funny it was and how they acted out the rugby and everything.' His face smiles as he speaks. He's happy and he's kind. I can feel it in my bones. It is our third date. We had dinner, went to the cinema and now the theatre. I feel like a proper 'dater'. Like I am being respectful to myself.

As I look at his face, side on, I feel a thrill move from my waist all the way up to my head. He is so hot. His lips, his hair, his eyes ... he is breathtaking. He looks at me.

'You're gorgeous!'

'I was just thinking the same thing about you!' I laugh.

He is smiling. There are no games here. He is open; so am I. He wants what I want. To be settled. To meet someone. To be free.

'Where to now?' he says as we stop at the traffic lights in Drumcondra.

'Back to mine?' I say, as I lean over to kiss him, letting him know that tonight is the night he gets to stay over.

I met Dave, officially, on Valentine's night in 2004. I had gone to an AA meeting, and he had been there with Rob, another lad I knew. We had gone for coffee in Rob's little apartment after the meeting.

I had known Dave before this. A year earlier, I had been having a casual thing with Dave's housemate, Carl. Dave had been serious about recovery. Focused on getting well. Not my type ... well, not back then.

I had done some healing since then: had a break from men, focused on healing my hurt heart, started studying psychology at Trinity College Dublin. Hoping psychology would give me some insight into my family and myself – it seemed like the best option for me. Deciding there needed to be some new boundaries around how I related to myself and men.

That Valentine's night, we sat in Rob's, talking about life, recovery, football – Rob, Dave, Robin (a girl from recovery) and me. At about 9pm, Dave went to get food and suggested I come with him. As we drove, he had talked about his family, how much he loved his mam, how he was trying to fix his mistakes. I was taken aback by his honesty. I went to the chipper and got two bags of chips. He went into the newsagent and, when we got back into the car, he turned to me and said, 'I can't believe someone like you was with someone like Carl!'

His directness took me aback. *Someone like me?* Did he think I was somebody? I really saw him then: blue eyes, broad shoulders from his carpentry job, dark hair. *He's cute.*

At the end of the night, I asked if I could borrow his jacket to go home in. I was driving a moped, and it had got cold. He took my number and gave me his grey Columbia jacket to take home. 'I'll text you tomorrow to pick it up.'

My ploy had worked – he had to see me again now!

The next day, I jumped every time my phone beeped. All day waiting for him to text. Hoping. All day I heard nothing. I went to bed disappointed. He hadn't texted me. *He must not like me.* I thought about texting him, telling him he could collect his jacket any time, impatient and insecure. I wanted to step in, force his hand, but I stopped myself. Working in therapy with May over the previous few months, I knew that it was better to let things unfold rather than letting my hunger, my fear, drive me. I said a prayer and went to bed.

10pm: Hi … it's Dave here. Can I pop over and collect my jacket tomorrow after work, maybe?

Don't answer straight away. Don't answer straight away.

10.10pm: Hey, Dave, how are you? Yeah, of course. Could you come after eight, maybe, when John is in bed?

10.15pm: OK, I'll be there at eight. Night.

Jesus, that was short and sweet. I asked how he was. I gave him an opening to chat, and he didn't take it.
Maybe he's not into you.
There is no way he isn't into me!

'Hi … do you want to come in? Sorry about the mess – I only just got John to bed. He had to do homework.'
'No worries at all. Yeah, I will come in.'
He comes into the living room of the little two-bedroom house I now share with John.
'Do you want a cup of tea?' I ask nervously, not sure if he wants to just get the jacket and go.
'Yeah, yeah, that would be lovely.'
He sits down and I make the tea. Four hours pass in the blink of an eye. We don't stop talking, no breaks, no awkwardness, just lovely conversation about life, family, football.

He looks at his watch and says, 'Jesus, it's midnight! So sorry for keeping you talking so long and smoking all your smokes!'

'Don't worry about it – it's my pleasure. It's nice to have some company,' I say shyly. Not really sure if it's too personal to tell him that being home most nights with John gets lonely.

'Here is your jacket. Thank you for the loan – it was freezing the other night.'

He takes his coat as I walk him to the door. We stand awkwardly facing each other, and I lean forward and give him a hug. That's what we do in fellowship, so why not? He hugs me back and says, 'Goodnight, thanks again for tea.'

I stand at the door and watch him drive off, my cheeks flushed, my heart beating. He is the kindest, sweetest boy I have ever met. I sit quietly after he leaves, asking myself what just happened. Most fellas who come to visit me try something on. Most fellas give a sign they are into me. Most fellas are sexual. He isn't like that. I can't read anything from him.

Maybe he's not into you!

As I wash up the cups, I hear a car engine outside the front door, and I go to the front window to look out. It's his green Mitsubishi Lancer outside. My heart misses a beat. He must have forgotten something. I open the front door as he gets out of the car. He hands me an unopened packet of John Player Blue.

'I was at the garage and thought it wasn't fair to have smoked all your smokes and left you with only a few. I got you these. Thanks again for the tea.'

I look down at the smokes and back at him and back at the

smokes – it is possibly the sweetest thing anyone has ever done for me.

'Thank you ... that is so kind of you. Will you wait? I'll get you some cash ...'

'No, no, please let me get them for you. Thanks again for the tea and the chat,' he says as he walks towards his car, hardly even looking at me. My heart is beating so fast I think it will jump out of my chest

I hope he is into you!

'Two days have passed since he was here, and I've heard nothing from him!'

I am bemoaning my situation to my recovery friend Robin.

'I thought he might have texted me at least!'

She is laughing down the phone at me. 'From what I've heard, he doesn't chase women. He isn't like that. He's really quiet – the fact that he came to your house is a miracle. He's called "spiritual Dave" because he's so focused on his recovery!'

I don't want to hear this. I want her to tell me he fancies me, and will be in touch.

'I think he must like you to even have come to your house – he hasn't been with anyone since that girl Ella that he had a quick thing with. Well, that's what I heard, anyway!'

I don't want to hear about other girls. I want him to text me. But I know that I can't force this, that I need to respect myself, that I need to practise the things that May, and I have been talking about.

'I'm not going to worry about him, anyhow. I'm going to get my nails done for myself and I will have myself a nice bath with some smellies tonight.'

'That's my girl!' Robin says.

I don't know her well, but I know she has struggled with messy man situations too, and we have bonded recently, trying to be better versions of ourselves. The great thing about being in recovery is that you can connect with people on a deeper level. You can share your pain and struggles more openly.

'I'm not going to get in the way of this. If it's meant to be, he'll get in touch. I'm not going to hurt myself any more or sell myself short ... I just hope he texts me!'

Robin laughs and says goodbye.

Two hours later, I am lying in a steaming hot bath with the CD player on, playing classic love songs, when my phone beeps. I jump out of my skin.

Dave: Hi, how are you? I'm football training in O'Devaney Gardens tomorrow night and thought I could pop in and have a cuppa if you're there.

Me: Oh, that would be nice. I was wondering if I would ever hear from you again now that you don't have a reason.

Dave: OK, I'll be there at about 9pm.

Wow, he is a terrible texter. There was an opener from me to be a bit flirty, but he either didn't respond to it or didn't recognise it. I don't know if this is a good or a bad thing.

He comes around for tea and chats three times that week.

Every time he leaves, he pops back with some smokes or some sweets for John for school the next day, even though he hasn't met him. Every time, we sit and chat and I feel myself liking him more and more. He is honest and good and kind. He wants a family and a career. He is normal, as normal as a recovering person can be. His friends in recovery are good men – Paul, Dan, Ger. They are settled and kind.

'Wow, it's midnight again. I'd better go. I've had you up late for the last three nights.'

He stays sitting when he says it this time. He looks nervous.

'Don't worry,' I say, 'I'm a late bird anyhow. It's nice to have company. I would only be watching TV or doing extra study for my course in Trinity.'

'Um ... I was going to ask you, like, what is this? I mean, do you see me as a friend?'

Thank God, he's finally saying something.

I knew he liked me. It was in his eyes, in his flushed face, in the glances at my body when I made tea for us in my little kitchen.

'I have enough friends,' I say. 'I don't need any more.'

I look him directly in the eyes when I say this, so he knows that this is an invitation.

He stands up.

He walks towards me.

He sits next to me on the sofa.

He reaches for my face, taking my hair in both his hands. He leans forward and kisses me, softly at first, gently opening his mouth, his tongue darting in and out.

He gives me my last first kiss.

It's the kiss of my lifetime. It is soft and passionate and hot, so hot. I let him push me back on to the sofa. I can feel him pressing against me, his groin hot. His hand moves to the strap of my vest top, but I pull it back to my face. I like him, I want him, but I want to wait. He continues to kiss me without pushing for anything more. We spend hours there, kissing and talking and smiling and then kissing again. At 2am, he stands to leave. I stand with him, not wanting to let go of the night, the connection.

'Will you come out on a date with me tomorrow night, to dinner?'

He is nervous asking. His hesitation fills me, and I jump into it and say, 'Yes – yes, I would love to.'

He wants to take me on a date – a real date! My heart hurts with the joy of it all. This good man, this kind man, this hot man wants to take me on a date. Me, broken me, hurt me, tarnished me. He wants to date me despite knowing some, not all, of my past. He leans in to kiss me one more time – 'I'll pick you up at eight sharp!' – and he is gone.

*

And now, as we head up the stairs, I feel his hands on my waist and his heart beating through his fingertips. Is that him or me? I can't tell. I want him. Not just his body, but his heart too. I've never felt like this before, never felt so much for one person. Seeing a future with them. His stability, his ability to stand in himself – it's what I have always needed but never been able to live with. There is no doubt in me. He is mine and I am his.

You've thought this before. He might not respect you tomorrow.

No, I know it's different this time. I'm different!

Before I know it, my skirt is around my waist. Joy courses through every vein.

There is no doubt in me.

He is mine and I am his.

We enter the bedroom locked on to each other, kissing and touching, hands and hearts all over the place. It doesn't matter that the floor is covered in my clothes from the night before or that I'd let a cup of tea go cold next to my make-up bag or that the ashtray is overflowing. He only sees me.

The lovemaking is hot and fast, very fast. It is passionate and raw and honest. Finished, he rolls over, smiling, his eyes glistening. I look over at him. I feel happy because he is happy, happy that he's pleased. I am also acutely aware that I am nowhere near finished. I hadn't come, hadn't orgasmed, hadn't reached my end – and I still feel that familiar longing.

Don't get me wrong: I enjoyed the connection, the passion, the fire and the fact that he wanted me so badly. But I hadn't finished in the way that he had.

In that moment, I know I have a choice to make – I could say nothing; I could lie here, half-satisfied, half-frustrated and push my needs aside; I could do what I have always done and choose a man's needs over mine. I could continue to act in line with what's taught to all women – that our sexual needs are second to a man's. That we are not supposed to want to come, to explode, to feel every single nerve-ending alight with passion. I could say nothing and succumb to the patriarchy and the lifetime of abuse I have endured. Or I could say something.

Speak the words.

I smile over at him as he takes a drag of his John Player Blue.

'Did you enjoy that, babe?' I speak.

He reaches over and kisses me. 'That was amazing.'

His blue eyes are full of love. They are open and wide.

The pause feels long.

'I'm really glad that it was amazing for you, but we're not quite finished yet ...'

My face reddens as I say the words. I watch his face drop. The light in his eyes dim slightly.

Sadness and embarrassment fill the air between us.

'Don't worry,' I am quick to assure him, 'it was amazing ... I really enjoyed it! The connection is there and everything else. You are so hot. But I think I need to show you how to please me now because ... there are two of us in this.'

The silence deafens us both. I hear my heartbeat.

He looks at me now with an honest heart.

'I've never ever had a woman say that to me before ...' He hesitates. 'In fact, I've never had a woman talk to me about her own pleasure before.'

I'm not going to write negatively about Dave. When he was a younger man, I know that he was driven by sex, like lots of young fellas. As a young man, he was as influenced by the world as I was. He was taught that his value was measured by how many girls he could fuck. And, apparently, he did his fair share of fucking as a young man. I know this from his friends and family and his occasional boastful moments where he forgets who he is talking to. He was Smokey Brennan with deep-blue eyes and a mop of black hair and girls loved him. Lying here next to me, having the realisation that he might not have been 'all that' in bed, is hard for him. I can see and feel his struggle.

'Oh, my God, like, how many other women have gone before you and never told me?'

I want so much to take the words back now, to say, 'No, actually, it's fine. I'm sorry, I shouldn't have said anything ... it's my fault, not yours.' But I know that it would not be OK to cancel my feelings in favour of his. That is never OK.

When I look over at his face, I see the embarrassment, the shame – and an admiration for me.

There is no anger. He isn't angry. His hand reaches for mine and there is that heat again. 'Most girls I know do the work for themselves. Honestly, babe, I've never even asked a girl if she was done too.'

I hadn't thought my heart was capable of more love for him until he said that. Despite the shame he felt, and the realisation that his stud status was in question, he was reflecting. He was trying so hard to reach for me and be better.

There's such a big lesson in that for men and women. This man, who had been with many women, had spent most of his adult life never talking about sex, never asking questions of a woman or her body. This man had assumed that because she opened her legs, and it was wet and warm, that she was ready and that that was enough pleasure for her – and him.

The lesson comes in questioning the assumptions we all hold about pleasure and sex. In being open to asking, to listening, to working together to make sure both people get as much from their bodies as they can. The lesson comes from the bravery we showed in that interaction: me in telling my truth and him in being open and brave enough to hear it and care.

That moment didn't come from nowhere. Six months before meeting Dave, I had decided, with May, that I would never let my body be used again. That I would never allow a man to use me for his pleasure and not think about my own pleasure too. Through my childhood experience, through abuse, rape and putting men's needs ahead of mine over many, many years, I had somehow lost myself and the pleasure that could be derived from sex and my body. I had spent so long denying my body pleasure and power that I had become someone I did not know, a vessel for men to use. I had lost my own sensuality.

In my therapy sessions with May, I talked about this. I cried about it. I committed to respecting myself and my own body and that, in turn, led me to this moment: to risking being rejected by Dave because of my refusal to ignore my needs. Luckily for me, Dave was and is the man that I was able to talk that through with. I'm not going to detail how wonderful our sex life is or how great that night was. But I will tell you that there has never been a moment in our relationship since then where his pleasure has come ahead of mine, where his body has been more important than my body.

There have been times when I've thought, *I'm just going to please him because I love him.* And that's what I want to do. And there have been times when he has thought, *I'm just going to please her because I love her.* And that's what he wants to do. (For the record, that happens much less.) But the reality is that the decision I made twenty-odd years ago – that my body was worth something and that I would never ever disrespect it again – has led to a marriage and a connection between me and my husband that is based on honesty and truth. That has stayed strong.

This decision, to respect me, laid a foundation for us to respect each other's needs. I think telling him that he was shit in bed has been one of the many reasons why we've stayed happily married, and stayed connected. The honesty from me, the desire to respect myself, and his willingness to be better, set a foundation for our love to grow from.

I've also learned there's a distinction between hating how you look and being able to trust another with your body, accepting that someone else truly loves how you look.

Throughout my life with Dave, I have continued to struggle with the same pathological hunger that has consumed my entire life. I remained driven by the idea that I would arrive at the ideal place physically, that my body would be the right size and meet the standards imposed on it by the world. Yet this struggle existed separately from my ability to connect with Dave emotionally and sexually. Even in the darkest of my body moments, where I was searching for answers in surgery and extreme solutions, the emotional connection with Dave has remained intact. Trust. Care. Honesty. Respect. Dignity. Talking. They created a foundation that enabled me to let someone else love me. Through this love, I have discovered that learning to love my own body and allowing my body to be loved and respected by another person are completely separate things.

And that accepting love from someone else requires far less work than learning to love yourself.

What I Was Made For

He is frantic. Running from room to room. He has checked the back door lock three times already.

I sit.

I wait.

Bag at my feet.

Heart full.

'Come here, babe, sit down for a minute.' I pat the sofa next to me. 'Sit down, babe ... please.'

He concedes. As he lowers himself into the seat next to me, I smell his warmth, a mixture of Lynx Africa, Issey Miyake and heat. I love his smell.

'Babe, look at me please.' I take his face between my hands. Gently, I move it towards mine. His silver-blue eyes shine with fear. And hope. And love. 'This day is going to be wonderful. He's coming, he's finally coming! We need it to be perfect for him, babe; calm and easy. Can we make it easy for him?'

His eyes brighten with recognition. The shadow lifts.

'Yes, yes ... of course ... let me check the back door is locked one more time and we'll go. OK? OK?'

I laugh.

This is his first time.

'OK, you do that, and I'll get the baby bag into the car.'

'No!' He grabs the bag from beneath my legs before I have a chance to move. 'Don't carry that, it's heavy. Let me do it. Let me do something.'

'You've done enough!' I pat my massive belly and we laugh.

He bends in and kisses me fully on my lips. 'You're amazing, babe!'

He means every word.

I know it.

And our baby knows it too.

It has been a year since we met, a year and eight days. This baby came quick – but when you know, you know. I continue to succeed in college, a first-class student. I don't know how not to be first class. I work hard at everything. Our love. My grades. The home we are building. It's February and I will sit my second-year exam in May, take the summer off and then go back in September. If I stop college now, I may never go back. I'm not stopping.

'Can you call your ma, please, and check on John?'

His eyes widen. 'I can't believe you're worrying about John now, love. He's fine. He's in me ma's since last night.'

As he speaks, I feel another wave of pain engulf me. The induction started four hours ago and the machine they have me hooked up to is measuring the strength of the contractions. I don't need to look at the reading – this one is bigger than the last.

Breathe.
Go inwards.
Feel him.
Breathe.
This is what you are made for.

'I want to talk to him. This has to be hard on him,' I say as the pain washes away. 'It's been just John and me for years. And then there was you, only last year, and now a new baby, a new person. He has to be feeling it.'

He puts the phone to his ear.

'Ma ... no, no, nothing yet. She's still being induced. Yes, yes, the pains are coming now ... She's good, Ma, amazing ... I know, I know, I will. Is John there? She wants to talk to him.' He smiles at me with his eyes.

I love how he loves Steph, his mam. She can do no wrong. Even when she does wrong, she can do no wrong.

He covers the phone and whispers to me, 'He's playing the PlayStation with Lee. She kept Lee home from school.'

'John, son, are you OK? Are you feeling OK?' My voice sounds level to me. I hope it does to him.

'Yeah, Ma – why? What is it? I'm in the middle of a game here with Lee.'

He isn't bothered at all. My eleven-year-old boy has no clue everything is about to turn upside down.

'Can I go?'

'Yeah, yeah, of course, son ... I love you.'

He's gone before the words hit him.

'Hey Kat,' says another voice on the line, 'it's me, Steph. Sorry, he missed you there. Don't worry about him. He is grand, not a bother on him. How is it? How are you doing?'

'Yeah, Steph, I'm doing good. They broke my waters about four hours ago. Jesus, it was like I was pissin' myself for hours. Then they put me on the drug to bring on the contractions; they started about an hour ago.'

'Walk around, now, don't just lie there. It will bring it on quicker. How is David doing? Jesus, back in my day, we would go in there for a break from the men. The Rotunda was the best craic; we'd sneak in little naggins of vodka and have a party after the babies were born. It's not like that now.'

'No, Steph, no naggins here.' I laugh, imagining her having a party in the ward with all the other women; no men around to ask them to cook or clean, babies being minded by the midwives while the women got their strength back. 'He's OK, a bit scared. I can't say much 'cos he's right here. We're good though. Can't wait for him to get here now. Thanks for taking John, Steph. My mam and dad will come up later if you need a break.'

'A break? Shut up – he's grand here. Let us know how it goes.'

'Thanks, Steph, we love you!'

She hangs up without replying. She hates all the soppy talk.

'Katriona, can you please lie down in the bed rather than walking around and bouncing on the birthing ball? It's the best way for us to keep track of the baby's heart rate.'

I don't like this midwife. She is prim and modest and has no concept that this is my body and my birth.

'I will move around for a few minutes and then lie down and put the monitor back on. It's easier for me if I move around – and I know gravity helps it along.'

'Oh, OK.' She sighs. 'I suppose that will have to do.' A minute later: 'Can we check it now? Baby's heart rate.'

It's my turn to sigh. 'Of course.'

I jump on to the bed and watch as she places the heart monitor across my belly. The overhang of loose skin from my first pregnancy means that my bump is not neat. It definitely wouldn't be featured on the cover of *Vogue* or even *Motherhood* magazine. I have stretch marks – silver and purple slashes, new and old ones, from my pelvic bone all the way up to my belly button. I hate looking down at the war zone that is my belly. Even in the throes of labour, I'm conscious that my belly isn't good enough; doesn't fit the standard of beautiful baby bellies.

As quick as that thought comes, I push it aside.

Breathe.
Go inwards.
Feel him.
Breathe.
This is what you are made for.

There's a song playing in the background, its soothing tones familiar from the radio.

Friday night, I'm going nowhere
All the lights are changing, green to red
Turning over TV stations
Situations running through my head
Looking back through time
You know it's clear that I've been blind, I've been a fool.

'Babylon' by David Grey. Then there's another voice in the room, alongside David's soft tones.

'Hi Kat-ree-ona! My name is Maggie. I'm the new midwife on duty, and we are going to get this baby out of you tonight – what do you think?' She is smiling. I like her.

'Hi Maggie ... it's Katriona ... my name is Katriona.'

'Oh, I'm so sorry. I'm Aussie, can't get my head around these Irish names. Thank you for teaching me something.'

Friday night, I'm going nowhere
All the lights are changing, green to red
Turning over TV stations
Situations running through my head
Looking back through time
You know it's clear that I've been blind, I've been a fool.

She is the fifth midwife I have had since I have been here; she has red frizzy shoulder-length hair, bright-green eyes and freckles are the central feature of her face. She looks more Irish than any Irish person I have ever met.

'OK, so I understand this is your second baby. Do we know the gender?'

'Yes.' I like her. She sees me. 'It's my second boy; he is going to have a big brother.'

'Oh, wonderful, and how is big brother about the whole situation?' She talks as she checks me. She checks my fingers, my toes, my arms, my face. She checks the printout from the heart machine. She has the uncanny ability of making me feel as though I am her only focus when she is, in fact, doing twenty things at once.

'He is at his nanny's playing PlayStation, as we speak. He's eleven and, honestly, I don't think he cares.' No need to say step-nan; she is his nan now.

This stranger doesn't need all the details.

'Eleven – wow, you have a eleven-year-old! You don't look old enough.'

Shit. I forgot. This reaction is always the same.

'To be honest, I am not old enough. I was sixteen, a baby myself. Long story.'

'And how was that birth ... easy, hard?'

As she speaks, a wave of pain washes over me. Dave stands from the chair he has been resting in and grabs my hand. 'OK, babe, you're OK, babe.' Fear stains his blue eyes.

'Aaaaaahhhhh ... fuck, fuck, this hurts.'

Friday night, I'm going nowhere
All the lights are changing, green to red
Turning over TV stations
Situations running through my head
Looking back through time
You know it's clear that I've been blind, I've been a fool.

She waits patiently for the pain to recede. Holding on to my other hand, she smiles down at me. This one actually sees me.

'How was your big boy's birth. Was it natural, easy?'

Tears prick my eyes at the memory of it.

The fear.

His heartbeat. The horse.

How they ignored me. And my poor body.

'It was a forceps delivery. He was angel-faced, my John. I lost blood, a lot of blood. It was scary.'

She takes a moment to compose herself. She squeezes my hand as she speaks.

'I am so sorry to hear that, Katriona. I promise you this won't be like that for you. I will do my best for you both. And for you, Daddy. What's your name?'

Dave looks up sheepishly from the chair. He isn't used to being so useless, to feeling so powerless.

'I'm Dave. David.' He puts his hand out to shake hers, then pulls it back as quickly. She smiles.

'Well, Dave – can I call you Dave? We're going to get this baby out in a nice relaxed fashion – are you up for that?'

He nods, wiping his hands on his leg as he looks from her to me and back again.

Friday night, I'm going nowhere
All the lights are changing, green to red
Turning over TV stations
Situations running through my head
Looking back through time
You know it's clear that I've been blind, I've been a fool.

'Ahhhhhhhhhhh! This really hurts ...'

The words escape me. I am trying to be positive, but it fucking hurts.

And he isn't moving.

Is he stuck?

IS HE STUCK?

I bite down hard, listening to his heartbeat. It's stable, steady.

'That's it, now, it looks like it's slowing up now, Katriona. You're doing amazingly. Well done.'

I try to smile at her. I grimace instead.

'With induction, the pain can be worse. That's why we suggest the epidural at the same time as the hormone drip. The pain is higher when we induce it. Is there anything I can do for you?'

Friday night, I'm going nowhere
All the lights are changing, green to red

'YES, YES, YOU CAN! CAN YOU TURN OFF DAVID FUCKING GRAY?'

She steps back, startled at the intensity of my request.

'I'm sorry,' I explain. 'I've been on this labour ward for eight hours now and David Gray has been playing on repeat for the whole time – *the whole time*! I cannot listen to him for another second.'

Tears prick the corner of my eyes.

I know I am being unreasonable. I know I sound crazy.

But I don't care. Right now, I HATE DAVID GRAY!

'I planned for this day. I know what I am made for, what my body should do ... but I can't do it with David Gray playing over and over again in the background! He's depressing as hell. This song, the words – please just make it stop. Could someone please TURN HIM OFF?'

Maggie and Dave look at each other, look at me and look at each other again before they burst out laughing. Their giggles are contagious and, even though I am in pain and tired and I know there is worse to come, I laugh too ... I laugh harder than I have laughed for a very long time.

'Katriona, I can definitely do that for you,' she chuckles. 'I thought you might want ice cubes or food or drugs even ... but the music? No one has ever requested a change in the music before.'

The back of her head is smiling as she walks off to change the soundtrack of our baby's birth day.

The lights in the room are brighter. His heartbeat and mine perfectly aligned.

Hot fire burns through me every minute. The pain comes from within me and outside of me. It fills every ounce of me.

There is no escape.

No stopping it.

No end.

This is what I am made for.

Dave's face is next to me, and it is far away too. His eyes shine a colour I have never seen before. His jaw is tight, his arms ready to grab me or him or all of us.

In the distance, I hear whale sounds playing. We have gone from David Gray to the sound of the ocean. Maggie took my plea for peace literally, introducing whale-birthing sounds to the room. I haven't got the heart to tell her I'm not that hippy-dippy. But anything is better than David fucking Gray.

'Maggie, Maggie ... is it possible he's facing upwards too – that he's angel-faced too? It is taking him so long to arrive ... it hurts so much.'

'It would be rare, Katriona, but I think we should check. Mam usually knows best. Let me ask a doctor to come and have a look.'

She hears everything I say. She puts me in charge of me.

I am leading this.

Not her or them.

My body is in charge.

'Katriona, this is Dr O'Brien. He is going to examine you now to check why baby is taking so long to descend.'

He has kind eyes. He smiles at me. 'Hello, Mrs O'Sullivan. I'm going to take a look now. Is that OK with you?'

'I think I'll wait outside.'

Dave is halfway to the door before the doctor has even got one glove on. He decided months ago that he would stay away from the 'business end' of the birth. His neck is fixed at a ninety-degree angle at the top of the bed.

'My son was angel-faced, and I'm convinced this boy is too.'

He smiles and nods at me from between my legs. 'Well, let's have a look-see.'

He pushes and pulls and lights and looks.

He whispers something to Maggie and she smiles at me.

'It looks like Mammy knows best. You're right, baby is facing upwards. This is what is stopping him from coming along by himself.'

Relief.

Fear.

The beeping on the contraction machine begins to quicken, and the burning begins. I bite down on my jaw, waiting for it to stop. She grabs my hand. The whiteness in the room glows brighter. 'Ahhhhhhhhhh!'

Breathe.

Go inwards.

Feel him.

Breathe.

This is what you are made for.

'Come on now, come on now, push, Katriona, push …'

Maggie is pulling me along now. I press down on myself. Pushing into the darkest parts of myself. Willing him to come out.

'Keep going ... keep going.'

The beeping is louder with every push.

Dave is standing now. There is no more time to sit down. His face is red. Eyes are grey. Scared. Alive.

'You're doing great, babe. Keep going, keep going.'

Is he speaking or am I imagining the words?

Breathe.

Go inwards.

Feel him.

Breathe.

This is what you are made for.

'OK, again, Katriona, again. Focus now, focus on your baby. He's coming, I can see him ... PUSSSSSSSSHHHH.' She is between my legs, her red hair growing out of me. 'Keep going, don't stop, you can do this!'

She looks at me with love and light. She has me, she has us. I bear down on my soul. Pushing, pushing, pushing. *Come on, baby – we're waiting for you. There is so much love waiting for you.*

Breathe.

Go inwards.

Feel him.

Breathe.

This is what you are made for.

'Stop pushing, Katriona, stop pushing ...'

This is another voice. I open my eyes. It's him, the doctor, O'Brien, O'Reilly – what was his name again? Why is he here?

'Katriona, look at me now, look at me.'

He looks serious. I open my eyes wide. 'What's wrong? Is he OK? Is the baby OK?'

Dave's eyes are wide open. His face full. Fear, hope, hurt, all of him laid out in front of me. 'Dave, is he OK?'

He takes my hand. 'It's OK, babe, the doctor's here. Just listen to him now. Do as he says.'

He sounds uncertain.

'Katriona,' says Maggie, 'Dr O'Brien is here alongside my colleague, Jenny. We are going to help baby out as he's getting upset now. He's tired, and so is Mammy, so we are going to have to help – is that OK?'

I nod.

He's stuck.

HE'S STUCK!

'Katriona, on your next contraction we are going to use a machine called a ventouse. It sounds loud, like a vacuum cleaner, but don't be afraid. We need to help him out. Is that OK? On the next contraction we need you to push as hard as you can ... and then stop when we say stop. Can you do that?'

Is it him speaking or Maggie or Dave? I can't tell.

I feel everything cracking.

All my strength gone.

Heartbreak.

I am failing him.

This is my job.

I am failing him.

I can't do it.

I can't do this.
I can't do this!
I say it over and over again. Inward and outward. I surrender. Let go.

And then, he is there: Dave.

My love.

My only love.

He rises above me. The tallest he has ever been. His eyes and heart open, on show.

'You have to do this, Katriona! Now! You must do this for him and for us! YOU WILL DO THIS NOW.'

His face.

His fear.

His love. Everything is on show for us all.

And then I find it.

My last resolve.

My last push.

I find it for him. For our dream. For the life we have built. For his heart and mine. For John. For Steph. For our future. For my past. I find a place to pull from, the deepest part of me, the place I never knew existed. I visit there, and find the power to push our boy, our baby boy made from love and light and life. I find it for all of us.

'AAAAAAAHHHHHHHHHHHHHHHHHHHHHHH!'

A baby cries.

Just Like My Dad

'Do you want to stop the car and get her number?'

I can't keep it in. If I have to sit through another car journey with him ogling every pair of boobs that walks by, I'll explode.

I just did explode.

I hate myself. Baby two has taken away any hope I had of being slim. I have tried my best to shrink again every day since he was born. I have planned for my calorie deficit; sugar-free jellies and purple Snacks fill the fridge. The struggle started as we left the hospital to come home. I didn't fit into the size twenty velour tracksuit I'd bought from Dunnes for the occasion. I had an image of myself walking out of the Rotunda, hand-in-hand with Dave, with my flat stomach and peachy arse protruding from my fake Juicy Couture tracksuit. Like Victoria and David Beckham after baby Cruz was born.

Instead, I had to squeeze myself into the T-shirt and trousers I'd arrived in three days before – my maternity clothes still too tight around me despite having birthed a ten-pound baby.

That was the first of my many meltdowns about my body. The overhang is a fully fledged apron now. And it is affecting both of us. The stress of having the baby in February, then studying for exams, sitting the exams in May and trying to bounce my body back to what I wasn't happy with before I had my baby is beyond me.

Every car journey, I notice Dave ogling someone from the car window. The worries that I am not giving him enough sex, that I am not slim enough, that I am not the girl he fell for, fill me to the brim. I watch him watching other slimmer, prettier, sexier women and I want to cry or fight.

'Seriously, Dave, do you want to stop the car and get her number?'

'What ... what do ... you mean?'

He can't get his words out. Shame reddens his lovely cheeks. His eyes tell it all: he knows I know, and he wants me not to know.

'I am not sitting here every day feeling like a fat idiot while you look at every pair of tits walking by!'

I can't hold it now. In for a penny, in for a pound. I glance back at Sean, sleeping in his baby seat. Our beautiful boy is not even six months old, and he almost fills the car seat already.

He is a bouncer.

And he is so good, sweet and soft.

Like his dad.

When his dad isn't ogling other women.

'Babe, I don't know what you're talking about. I don't know who or what you're talking about.'

I can't help the jealousy. I am trying so hard to keep it in, to be happy, but whenever we go out together it's there. Ever since I had the baby, I feel different.

Afraid.

I am fat. I feel horrible. My body and heart feel changed. The new dependence on Dave and the life we are creating has opened wounds I thought were long gone. Being left by my dad, being abandoned holding John. These events have left their mark – men having power, the power to leave, to hurt, to abandon, stirs up the old darkness.

The lack of control over Dave and my future resurrects these feelings and thoughts about who will love me. I'm not sure if this darkness is depression. Or if this is just my life, issues I always have to battle. Being a new mother, with my past and my inability to control my body or him is destabilising. Unsettling.

I know now that vulnerability, fear and jealousy are the other half of the love, happiness and hope that I have found. I can't let one in without feeling the other. I can't have one without the other. To feel deeply, I must heal deeply.

'Babe, I'm sorry ... I'm sorry.'

He sees the tears.

'I don't even realise what I'm doing,' he says. 'I am a man, a red-blooded man.'

Just like my dad.

They are all like my dad.

'May, I don't think I can do this. I feel so open and hurt. He can't speak about things without shouting or storming off. He's emotionally broken, I think. Like ice sometimes. If I try to talk, he clams up. I'm not going to live a life like this ... I have worked too hard for this!'

I get louder with every word. Dave has pissed me off again. He won't or can't talk about hard things. He wants it easy. For there never to be issues. For us always to feel good.

'OK, Katriona, it sounds like you're clashing on things that you have differences on. Let's focus on you for now and what you are bringing to the relationship and how you might be contributing to things.'

Her calmness, our history, my unwavering belief that she wants the best for me make it easy for me to hear her say this.

She challenges me to think about me and my role; she asks me what is good and true about us. She points to the love and the happiness we have created. She sends me home with plans to communicate properly, to hold back my jealousy, to be the person I was born to be.

Loving Dave and staying in love with Dave has not always been easy. At times, it felt near impossible to get through, to keep going, to keep reaching for him.

It was made possible by May, and by the work we were both willing to do. I am asked by many people, 'How did you do it? How have you found and kept love?' And my answer is always the same – through work.

Not hard work but good work.

My hunger as a young woman, the drive to connect, to be loved, sent me into the darkest arms. It pushed me to seek out what I knew, the uncomfortable comfort. When I took a break from men, from the hunger, when I let in a new light, a new way, I opened the door for Dave. I allowed myself to see something new.

A good man.

A calm man.

A consistent man.

Up until then, I had been attracted to people who were not available. And that drive was deep, ancestral. By taking a break and working on my value, on self-love, on my heart, I was able to see the good men. For the first time, I was able to feel attracted to them.

Dave was, and is, the perfect man for me.

Not because he is cute or kind or calm, but because he was also hungry for love, for connection. He came from a broken home. He sought relief in drugs and sex; he lost his light for a while. And he was willing to work with me, to stay connected.

To build a connected life.

When the fire of passion had died down, we had to work to stay in love, to stay connected and focused. I did that with May. I spoke about all the hurt that had emerged because I was vulnerable. I shared with her and with Dave my fear and my doubts. I said sorry quickly for my failings. I sought him out; even in the worst fights, even on the worst nights, I sought him out. To keep trying. To keep finding each other.

Having May in my life, in those early years, was an essential part of my seeing Dave for all he was and letting him love me the way I deserved.

The way I should have always been loved.

Motivation

'OK, so the cost of the programme for twelve weeks sounds expensive but think of it this way: you're probably spending that on takeaways at this point, so you need to see it as an investment.'
She laughs.
'We also advise that you buy our protein support products. They are an essential part of the weight-loss plan. There are soups and bars to keep you healthy. Protein is the key to this. We are low-carb and high-protein focused. This is how you lose body fat. This is how you ensure you don't lose muscle mass ...'

I am sitting in a little cottage in Blanchardstown village. The 'Motivation' advisor is named Laura. She is blonde and very beautiful. I can't help wondering if she lost weight with the programme. I don't want to ask, as I don't want to assume she was a fat loser too at one point in her life.

I think about telling her about who I am and what I'm doing, about how ashamed I am of myself and my body. I want to tell her that I'm not a complete failure, that I'm studying psychology at Trinity, and am a first-class honours student. That I'm brilliant at loads of other things . Except this, the one thing I want to be good at – shrinking myself.

'... the protein bars are twenty-five euros for a box of six and if you buy three boxes you get one box free. We advise eating one or two bars a day to stave off the hunger.'

The many hundreds of euros she's asked for *is* a lot of money. I will need to get an overdraft to pay for this, but I think about Sharon and how good she looks. Meeting Sharon in Lidl and her telling me about this place was a sign. I had been toying with the idea of rejoining Slimming World or WeightWatchers, but this place sounded amazing. One-to-one appointments and they measure body fat, not just weight. Perfect. She said she had lost two stone in three months doing the Motivation programme, and she seemed so happy.

'Honestly, I don't feel hungry at all ... I can fit into my old jeans, the ones I had before I had the baby. I feel great!'

She smiled, and her cheekbones were prominent. She was glowing.

'My hair feels great and, honestly, he cannot keep his hands off me. It's given us a new lease of life. I didn't even want to have sex while I was feeling so fat.'

She laughed conspiratorially. And I know that feeling so well. I cannot imagine letting anyone touch me when I feel like this. My belly is hanging over my jeans; my hips are burgeoning.

I really have no more excuses. Sean is nearly eighteen months old; he is nearly fully grown! And I'm still telling myself it's baby weight – 'baby weight' when it's actually 'lazy weight'. I just haven't been able to find the motivation or plan that gets me to stay on track. I am living in the cycle of hate and hurt. Today is the day I will succeed; today is the day I fail. The planning to succeed, the feeling of failing go around and around and around in my head.

It doesn't help that I have so many other things to manage. To worry about.

I am heading into my final year of my psychology degree at Trinity. My grades are good; in fact, they are great. My hunger for achievement is in full flower. Nothing stops me getting the work done. I have never requested an extension. Never taken maternity leave. Everything is completed to a high standard. I'm scared to let go of this new life. The success. The hope it gives me. Even though I am tired. Really tired. And I have no time to rest. I keep going on and on and on.

My body comes last; food planning and exercise don't fit around the work ... and then there's my family. My fucking family. Matthew is in prison again; the baby's babies are in care. My mum is relapse incarnate. She can't get clean or sober for long enough to see herself or the wonderful life I'm building. She crashes cars, hurts and hits, and takes whatever remnants of peace I have. My dad uses me as his wife, asking me to pick up their pieces every time there is a drama. And that is every week.

I can't find time for me and my body. I feel fat. And a failure. And the pathological desire to be a good girl, to fix my body, to fix *me*, keeps pushing me further and further towards new, crazier weight loss solutions.

I smile at the pretty blonde, Laura. 'Where do I sign up?'

Many hundreds of euros plus more for soups and bars? She could have told me to spin around five times and jump through a hoop. At this point, I was well and truly caught in the fat cycle. There was no other answer to my hunger for acceptance and self-love than being skinny. I had found the new solution. And now I'd found a better tool, one focused on motivating me with mental exercises to help me reach my goals.

She tells me the exercises are built by a world-renowned psychologist whom I have never heard of. I don't mention that I am a psychology student at Trinity. I just smile and ask her, 'How much can I pay today to get started?'

Achievement

Dear Katriona,

Offer of PhD Studentship at Trinity College Dublin

I am pleased to inform you that you have been selected for a PhD studentship in the Psychology Department at Trinity College Dublin. This studentship is awarded based on your academic achievements and your potential for significant contributions to our research community.

Details of the Studentship:
- *Title of research project: Implicit Cognition and Addiction*
- *Supervisor: Dr Michael Gormley*
- *Duration: 4 years*
- *Stipend: €8,000 per annum*
- *Tuition fees: Covered for the duration of the studentship*

We look forward to welcoming you to Trinity College Dublin and supporting your academic and research endeavours.

Yours sincerely ...

*

'Dad, Dad, it's me ... can you talk for a minute?'

'Yes, of course, Katriona, everything OK?'

'Dad, you won't believe it. I got offered a scholarship to stay on in Trinity, to do a PhD in Psychology. They are going to pay my fees and everything ...'

The silence on the end of the phone fills me with dread. I still need his approval. Even after all the work. And all the hurt.

'Dad, are you there?'

'Yes ... I can't speak ... I ... I ... I'm so proud of you, my Katriona. Wow ... this is a real achievement; your grandad would be so proud of you. We are so proud of you.'

I hear Tilly in the background.

'Hold on a minute, let me tell your mum ... Yeah, she got a scholarship ... She's going to do a PhD in Trinity.'

I hear her ask what that means.

To be honest, I don't even know what it means. I had only applied because Dr Michael Gormley, my undergraduate thesis supervisor, had suggested it to me. Before that, I was leaving. Taking my first-class honours degree and getting the hell out of there. Going to get myself a 'real job', as Dave called it.

He wasn't sure what I was doing at Trinity. His lack of academic knowledge made him suspicious of that world. And a bit jealous. On the darker nights of our relationship, he would worry that he wasn't intellectual enough for me. That he wouldn't stimulate me like the Trinity men. I could never imagine anyone else in my future but Dave, and couldn't fathom that he didn't know that.

But, this time, I listened to him and applied for a job in a care home. I got the offer last week: social-care manager in a children's care home. I was going to leave Trinity and get myself a real job, start earning and doing what normal working-class people do.

But now, maybe, just maybe, I can stay in Trinity. Maybe there is more to this, and to me. Maybe I am good enough.

'Dad, are you there still?'

He's crying now. Silent tears of hope and forgiveness for himself.

'My Katriona, a PhD from Trinity. Wow, we didn't do too bad, now, did we?'

Before-and-After Pictures

I'm having lunch in Trinity, taking a break from my work as a tutor in the Access programme. Coffee in one hand, phone in the other, I'm scrolling.

Facebook first. Kirstey looks well! My old pal from Dublin 1 has posted a 'before-and-after' picture. She is tanned, face beaming, hair done in the 'after'. I screengrab, worry for a second she will be notified of this. Then open it, and zoom in.

Wow, she's lost at least two stone – three dress sizes down, she claims. It's more like two with a two-stone loss. A stone equals one dress size, according to the Slimming World leaders. Her abs look great, though. And she seems happy. I heard she's bagged herself a new fella too. Probably all due to the newfound confidence in her body!

I browse back to Facebook, read her post. She has been working with Pure Fitness. She is thanking someone called 'Ger' for her new body. I note the roll of fat hanging over my jeans. I catch sight of my double chin in the reflection of my phone.

I screengrab Ger's details.

I will follow up with him later.

I live in the grip of the fat-girl algorithm: Instagram, Facebook and 'before-and-after' pictures are my daily dish. Everywhere I look, women are posting their 'before' pictures, their fat pictures, their failing pictures, alongside their 'after' photos: their thin, successful pictures. Women are talking into my screen about how they did it, how they succeeded in their transformations. So many year-to-change-my-life stories. I feel sick and alone, and like I need so much more than a year to change my life!

The side-by-side images remind me of pictures I have shared: a middle-aged woman standing in her bra and knickers, showing her failings and her successes to the world.

Rolls of fat and cellulite and sadness appear in the left-hand pictures, the 'before' pictures, and the left-hand life. In the right-hand pictures, the 'after' pictures, is the woman who has 'done the work', 'committed' to herself, stayed 'on plan'. She stands tall: taut, toned abs, fake tan and curled hair – success in the form of skinniness.

All the comments are directed at the woman in the right-hand world – encouraging the 'after' girl, telling her, 'That's awesome' ... 'very inspiring' ... 'your waist is so tiny 😍' ... 'Way to go!!!!!!!!!' ... '👏 👏 👏 👏 👏 👏 👏 👏 ... Keep up the good work!!!'

The woman's face is always sad in the left-hand world, in the 'before' pictures. Even if she's not 'fat', if her body is smaller or curvier or bigger, she is sad in the left-hand world. The thing all 'before-and-after' women all have in common is the desire to alter how they look. To fit. To get to that place where they feel thin!

Where they feel like they are enough! Everyone in my algorithm is trying to buy a ticket to the right-hand world.

'Hi, Jenny, how are you?' I hear them chatting, look up from my phone, watch their interaction.

'Hey, Mel, I'm good ... yeah, good ... busy with marking. You know yourself ... but good.'

I avert my eyes, try to hide. I don't want to have to exchange niceties. Mel orders her skinny cappuccino, Jenny an Americano with no milk. I watch them move, my colleagues from the department. One a postdoc, the other a lecturer. They walk to a table together, at ease in themselves, smiling, chatting.

'You look so well, Mel ... you still doing the Yoga with Lucy in the sports centre?' Jenny looks her up and down, smiling in approval at the tightness of her friend's body.

'No, I'm with a private instructor on Camden Street now, 5am starts, but I feel so connected to myself – and the practice ... Ashtanga ... it's changed everything!'

They smile, more words, something about the benefits of spending two hours a day before work in yoga poses. I can see the benefits: their tiny frames, the sinewy veins that protrude from their necks and arms. The shadow of muscle definition in their legs. The way they fit perfectly into the modest uniform women in academia often wear: Oasis or Warehouse dresses, tight enough to skim their perfect forms, but not too tight to be considered sexy or slutty.

I self-consciously tug on my River Island jumpsuit, aware that the square neck is revealing just a little too much tit-line. I wish I had the commitment or the command of my body to over-yoga myself into thinness like most of the women in this world.

A picture of a friend pops up on Instagram. She looks different, lopsided. Her lips changed, puffier. One side a tad bigger than the other. Her eyebrows dip in the centre – forehead smoother than I remember. Her post reads: 'Jen's injectables have transformed the way I feel about me and my body.' She tags Jen. I click through.

Swaths of women's faces open before me. Rows and rows, columns and columns of lips and foreheads, 'befores-and-afters'. I click the reels. A half-famous Instagrammer from Tallaght is getting gifted some lips and eyebrows. I turn it off as the needle goes in. It looks sore. First time I have felt grateful for my 'blow job' lips!

It's the norm now for my working-class friends to be poking and prodding themselves with needles and fillers; to be getting facials and starting restrictive food plans. Last week, one of them stopped me, pointed to my sun-lined forehead and said, 'Have you thought about getting Botox before that gets worse?'

I watch them transform in front of me. Not just their bodies but their faces and features too – plumper lips, higher cheeks, smoother brow lines, tattooed eyebrows. Nobody looks like themselves any more.

The contrast between my people and the people I meet in the university is stark. Academics don't get lip-fillers. Their eyebrows are mostly their own. They are not posting before-and-after pictures on Instagram. Or on LinkedIn.

But they don't escape the fat algorithm – they just respond in a different way. The university women stay extremely thin. They over-yoga. They eat rice cakes or salad or couscous. They run. They have been taught to control their bodies too, but in ways that seem healthy and are masked in wellness and achievement.

They don't fly to Turkey in groups to get cheap surgery, to fit in. They don't let their newly qualified beautician pals pump chemicals into their top lips to fit in. The pressure to be slim and young, thick and curvy or thin and waif-like affects all of us – but what we do to get there differs based on where we are from.

Tadhg

'It's positive, babe ...'

I know it before we even take the test. My boobs are huge; my head feels as if a dark cloud has moved in.

'I didn't even need to take the test!'

Dave takes my hand, gives it a little squeeze, reminding me I am not alone. We are in this together.

'Well, we did say we wanted another one for Sean to play with. Remember that one night after we were in my ma's? We said that night that we would try. This baby is determined to be here.'

Dave is right: we had had one night of weakness a month ago. While visiting his ma, his brother had announced that he was having another baby. We had gone home on a high and said we should try too. One night was all it took. The next morning, we both woke, sobered from the emotion of his brother's news, and we retracted. 'What were we thinking? We're not ready for another baby!'

But baby Tadhg has different ideas. He arrives in July 2008 during the first year of my PhD. His eleven-pound, four-ounce arrival adds another element of love and stress to our already full lives. But a newborn doesn't stop me. If anything, adversity pushes me more. I stay in college, don't defer, still determined to finish in four years, to be as good as them: those 'imagined' Trinity students who do everything perfectly.

It's the same as when I had Sean in 2005. The achievement train is as addictive to me as the drugs, the men, the diets – all of them fill my head with noise.

At first, achievement seems like a more positive addiction. I am becoming socially mobile; I am learning how to move my life, and my family's life, out of the trenches. There is something magical about achieving things when you fundamentally believe that you are no good. Every success is a sign that you are wrong.

Every high heals.

Being good in university, getting good grades and being a good student, helps. It changes how I think and feel and how I see the world. It teaches me that even in a world where people hurt you, where food is scarce, where men leave, where addiction dominates, there are things about me that are good. There are things that I can be good at.

I can achieve.

The pathological drive for connection, for fulfilment, is flipped: applied to good, used for success. I transform life's horrors into academic strengths, my trauma into triumph. I flip the script and use my history to help me succeed. When I was a traumatised girl with no support and no therapy, I spent my time reacting to the world. The impact of my past drove every response. I had an incessant need to control my environment, to read everything and everyone, to never rest. My body was constantly preparing for an attack. Living near the coalface of crime taught me cunning, taught me to be able to navigate the toughest situations. I could buy and sell most people.

All these pieces of me, everything that had driven me to hurt and harm myself, become my superpowers in academia. They become the tools I use to succeed in Trinity.

In lectures, I use this awareness, my hyper-vigilance, to 'read' the lecturers, noting the inflections in their voices when telling us what to prepare for in exams. The fear, the bubbling in my stomach, the drive for control is tempered by study plans, by index cards, by reading and revising everything. My resilience, my capability to survive even at the highest threshold of stress, carries me through my third pregnancy and final baby while I'm still studying for my PhD.

The problem with becoming dependent on anything outside of yourself to feel good is that it never ends. The drive is insatiable. For good or bad, there is no end to it. And even though I am succeeding in the college, and my life with Dave and the kids is flourishing, my relationship with myself, my body, is descending into the darkest, most hellish place it has ever been.

A Wedding

'We can't do the date now as Noel has lost his job, and the stress of the cost is too much for us right now. We were thinking that maybe you might want to take the date instead, so we don't lose the deposit.'

It's December 2008. Tadhg isn't even six months old. We have just had our dinner handed to us by Dave's mam, Steph. The recession has hit Steph and Noel hard. Even the dinner is less now. Dave's stepdad, Noel, a big-skip lorry driver, is more badly affected than most. His whole job is dependent on the building industry. Now that industry has collapsed, they have nothing coming in.

Steph is asking if we want to take their wedding date in April next year. She's asking if I want to plan a wedding in four months while nursing my baby, while I'm in my second year of my PhD and, while I'm helping my mum, who has just been diagnosed with liver cancer.

'Let's do it!' I say.

Nobody knows the real reason I agree. Nobody knows that the idea of planning a wedding for a year or more fills me with absolute dread. The idea of having to spend that long worrying about what my body will look like on what's supposed to be the most beautiful day of your life is unpalatable to me. I would not survive. My mental health and my body image are on the floor. Since giving birth to Tadhg, my ability to apply any dieting knowledge to my body has left me.

I am fat.

I hate myself.

I am fat.

Having a wedding while he is under the age of one, in four months' time, gives me an out. An excuse. A reason not to be the skinny-perfect bride. It provides an out from years of diets and shrinking and comparing and worrying.

I am so low right now that I have agreed to plan a full wedding in four months, just so I don't have to face two years of the constant body-obsessing that goes with bridal life.

'Are you ready, my Katriona?'

He is here for me, my dad. He looks so well: his suit and buttonhole, his smile. He is here for me.

'Dad, do I look OK?'

I hate myself. I hate the dress. I hate the way Leigh made me get eyelashes on yesterday and how I am slow-blinking like a dairy cow. I hate that everyone is going to be looking at me – my body, my dress – judging me.

I am not a beautiful bride.

'Katriona ... my Katriona, you have always been and will always be the most beautiful girl in the world.'

For a minute, just a minute, I believe him.

The music begins. Anita Brogan, my lovely friend from my psychology degree, who has talent in abundance and kindness on tap, has offered to play me down the aisle as a gift, and, while I have no experience of classical music, I say yes! *She* is a gift.

She plays her violin, and I cannot feel my feet. Anxiety, fear of the eyes, the judgement, take over. Dad squeezes my hand. 'You're the most beautiful girl in the world.'

And then I see him. Dave, my Dave, my heart, standing at the top of the aisle, his eyes alight. Open. Warm. Wanting me. I see our Sean standing next to him and John at the edge, Tadhg in Steph's arms. And, for a moment, I don't care. He is mine and I am his. This day isn't about how I look. It isn't about the wedding. It's about the marriage, our life, our love.

I walk towards him and think about all the years of love we have had. The boys, the Mitsubishi Lancer, the night John asked Dave if he could have a chicken burger from the chipper instead of a battered sausage because Dave ate chicken burgers and John wanted to be like him. I think of Sean's birth, one of the best days of my life, and Tadhg's bright-blue eyes, how they reflect the love we all have for him and each other.

My dad holds my hand for too long when we reach Dave, not wanting to let me go, not wanting the moment we had this morning to be over. I kiss his cheek. 'I love you, Dad ... thank you.'

He lets go; so do I. For a minute, I forget that I am on show; that they are looking at my shape, my dress, my size. I hold Dave's hand and we both say 'I do'.

A Funeral

'Thank you for coming, Michael. It really means a lot to me ...'
The crematorium in Mount Jerome feels cold.
My dad.
Tony.
My hurt.
My hero.
Lies in that pine box waiting to be burned.
It is over.
Two years after he walked me down the aisle.
I look around at the faces, and shame burns hot. My Trinity colleagues have come to pay their respects. Privileged people know the rules. The lecturers, the PhDs and the admin staff sit at the back of the chapel. I can't look at them. Aware of my family. Conscious of the bandits that surround me. What a contrast we make: the poor and the posh.
Something cracks.
'Did you hear that?'
I look to Dave. He smiles and takes my hand. 'It's OK, babe. Sit here.'

I wanted to keep them apart, the two parts of my life. Forever.

I wanted to be allowed to escape. To be allowed to feel comfortable wearing Oasis dresses, modest shoes; to teach psychology without anyone knowing what I am.

That is all gone now – another dream, up in smoke, like Dad. My brother is over there with his pals from rehab. Wearing Nike tracksuits and gloves, they look as though they are going earning. The baby is drunk and late, shouting that she had to stop to get a new dress on the way here, she didn't like her old one. My mum carries the scars of her life in her face and on her hands; the small pockmarks where the needles went in are visible to anyone who looks closely. Visible to the inquisitive psychology graduates scattered around the room.

Why am I not allowed to escape?

Whitney Houston's 'I Will Always Love You' plays as the curtain opens, as he leaves us forever. The crack widens. I can't look up or down, forward or back.

I am stuck.

I find myself on the Wooden Bridge in Clontarf in Dublin one day, the statue of Mary in the distance. I want to feel close to Dad. I have this urge to see him again, to hear one of his many stories.

I think back to when I was a kid. On the rare occasion that my dad gave up the gear, he would turn to drink. Bottles of cider would appear around the house. He would sway back and forth to music, burning holes in the sofa with falling cigarettes.

'Come over here and have a look at this!' he would say. Then, he would pull out an old photograph and keep me up to sit with him late into the night, telling me stories of when he was a kid in Ireland, of riding his bike along Dollymount Strand and visiting the Virgin Mary statue at the end of the old wooden bridge in Clontarf.

'They erected that statue on the day your brother Michael was born, you know. I should have been here, but I left Tilly and went home to Ireland. I remember watching the statue being pulled up straight with Ma and Da, not even knowing I was becoming a dad on that day!'

I'd heard this story many times. And how he had met my mum at a bus stop, asked her for directions; how she had taken him home that night and they had fallen in love. When she fell pregnant within three months, he had run back to Ireland terrified, leaving her to deal with the pregnancy on her own. He'd returned when Michael was a few months old – and she insisted he marry her!

Tony was so prone to making up stories that I often had to check with my mum if they were true. The one about him leaving her was true. She had ranted about that many times.

As I walk the two kilometres down the Wooden Bridge towards the statue, close to the good memories, my nerves grow.

I am scared to look at the plaque at the base of the statue.

I fear the truth of who my dad was.

I could take his lies while he was alive, but I am not sure about how it will affect me in death.

The plaque reads *Réalt na Mara* (Star of the Sea) and the date that the memorial was blessed by the Archbishop of Dublin.

I cry hard that day.

I take a photo and WhatsApp it to Dave, my husband, waiting for me in our loving home.

He didn't lie about everything.

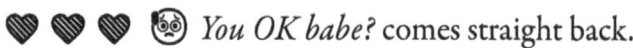 *You OK babe?* comes straight back.

This means so much to me in the instability of my grief. Knowing that some of it was true means something.

Driven

31 August 2012
Dear Ms O'Sullivan,
The examiners of your thesis have recommended that, subject to your successful completion of the recommended corrections, the doctorate degree should be awarded [...]
Following submission of your final copy, your name will be put forward for formal approval by Council and Board, after which you will be eligible to graduate [...]
Congratulations on your achievement.
Yours sincerely,
Professor Veronica Campbell,
Dean of Graduate Studies

Tony died in May 2011; it didn't stop me.
Nothing could stop me.
I continued my PhD studies.
I got a job covering someone's maternity leave in University of Limerick from January to May 2012, taking a bus twice a week,

200km each way, to lecture on developmental psychology to Limerick students.

I got my PhD in August 2012.

I passed.

It meant nothing.

I just kept going, kept achieving.

I started a full-time lectureship in Dublin Business School in September 2012: twenty hours a week of teaching and forty hours a week of preparation.

My heart and soul were poured into this new hunger to be better, do better, feel better. I turned my adversity into opportunity. I was successful. I was good. I was a good girl. Finally.

Except in the silence.

Except in the dark nights when I would cry into Dave's arms; unable to quell the hurt of my dad being gone, of my kids never knowing him, of continued body issues and the tiredness of having to keep on going.

There was no balance.

There was better.

I was able to love the boys, cook and clean. We bought our house and got a new dog, Buddy. I powered on, but at what cost?

Using all my skills to progress academically and professionally was equally good and bad. The bad was not knowing the difference between my pathological hunger to feel whole and the normal drive to be successful. I got into situations that left me drained and almost drowned. I said yes to everything, even things that were not good for me. *Yes, I can supervise that student. Yes, I can teach an extra class. Yes, I can collect that data.* All of it driven by the insatiable need to be whole, to be good.

The good was that we got out of the gutter. I got a car and a house, and we could breathe financially. We could fly to Turkey for holidays and pay the crèche fees. I stopped claiming my welfare. I had been on welfare my whole adult life. I let go of it, forever.

The good was being able to look people in the eye. *Dr O'Sullivan is in the house* – not pissy pants me, not poor me. Doctor me. Clever me.

The mixture of good and bad, hurt and hate, was better than just feeling awful all the time. But the voice inside that criticised my body kept shouting, *You are not enough, your body is not enough.*

It was as though I existed in two worlds.

In the good world, the happy world, I was a successful academic. I was a lecturer in psychology. I was a good wife and mother. I loved my family and my home was stable.

In the bad world, the world where I and my body exist, I was dying. I heard only negative words. A constant low hum followed me around, even into the joyful moments. It said: *You are not small enough; your belly is too big; your arms too fat; you need to shrink. You need to shrink.*
YOU NEED TO SHRINK!

*

Dear Dr O'Sullivan,

I am delighted to inform you that your grant application for the project titled 'An International Examination of the Impacts that Different Access Routes to Higher Education Have on Students' Capability to Participate' has been successful [...]

[...] highly impressed with your proposal and the potential impact of your research ...

We are pleased to award you a grant of €100,000 to support your project [...]

We believe your research will provide valuable insights and contribute significantly to the field of education policy.

Irish Research Council

'I got the grant, babe. I got the grant!'

I call Dave as soon as I receive the email.

'Great ... I think ...'

He's laughing. He has no idea what I do, what the grant is ... what it all means. I have to call someone, though.

'It means I am fucking great!'

He laughs again. 'Does it mean more work?'

I feel the fire in my pit. He knows what's happening. Since I started my new postdoctoral position at Trinity, he has seen me grow and grow in confidence and busyness. I am filling the days with things that feel good.

In academia, there is no end to the goals, the achievements, the things you must strive for to be deemed 'good enough'. This was one of them – a grant from a research council. I am meeting the standard, getting the gold stars.

There are also publications, promotions and permanency all within my sights, all of them sitting just ahead of me – like my size ten jeans and perfect body!

Enough.

I am enough.

*

Dear Dr O'Sullivan,

We are pleased to announce that your article, 'A Just Digital Framework to Ensure Equitable Achievement of the Sustainable Development Goals', has been scheduled for publication in Nature Communications [...]

No matter how many grants, promotions or publications my work appeared in – even *Nature Communications*, one of the best – nothing fixed me. Nothing gave me what I was looking for. Connection. Ease. Calm. Relief.

All the driving ambition meant I couldn't fully experience the joy that was happening in front of me. Always striving, looking for the next big thing, made it hard to stop and appreciate what I had achieved in my personal life: my home, my lovely kids, my marriage to Dave. Being present for any of it was hard. I couldn't fully absorb the life I had built.

Dave – with his easy nature and his desire to keep the peace –

let me chase my dream. Happy to be pulled along by my incessant drive.

Until, eventually, it caught up with me.

Until, eventually, I was forced into the present.

'It's OK, Katriona. It's OK. Nothing is stuck in your throat. You can breathe, you can breathe.'

Panic rises.

No rational thought.

It's stuck.

It's stuck.

I can't breathe.

I pant for breath, lying on the floor of the kitchen in the Trinity Access office, surrounded by a sea of female faces. All looking on with concern; some have realised I am not choking on an apple after all. This is panic. Pure panic.

My day had started the same as every other day since returning from Tilly's funeral in England four weeks earlier. My throat has been swollen with a lump that stops me from sleeping and eating properly.

Just as when Dad had died three years earlier, I force myself to go back to work as soon as I get home. I can't let them down. But, with each passing day, the sensation of my throat catching or closing is getting harder and harder to manage.

After eating nothing for two days, that morning in the kitchen at work, I tried a small Granny Smith apple to keep the food dizziness at bay. As soon as I took a bite, I begin to choke.

It's stuck.
It's stuck.
I can't breathe.
'Katriona, lie down.'
Carol helps me on to her yoga mat where I lie on my back, gasping for breath. The apple is stuck in my larynx, blocking my airway.

'It's OK, you're OK, the apple has passed through your throat now ... you're breathing.'

Carol is using her yoga voice to bring me out of the terror. Somewhere in distant parts of my mind, I know the apple is not stuck, but I can't tell this to the side of my brain that's closer. The side that manages my heart rate and my palm sweat. It won't listen.

It's stuck.
It's stuck.
You're going to die!

Ever since Tilly bled to death, since she left me, since I got home from her funeral, I've felt as if I am going to choke to death. Ever since Tilly, I have had this hard lump in my throat and this empty space where all my anxiety used to land.

I have dropped two stone in four weeks. No food can pass the lump.

That night, on our soft walk down our country lane, I tell Dave that he will have to look after our boys properly when I'm gone. That I will either die from choking or I will kill myself. His eyes hurt. His arms wrap around me.

'Please don't leave me alone, babe.'

*

I am prescribed antidepressant medication, an SSRI. The doctor says that, with my history, it's a miracle that I haven't been on medication all my life.

I am a miracle. She doesn't understand how I am still alive; how I am a doctor, a lecturer, a postdoctoral research fellow. A wife. A mother. She is fascinated.

I can't explain the hunger, the drive for achievement, how it hurts me as much as it helps, how balance evades me. The doctors only see 'success against the odds'. They don't want to hear about how fucking tired I am. How I would love to just snuggle into someone and sleep, feel protected and whole. To have peace.

I take the tablets and, eventually, the lump moves from my throat back down into my heart.

Gastric Solutions

'Heya, how are you? You look amazing!'

'Aw, thanks, love. I feel great!'

She looks over her shoulder before she leans in and whispers, 'I went to Turkey in July. I couldn't take it any more – couldn't face going back to Slimming World again. I got meself a credit-union loan and said fuck it. I got the sleeve and have lost four stone since then. I swear to God, it's saved my life.'

We are standing in the queue in Kay's Kitchen in Blanchardstown Shopping Centre. I haven't seen Michelle since January last year, when we were both at Slimming World, rejoining again, full of our usual New Year diet gusto. I didn't last a month that time.

It's December now and she looks half the size she was eleven months ago. I grab a tray and order a goat's cheese salad. I am raging. I look a state. I didn't even wash my hair this morning and I have an old tracksuit on. She is glowing.

She is glowing because she got a sleeve.

'Oh, my God, no way! How much did it cost? Where was it done? Sorry, I have so many questions.'

'It cost me €3,200, but I got a discount as I said they could use my pictures on the website for promotion. My ma went with me too and so we got more off it, like a two-for-one offer. I had some Botox thrown in for free too. They do teeth-whitening as well.'

She tells me the name of the clinic in İzmir she used. 'Oh, my God, the place was immaculate.'

I don't know whether to laugh or cry. She looks and sounds so happy.

'That'll be €15, love.'

'Oh, yeah, sorry ...' I tap my card and turn back to Michelle. 'You look fab, hun. Congratulations, chat soon.'

I feel sick with envy and shame. I feel fat. I sit down and get my phone out and Google 'gastric sleeve'. I go on Instagram and follow the clinic and several gastric-sleeve bloggers and dive into the world of all things gastric.

*

From: Katriona O'Sullivan
Sent: 11 February 2019, 11.12am
To: Bren
Subject: Re: Gastric Band Enquiry
Hi Bren,

Thanks for replying to my enquiry. I have been battling with my weight for over twenty years now and am currently at my heaviest weight of 225 pounds. I am five feet six inches and am finding that I am getting bigger rather than smaller as I age. I am 41 now and will be 42 in April. I am not sure of what my expectations are. I am very good at sticking to a diet plan initially but find it hard to maintain and I exercise regularly. I have found in the last year that my health isn't as good as it was; I am tired, I am getting colds and have been feeling less healthy, and I think this is related to my weight.

My goal is to feel healthy in my own body; this does not relate to a number on the scales. I do not aim to be a size ten, just a healthy size twelve and to have energy and feel better about my body. My hope is that the surgery can support me in my weight loss journey, and that this, along with exercising and eating better, can get me to a healthy place. I just cannot seem to do it on my own. I have been considering weight loss all my life, but I have been considering surgical help for the last year or so. I think I need something else to help me reach my goal and to be healthier.

Kind regards,

Katriona

*

From: Bren
Sent: 11 February 2019, 11.35am
To: Katriona O'Sullivan
Subject: Re: Gastric Band Enquiry

Hi Katriona,

Many thanks for your reply. I fully understand your thinking. After many years, it can become quite a negative process of trying diet after diet without long-term success. For patients in these circumstances, weight loss surgery can be a great option as, ultimately, it controls the portion size of your meals. Your goals are very realistic, which is great too!

I have posted out our information pack today. Please feel welcome to ask me any questions which may come up once you've read through it.

Bren

*

From: Katriona O'Sullivan
Sent: 11 February 2019, 11.37am
To: Bren
Subject: Re: Gastric Band Enquiry
Hi, Bren,
I have read the information online. Could I arrange a consultation?
Katriona

*

From: Bren
Sent: 11 February 2019, 12.10pm
To: Katriona O'Sullivan
Subject: Gastric Band Enquiry
Hi, Katriona,
Many thanks for your fast reply. Of course, that's no problem. All consultations take place every Monday, Tuesday and Thursday in our Dublin clinic. Currently, the next available appointment would be:
19 February 2019 3.00pm
21 February 2019 12.00pm or 1.00pm
The appointment should take about 45 minutes. Would any of the above suit?

*

From: Katriona O'Sullivan
Sent: 19 February 2019, 2.30pm
To: Bren
Subject: Re: Gastric Band Enquiry
Dear Bren,
My car has broken down on the M50 and I will not make it for three today. Could you reschedule, please? [This was a lie.]

*

From: Katriona O'Sullivan
Sent: 7 May 2019, 11.06am
To: Bren
Subject: Re: Weight Loss Surgery Enquiry
Hi, Bren,
I am sorry I could not attend in February. I was awaiting approval from the finance crowd [not true – I have the cash], which I got recently. Could I reschedule the appointment for this week? I work from 9–5, so find it hard to get there in the daytime.
Kind regards,
Katriona

*

From: Bren
Sent: 7 May 2019, 11.38am
To: Katriona O'Sullivan
Subject: Re: Weight Loss Surgery Enquiry
Hi, Katriona,
Many thanks for your reply.

That's no problem. The appointments take place during the day, from 10am onwards every Monday, Tuesday or Thursday. The only available day this week would be Thursday. Alternatively, all three days next week are available. The appointment usually takes about 45 minutes. Would a particular day suit?

*

From: Katriona O'Sullivan
Sent: 7 September 2019, 12.08pm
To: Bren
Subject: Re: Weight Loss Surgery Enquiry
Hi Bren,
I messaged you earlier this year for an assessment for a gastric band but wasn't well and couldn't attend. I am ready now – could I get an assessment?

*

From: Bren
Sent: 7 September 2019, 12.38pm
To: Katriona O'Sullivan
Subject: Re: Weight Loss Surgery Enquiry
Hi Katriona,
Many thanks for your enquiry. We will require a deposit of one hundred euros for the assessment due to the two missed appointments. We have Monday, 7 October available. If that would suit, let me know, and I will get Accounts to call you to take the deposit.

I eventually attended an assessment for the gastric band on 21 October 2019. I had enquired and booked an assessment three different times, and each time I didn't turn up, making some excuse for not going. The truth was, I was terrified and had an inkling, even back then, that this wasn't the solution to what was wrong with me. But I was well and truly trapped in the fat, hate-myself, looking-for-a miracle-cure cycle.

There was no space in that cycle for me to stop and question the feelings I was having. There was little or no body-love. If I had a thought about a diet or an exercise plan or a gastric solution, there was no pause afterwards. No moment to question it.

The shame I felt about my body had become entwined with the shame I felt about being abused. Fixing one was unconsciously attached to fixing the other. But chasing the dream of being skinny was easier than listening to the voice that said I was to blame for what had happened to me; easier than stopping and feeling the deep sadness that goes along with being abused in childhood and adulthood.

Even though I had learned how to love Dave, how to stay clean and sober, how to achieve in education and work, I had not learned how to heal my relationship with my body.

I had not learned how to process the neglect and the hunger of poverty; the men who hurt me; the ideas about myself that swum around in my head unprocessed, unhealed.

I still believed, beyond a shadow of a doubt, that shrinking would fix the way I felt about myself.

'Thanks for coming, Katriona. In this clinic, we're committed to providing our customers with the highest standard of care and support.'

I am in Bren's office. He is the front man for this gastric-band-weight-management programme. He is a robust man, chubby to say the least, which throws me. Why would a man who looks clinically 'obese' be the face of a weight-loss programme?

If this procedure is so great, why hasn't he had it done?

'Sorry about missing the assessments before; I wasn't sure whether this was for me really,' I say. I can't lie, even to a complete stranger. I have to tell him I missed the appointments on purpose.

'Don't worry about that now. We understand that this is a big decision and there will be doubts. Doubts are part of this ... so tell me about why you're here.'

'I'm fat!' I say in my best joking voice.

He doesn't laugh.

'Honestly, I hate myself. I hate my body, and I can't seem to get it under control – my eating, that is. I'm in a cycle of lose a few pounds, gain more, lose a few pounds, gain more. It's like I cannot get a grip of myself, not like I used to.'

'Katriona, this is totally normal. We see this all the time with women who are your age. Their bodies change, and it gets harder to lose the weight. We're here to help you with that. Do you know anything about the gastric-band procedure?'

I shake my head.

He pulls out a white plastic circle yoke, about ten centimetres in diameter, with a wire hanging from it and a type of button hanging on the end of the wire.

'This is the band. We do keyhole surgery and place this ring around the top of your stomach. See, it wraps around?'

He is holding up a plastic cast of what looks like a large swollen testicle that has drooped. He places the band around the drooped bit. 'This is your stomach.' (The testicle.)

'And this is where we place the band. When it's placed, this part, which is called the port, is stitched into your tummy.' (That's the button.) 'When the band has settled, we place a small amount of liquid, up to ten millilitres, into the port, which fills the band up and restricts the amount of food you can eat.'

'Oh, I see. And how fast do you lose weight?'

'It comes off steadily, but we don't recommend weight loss to be too fast, as we know there can be loose skin, and it isn't good for maintaining that loss. We want you to keep the weight off!'

'Yeah, yeah, I know. That's why I'm here – so many yo-yo diets. I just need that extra bit of help.' I'm saying the words he wants to hear. 'Are there any side-effects to this?'

'Well, there are some, but they are rare. The band can 'slip', which means you get a reflux situation. This is very rare and, if it happens, we will get you in and take it out. The band is great because it's an adjustable tool. You can adjust the level of restriction you have by getting fills and de-fills. This port is positioned in your stomach, and you can get a millilitre of fluid put in or taken out on each visit to the clinic. We fit the band, we let it settle, and then we build up the restriction. It takes different amounts for different people to get restriction. When it's restricted, what happens is food will be harder to eat, as in, you will literally not be able to get the food to fit into your stomach. Smaller amounts of food will make you feel full. It's a tool to help you learn how to stop eating.'

'That all sounds great. If I wanted to get it done, when could you fit me in? Could we do it soon?'

'We usually have a four-week turnaround for these things, depending on financial situation and the availability of the surgeon. Luckily, it's not too invasive, so you only have to stay in for one night in the clinic.'

'Sounds great. Can we start the process, then?'

'... the surgeon specialises in gastric procedures and is world renowned ...'

'Uh-huh, yeah, great, so can we get the process going?'

'We'll need to complete some assessment first. Can you fill in these health forms? I'll be back in a minute with the details of the finance options.'

'Oh, I'll pay cash – I have some money saved.'

I am lying. I completed some consultancy work with a tech company over the summer and have decided that I will use the money to pay for this. It's my money, so I should do what I want with it.

'OK, fill these in for me and we can get you weighed today.'

'Oh ... Do I have to be weighed now?'

He will find out how fat and lazy you really are now! And that you lied about your weight in the initial email.

'Yes, best to get it over with! It will be the last time you are this weight,' he says, laughing as he leaves the room.

I sit, filling out the questions.

Diabetes – no.

Heart disease – no.

Depression – *oh, no, should I tell the truth? Will they let me have it if I say yes?* I tick yes. Best to be honest.

Have you ever been diagnosed with an eating disorder? *Oh, no, do I tell him about my stint in the Rutland Centre where they claimed I had food addiction? Do I mention the secret eating?*

Eating disorder – no.

If I say I don't have an eating disorder, then I don't, right?

'OK, so quick review here. The depression answer – are you on any medication?'

'Yes, sertraline. Ten milligrams.'

'Great, well, this all looks OK. You say you don't drink alcohol – do you mean ever?'

They don't even care that you're depressed – should you really be here? Are they even good people?

'No, I'm in recovery, don't drink or do drugs!'

Why do you always overshare?

He looks uncomfortable and continues to scroll through the form.

'This all looks fine. Can you jump on to the scale there, and then I'll measure you?'

The scales are massive. Industrial-sized, square silver weighing scales for really big people. He measures me then with the measuring thing, which is fitted to the wall. I stand as tall as I can, knowing that, if I add an inch or two, my BMI will be lower.

He smiles. 'Put your feet flat on the ground for me ... Two hundred and thirty-eight pounds, and I have here that you're five feet, five inches – is that about right?'

'Oh, my, I must be shrinking!' I laugh, but he doesn't laugh back.

'OK, so your BMI is 37.5, which puts you in the obese category and you qualify for the band. You need to be over 30 to qualify. Next thing is to get a date for you and get you to pay a deposit – does that sound OK?'

'Yes, great!'

Gastric Lies

Weight: 238 pounds
Goal weight: 180 pounds
Date: 22 October 2019

'Do you get put under or is it just a local?'

'To be honest, I'm not sure. I stay in for the night, so I assume I'm put under.'

'And can you eat straight away or what?'

'I don't know yet. They're going to send me the details.'

'Will it be painful?'

'He said it won't be too bad.'

Dave is looking at me with wide eyes. He's worried about me and worried for the boys. Sean is fourteen; Tadhg eleven. They need me. I know he doesn't want me to do this. The questions are a mask. I lie about the pain not being too bad. I don't even know because I didn't ask. All I know is that I will lose weight with this and feel better. I don't know why Dave is even questioning that.

'How much is it going to cost us?'

'I'm going to pay it out of the extra work I've done, so it will cost us nothing!'

He pauses for a minute and looks at me. Softly.

'Babe, you know you don't need to do this. I love your body. You are beautiful to me.'

He looks scared as he speaks. He knows what I'm like. His fear makes me feel ashamed. *Am I that bad?*

'Dave, I hate how fat I am; I hate how I can't control myself – I can't even stand to be touched at this point. It's affecting everything. I try so hard to control myself – you see me. I just want it to be easier. I just want to lose some weight, babe. Please support me. I can't do this without you.'

I watch him suck it all up. I see him take all his doubts, all his love for me, all his desire to protect me from myself, and place them to one side. He reaches for my hand. The distance between us gets smaller.

'Of course I'll support you, babe. I want you to be happy. If this is the thing you need, I'm here for you.'

I want to cry in that moment. Tears of relief, not sadness. If he is with me, I can do this. If he had stood firm and said no or please don't, I would have yielded. My desire to stay connected to him is more important than everything else – except the boys!

But he relents. He stands back and lets my demon lead me.

'When is this thing going in, then? When is the op?'

'Next Wednesday,' I say quietly.

'NEXT WEEK? Next week, OK, OK, let's do this, so.

*

Weight: 227 pounds
Goal weight: 180 pounds
Date: 6 November 2019

'Oh, my God, it's only been eight days and I've lost eleven pounds, eleven fucking pounds – that's nearly a whole dress size!'

I feel high. Elation. Success. It's working ... It's actually working.

'Of course you've lost weight. You're not fucking eating, babe.' Dave's face is contorted with concern. 'You're supping on water and protein shakes and the odd spoon of yoghurt. How long will this go on for?'

'I can eat mushy foods next week. Stop being so negative – you're ruining this for me. I've been trying to lose seven pounds for a year, and I've smashed that in eight days. EIGHT FUCKING DAYS!'

*

Weight: 207 pounds
Goal weight: 180 pounds
Date: 24 December 2019

'Babe, babe, before we head off, will you take a photo of me? Don't pull that face, please. I want to compare what I look like.'

On the day of the surgery, I had asked Dave to take a picture of me in my bra and knickers. Thirty pounds down later, I want – no, I *need* – a comparison picture. I take my T-shirt off in the middle of the kitchen, showing off my new bright-pink sports bra that I got from Marks last week. I expect him to ogle me, but he is too focused on the phone. My being thirty pounds lighter has no impact on him or the way he looks at me.

'Hello!'

He looks up and smiles. 'Sorry, babe, you know I'm no good at this stuff.'

He holds the camera up and clicks away. I grimace.

'Higher, babe, higher with the phone, angle it a bit ... Jesus, Dave. Can you please just get one good picture?'

He hands me the phone and walks off. He's pissed off. I scroll through the photos, disappointed at what I see. The flab is still hanging over my leggings, my silver stretch marks visible. I note a roll of flab popping out over the bra strap under my left arm. I reach around and feel it.

'I need to go to the gym.' I say it out loud.

I find the best of the pictures, click 'edit', and resize the picture to cut out the background. Adding a sunshine filter makes my skin look browner and smoother.

The PicCollage app starts really slowly.

'Are you ready, babe? We said we'd pop to my mam's for a quick drop-off of the presents. What are you doing?'

My agitation and disappointment in how I look boil over.

'I NEVER SAID I WANTED TO GO YOUR MAM'S – YOU MADE THE FUCKING PLANS!'

As soon as the words leave my mouth, I regret them. It isn't his fault I feel fat. It isn't his fault I can't eat properly and am starving all the time. It isn't his fault I still hate myself.

I look down and load the old picture from the day of my surgery, the day I went in to get the band fitted. I'm wearing an old grey bra, hair in messy plaits. I add the picture of me today to the collage, widening and stretching the earlier pictures to emphasise the difference in my weight from before to now.

I hear the front door slam and his car start.

I look up for a brief minute, then back to my phone.

Elation fills every vein. I have lost weight. When the pictures are side by side, you can see a big shift.

I feel better.

I open Instagram, upload the collage and write underneath: *30lbs down in 30 days; 30lbs gone forever, baby! #weightlossjourney #gastricband #weightloss.* I click 'share'.

I stare down at my phone and think about Dave. *Shit!* Why am I so mean to him? Why does he stay with me?

If you keep treating him like shit, he'll leave you for someone else.

I open WhatsApp. I see he's online even though he's driving. I wonder if he's on a call to Ger telling him what a cunt I've been lately.

I type a message.

Babe, I'm sorry for snapping. I'm starving and feel stressed about Christmas. You know how sad I get this time of year. If you're still close by, will you come back for me? I'm sorry. Let's have a good day. I love you. X

As he pulls up outside, I check Instagram. Thirty-five people have liked my post. I look at the list of 'likers' to note who is watching. I have ten messages.

Babe, you look amazing!
Keep going. Well done you.
Wow, hot momma!

It's working!
I am enough!

I look at the photos again. I have lost weight. It's definitely visible. I zoom in on the pink bra and think, *tomorrow I join the gym.*

*

Weight: 187 pounds
Goal weight: 180 pounds
Date: 4 March 2020

'Excuse me, can you hold off on the mains for a minute, please? I'm just going to pop to the ladies."

The waiter points me towards the bathroom door.

'Back in a minute, babe,' I say to Dave.

He looks pissed off. This is my third trip to the bathroom since we sat down to eat dinner. We're in Rudy's Steakhouse in Blanchardstown village. We're celebrating sixteen years together. Sixteen years! He booked this place because it's where we had our first proper date. He took me here in early March 2004. He was dressed in his best friend's brown leather jacket, and I wore a black-and-red off-the-shoulder Morgan top and a short leather skirt. We ate, we flirted and we enjoyed each other. Tonight is a celebration of our success. Sixteen years on and we still love each other.

'For fuck's sake, love, you're spending more time in there than with me. It's embarrassing!'

I look at him with regret but still walk towards the bathroom.

I have food lodged in my band.

The ritual starts. I have to get sick before I can continue with the night. The spicy chicken wings we got to share for starters have lodged in my band and until I get the chicken 'out', I will keep burping and heaving. No other food will get in. Not even water will slip past the blockage.

This is my life now.

Food is my enemy.

I have to eat slowly and with focus or else it gets 'stuck', and I have to vomit.

I am vomiting every day.

At every meal.

But at least you are slim!

I wait until I know there's no one else in the bathroom, then I bend over the toilet seat. I wait. Sometimes, gravity does the work for me and the lodged food comes up and out by itself.

Nothing is happening.

I push my fingers down my throat and gag loudly. A small bit of wee leaks out at the same time as the loud gag.

Nothing.

It's still there.

I can feel it in my chest.

Stuck.

Goading me.

Reminding me of the bad choices I've made in the pursuit of skinny.

A tiny piece of chicken is causing all this commotion.

I push my finger down again and this time let out a loud gag and the chicken flies out of my mouth into the piss-stained toilet bowl.

Relief.

As soon as it's out, I know I'm free to eat again.

I check myself in the mirror. I look good in this dress – a short black velvet mini with red roses embroidered on the shoulders. The roses remind me of Cheryl Cole's arse tattoo. Penneys' best. Black tights and flat boots. I'm a size twelve.

I turn sideways and look at my stomach. It protrudes over my tights, and I can see a roll of skin bursting through the velvet dress, making my waist misshapen. I wear tights to hold it in, but sometimes it escapes. I yank the tights up higher, causing a tiny ladder in the top of my thigh. 'Shit!' I only bought these today.

I turn back to myself in the mirror, noting that the overhanging skin is still there. It has been there since I gave birth to John. An eight-pound, thirteen-ounce baby left me with an overhang of skin that is resistant to all abs exercises. I push my stomach in with my hand.

If that loose skin was gone, you would be happy. You would be finally where you want to be.

I put my face close to the mirror. There are burst blood vessels in my left eye from vomiting.

Being sick like that isn't normal.

I reapply my lipstick and ignore that thought. I'm a size twelve; I'm nearly there. I can put up with a small bit of sickness to be slim!

*

Weight: 177 pounds
New goal weight: 160 pounds
Date: 15 September 2020

'Kat, I'm over here with Kate, and the doctor recommended the gastric balloon for me, not the band. He says the band can slip and that if I get the balloon, I'll be able to remove it after six months when I've reached goal weight. He'll be able to fit it while I'm under and getting my tits done.'

'Leigh, I heard the balloon isn't great.' I'm an expert now on all things gastric surgery. 'I'm in this private group on Facebook, and there are girls on it who didn't like the balloon. I'll send you the link to the group.'

'I know. I know. There are bad reviews of everything, even the band gets bad reviews, Kat, but look at you – I've never seen you look so great! You're keeping it off, too.'

I flush with pride. I am nearly at my target weight, and Leigh complimenting me – my best friend and fellow diet junkie telling me how great I'm doing – is the ultimate boost. We never say how well we are doing. We always talk about failing or changing or being fat. Leigh saying I am slim must mean I am slim!

But why do you still feel fat, then?

'Leigh, you're there and you know what's best for you. If you think it's a good idea, go for it. Did you get a good read on the hospital and surgeon? There's a group on Facebook about dodgy Turkey hospitals. Are you on it? Send me the name so I can look it up.'

'It's fine, Kat. I know someone who got a BBL' – that's a Brazilian Bum Lift – 'here last month. It's immaculate, so clean – it would put East Birmingham Hospital to shame.' She laughs. 'I'm going to get the balloon and see what happens. Kate is too. We'll be a double act on the plane home – me with the tits and balloon and her with a tummy tuck and balloon.' She laughs again.

'OK, OK, keep in touch then. Text me when you wake up ... love you.'

I'm still shining from her compliment.

People are noticing.

I am a success.

*

Weight: 180 pounds
New goal weight: 160 pounds
Date: 25 September 2020

Instagram Messenger:
Amanda: Katriona, you look unreal. What are you doing? You look ten years younger.

Katriona: Hiya, Mandy – stop! I still have a few pounds to lose. I got a gastric band fitted last October – the weight is flying off.

Amanda: Wow, where did you get it? Was it expensive? You look great, hun.

Katriona: I'll send you the link to the place. It was eight grand and worth every penny. They do a finance option too. Couldn't recommend them more – great service.

Amanda: Yes, send me the link. I'm struggling. Need to do something before it gets out of hand.

I lied. The service wasn't great. I don't tell her that they put a band in me despite me being clinically depressed and having no capacity to control my food intake. I don't say that the band they placed around my stomach did nothing to stop the insatiable hunger for food. If I could reduce my food intake on my own, with self-control, I would not be asking for help from a gastric surgeon.

Telling my friends how great the clinic was, and how wonderful the experience was, was my way of telling myself that I had done the right thing. What was the other option? Being honest? Admitting that this 'tool' was harming me more than helping? Telling them that I was getting sick every day, at every meal. Telling them that I was willing to accept being sick, being weak, being unable to dine out with friends and family so I could fit into a size-twelve dress.

Would I tell them that I feel no different about myself? That my self-worth and self-esteem are only boosted by the comments of others. That, inside, I feel the same disgust with my body as I always have. That there is no rest for me, no peaceful body thoughts.

Do I share with them that I am posting more and more on social media just so the outside world can tell me I am OK – tell me I'm good, acceptable?

This Is Not Right

The party is full now and the DJ has hit the nineties classics. The walls are sweating. The tiny dance floor swells with ageing ravers. Indigo strobe lights blind my eyes and my feet hurt. My legs are getting bigger. My dress is getting shorter. The waiter walks by with a platter of food and, without thinking, I reach out, grabbing a sausage roll. Even though it's lukewarm and soggy, I eat it too fast. As soon as I swallow it, bile rises in my throat. I know it has got stuck, and now I am here – stuck.

I look around for Dave. He's chatting to Ger and his friends. I head to the toilet, panic rising in my chest. It feels as if the party has doubled in size. I swerve through the crowd, bile rising with each step, hoping the toilets are empty.

No such luck. Friends of a friend grab me in the queue for the ladies'. One of the women is about a size eighteen. Blonde and pretty, she smiles at me, while taking a long, sweeping look, examining me from top to bottom.

'Katriona, is it? Hi, hi ... I'm Lauren's pal. I heard you got one of them gastric sleeves. You look stunning – was wondering if you would recommend them?'

I smile. 'Oh, my God! Hi! Thank you ... thanks ...'

The bile feels like a volcano about to explode. I make a small involuntary choking sound.

'I still have a few pounds to lose, but I'm delighted. I can wear anything I want now.'

I point to my tanned legs. My black body-skimming River Island dress fits my curves perfectly. I forget how much I hated this dress five minutes ago.

'I actually got a gastric band, not a gastric sleeve. The band is reversible, you see. I can take it out. I was afraid of how permanent the sleeve is. Yes, I got it here in Dublin. I'm delighted with it.'

I glimpse my face in the mirror; a sheen of sweat is forming on my brow. The sausage roll sits on top of my throat, heating up my insides.

'Amazing!' the woman replies. 'Yeah, my pal got the sleeve, but she gets this 'dumping' thing. You know, when she eats bad foods, she can't keep it down. It comes out all ends of her. Do you have that?'

I wish they would leave me the fuck alone to get sick; the ball of pressure in my chest is becoming unbearable.

I smile. 'No, no, I don't get any of that,' I lie. Why do I lie? I'm standing here, trying not to suffocate in clear sight of the entire party.

'That's great!'

Another choking sound escapes my lips. She doesn't notice. Too enthralled with the idea of getting skinny.

'That's the thing with the band. You don't get the same side-effects as the sleeve.'

I wonder if my eyes are bulging. I want to tell her that you can't eat properly, that you get sick with every meal, that there's no more rice or chicken. That there is no more mindless eating. I want to grab her by the face. Scream at her. To tell her it's fucked up. *I* am fucked up. That it hasn't worked. It's the worst thing I have done to myself.

How can I admit that to her? I can't even admit it to myself.

I put my fingers down my throat for the fifth time, and the sausage roll stays put. Choking. Gasping for breath between heaves. Panic rises. What if I can't get it up?

I've been in this cubicle for fifteen minutes. The steady flow of women, coming in and out of the toilet, probably think I'm doing coke in here. Even Dave has texted me. He knows what's going on.

I'm worried this thing will stay stuck forever. I take out my phone, open WhatsApp and type, *Dave, bring a can of Coke to the door of the ladies' toilets, please.*

I wait.

Beep-beep. He responds. *I'm outside.*

I open the door and grab the can from him; catch his disappointed look before I head back in. I lock the door of the cubicle, open the can, squeeze my nostrils closed and gulp back the full can of Coke. Gas and the pressure of gulping make me projectile-vomit into the toilet; Coke sprays everywhere – the floor and walls. I pause to wipe my nose and mouth. Blinking slowly, gulping in the air.

Relief and shame fill the silence.

The remnants of the sausage roll float around the toilet.

It's out. Thank fuck for that.

I wipe up the mess and walk outside. Shame, guilt, pride follow me. A girl I don't know, who was probably in the cubicle next to me, stares at me as I walk by. I ignore her, and the niggling doubt that has me in its grip. I walk towards Dave.

THIS IS NOT RIGHT!

This gastric band makes me feel horrible. I'm vomiting every single day. I can't eat bread or chicken or rice or vegetables. I can't stand myself with food or without food. It isn't worth it! There is no joy in this. I'm a size twelve. I'm supposed to be satisfied. I've got here. Reached the goal. At target. If I were in WeightWatchers now, I would be getting my gold membership! There would be lots of silver sevens for me.

So why don't I feel happy? Why can't I look at myself in the mirror? Why am I still obsessed with the scales?

If I can just get these last few pounds off, then maybe, just maybe, I will feel it.

THIS IS NOT RIGHT!

Bren from the clinic says that getting sick is rare. He says that you need to find the sweet spot where you learn to eat slowly and can 'fit' food through the small space created by the band. The clinic says that you should chew food, every mouthful of food, at least ten times.

They suggest counting out loud while you're chewing. They recommend putting your fork down between each bite. Fork in, fork out, fork down. Chew for ten. Fork in, fork out, fork down. Chew for ten.

I am ashamed. I can't chew ten times. I can't put the fork down between bites.

Despite the success in my life, I can't control the body hate. The diet is beyond me. I am a lecturer now, working in Maynooth University, leading an initiative that aims to get diverse students into teaching, and I'm so good at it. I have agency and passion and joy in my work. My marriage is strong; the love has gone from strength to strength. Our boys are good, healthy, happy. But I cannot chew my food ten times or put the fork down between bites.

The 'stuck' brings everything into focus. It's like a microscope, magnifying my inability to control myself, highlighting my inability to follow the rules, to be a good girl.

I've only ever wanted to be a good girl.

In my secret moments of distress, when I am berating myself, my head hanging over the toilet bowl, a sobering thought emerges. Even if Bren from the clinic had told me about this, about the 'stuckness' and the sadness and the sickness – even if he had shown me the depth of grief I would feel at the loss of gorging food – I probably would have still gone through with it.

I hated myself enough to do this back then.

I hate myself even more now.

HUNGRY

From: Katriona O'Sullivan
Sent: 20 April 2020 10.12am
To: Chloe
Subject: Book for de-fill
Hi,
I am finding it really hard to eat since my last band fill. Could I come in and get a little bit of fluid out, please?
Katriona

*

From: Chloe
Sent: 20 April 2020, 10.36am
To: Katriona O'Sullivan
Subject: Book for de-fill
Hi, Katriona
We can see you at 3pm today in the clinic for a de-fill.
Chloe

*

From: Katriona O'Sullivan
Sent: 16 August 2020, 11.16pm
To: Chloe
Subject: Book for fill
Hi, Chloe,
I was in for a fill last week and have no restriction at all in my band. Could I come in please for it to be checked and filled? I am going away in a week and would like to have this done before then if possible.
Kind regards, Katriona

*

From: Chloe
Sent: 17 August 2020, 10.12am
To: Katriona O'Sullivan
Subject: Book for fill
Hi Katriona,
Many thanks for your email. This is normal to feel this way as you have had a de-fill in the past couple of months. It is going to take a few adjustments to get you back into the green zone. The next safe and available adjustment for yourself is 15 September.
  Let me know if this date suits you and I can confirm it for you.
  If you have any questions, don't hesitate to contact me.
  Kind regards, Chloe

*

From: Katriona O'Sullivan
Sent: 20 December 2020, 10.12am
To: Chloe
Subject: Book for de-fill
Hi, Could I come in and get fluid out of my band, please?
Katriona

*

From: Chloe
Sent: 20 December 2020, 10.36am
To: Katriona O'Sullivan
Subject: Book for de-fill
Hi Katriona
We can see you at 1pm today in the clinic for a de-fill.
Chloe.

I can't take it any more. My quality of life is so bad that I cry every day. The vomiting, the restriction, the loss of food, Dave's anger and disappointment – they are too much to take. I'm getting sick now in secret, so he doesn't know.

Even Sean and Tadhg, our beautiful boys, know something is wrong.

'Mam, are you OK?' Tadhg calls to me from outside the downstairs toilet.

I have chugged a glass of Coke in the hope that the stuck food will be pushed out. I know Tadhg's big blue eyes, which express all his emotions, are scared.

I have always insisted that we eat dinner together. Years ago, when I started my psychology degree at Trinity College, I read somewhere that families who have dinner around the table have better outcomes than those that don't. I took that home. If we eat together, we will do better.

This band, this drive for thinness, is even affecting that. I can't even enjoy a meal with my boys. During every meal, I have to get up from the table, head into our small utility room-bathroom and regurgitate stuck food. During every meal, I have to sit back down and ignore the concerned looks of my two sons and their dad. Ignoring the inner voice that is getting louder and louder until it is screaming at me.

*

Date: 25 March 2021
Weight: 192 pounds
Goal weight: 180 pounds

'OK, so you've put on twelve pounds since your last de-fill in December. Obviously that's a little disappointing, but we can pull things back.'

She isn't even looking at my face. She is concentrating on finding the spot on my torso where the port is, the entryway to the band.

'We'll put one mill. in today and see how it goes, OK?'

'Yes, that sounds good. It's really hard. As soon as I take any of the fluid out, I just start gaining again. I've started jogging, so hopefully that will help.'

'It's about balance, trying to find your sweet spot where you're listening to your body.'

I want to tell her that I cannot listen to my body. That it is emotionally impossible for me to take a moment out of this cycle to hear myself. The hunger, the hatred, the sadness would kill me. I think about dying more than I should. If I were to stop and pay attention to the world inside me, I am sure I would blow my own head off.

'OK, all done.'

The band is back to being restrictive. I feel it immediately. She hands me a plastic cup of water. I must drink this before I can leave. I take a drink and feel it pop back up my throat. I am too restricted. I know that food will not be able to pass by this level of restriction. I take a smaller sip and let it go down. She pays no heed to me, so I walk out of the clinic, throwing the half-full cup of water into the bin on my way out the door. I'll let the restriction be this bad until I am back down to 180 pounds, then I will come back to get half a millilitre taken out.

Healing

WhatsApp:

Katriona: Hi Máire, my name is Katriona. Jamie Judge, a counsellor I know, passed your details to me. I'm looking for a therapist, and he said you were really good. Could we arrange a session?

Máire: Hi Katriona, lovely to hear from you. I have an appointment available for tomorrow afternoon if that would suit – 2pm. We could talk and see if this is something that would work for us both. M

Katriona: Perfect, Máire. Can you send me your address and I will be there? Thank you.

Máire: Here is my Eircode. Looking forward to meeting you.

'Can I ask what your qualifications are ... like what type of therapy you do, and whether you have supervision? I'm a psychologist myself' – (cringe) – 'and I know there are some people out there who have no real qualifications. I went to a woman once in Blanch village, and she told me after my first session that I was being very hard on my mam!'

Stop talking so much ...

'Great question. I trained in Gardiner Street, and Jamie supervises me. I practise integrative therapy, so, really, I choose different methods to try to help us build a relationship and aid the healing process.'

She is so calm when she speaks. Her eyes are bright. Shiny. She is comfortable in her body. A large orange necklace around her neck, big orange balls. Her white linen shirt sits loosely over her khaki-coloured slacks. Modest shoes. But kind eyes. I am always trying to figure out if people are safe. If they are going to judge me.

If it is safe for me to share.

'Do you want to tell me a little bit about why you're here?'

'Yes ... and no. To be honest, I hate the first session of therapy. I dump out my whole life while you build a genogram of me and my family, and I leave feeling like I'm raw. Can I just share a bit today? Like, go slow?'

'Of course – you're in charge. I'm here to listen and check if I can be of help to you.'

'I'm here because I have no peace, really. I'm really successful in my life. I'm married. I love my husband, Dave. My three kids are good. I'm a doctor – PhD in psychology, lecturer, a great life. But I find it really hard to feel happy, always swinging from good to bad. I had a hard childhood. My parents were heroin addicts. They're both dead now, but it was hard. No food, no love, lots of heavy shit – sorry, I swear a lot – but I struggle to be happy. I explode at people – friends and family. More than anything, I want to be happy and good, but I can't hold on to it – the happiness, I mean.'

Tears fall. There are tissues on the table next to the large comfy armchair I'm sitting in. Behind Máire's head is a wall full of books. What feels like millions and millions of books. As I share my guarded soul with her, I look at the books. *The Road Less Travelled* is there, *The Body Keeps the Score* – I love that one. Lots of Ivor Browne. My eyes focus everywhere but her.

'OK, I see. And when you say you feel like you can't be happy and good, is there anything that makes you feel good now?'

I stop. The tears flow harder. I cry harder at the good stuff.

'My boys, Dave – I'm proud of us, of me, of the love we've created. We eat dinner together every day. Sean is such a good boy. Tadhg is a livewire. And then there's John, my eldest. He's in England, plays football. He's good too. My home makes me feel good. I wonder how I did it – escape, I mean. If I stop and think about them and what I have there, I feel happy.'

'That sounds wonderful, Katriona. Well done. It sounds like you had a tough start, so having a strong marriage and love in your home is wonderful to hear.'

The kinder the words, the more I cry. 'I can't stop, though, that's the thing. I am never happy. I'm driven, constantly looking for more – I am so tired. I'm only happy when I'm driving towards something. I run, you see. I mean, I started running last year to lose weight, and it's an obsession. I'm no good at it. I have these' – I point to my boobs – 'they stop me being fast, but I keep setting these targets to reach, not reaching them, then feeling crap. And I'm not happy with my body. I'm constantly dieting, aiming for a different body. I've done so much to myself that I'm tired, so fucking tired.'

I'm looking at her feet now. She is wearing sandals in November. I wonder if she buys them from FatFace or maybe Clarks. They are modest shoes, and it's cold out. This choice makes no sense. It's warm in here, though.

Her counselling room is a little side room off her big house. Walking into the hallway today, I noticed the plants and the paintings: a huge drawing of a hare on the wall alongside a painting of some balloons flying in the sky. *She's wealthy*, I thought. *I hope she's not wealthy-judgy.*

'It sounds like you're carrying a lot, Katriona – that you've created some really good things in your life, but you have some things you want to let go of, maybe?'

'Yeah ... yeah.' I'm still crying. This is why I hate therapy: so much crying. I grab a tissue from the box and look at the little clock on the windowsill. I'm anxious not to let the session run over. I would hate for her to think that I'm needy or that I want more time than I'm paying for.

'Your parents are dead, but can you tell me a little bit about them and your family?'

'Dad, Tony, died when he was fifty-six, about ten years ago, and my mum, Tilly, three years later. Both died from addiction. Well, the consequences of their addiction. Throat cancer and my mum, she bled to death – a variceal bleed, alcoholism. She went back on heroin when she was sixty – fucking sixty! If I'm honest I'm glad she's gone, but I miss my dad.'

Oh, she reads Philip Pullman too. I notice one of his books on the shelf. I wonder if she has read all these books.

'You've been through a lot, and you are still young. The death of a parent is hard, but when there are complicated relationships it can be extra-tough. What are you hoping to get from therapy?'

'I don't know. I just feel so tired. I keep trying, really trying, to be good, to be better, and then I lose it. I can't stick to a diet or exercise. I can't commit to things like I used to. I'm tired. And I keep exploding on people. I recently lost the head with someone in the running club I joined, a club I loved, and now I can't go back. It feels like my life is a series of failed relationships, apart from Dave, and I just want it to stop.'

I'm crying really hard now. I look her in the eye and say, 'I think I deserve to be happy. I want help with that.'

I see her flinch a little, not in an angry way. She wants to reach out to me. I see the kindness in her eyes and the softness in her soul.

'Katriona, I would be happy to help you with your journey. It sounds like you've achieved a lot that you should be proud of. I would ask that you take some suggestions on board if we are to work together. They might be hard, but to try to get to a place of healing, they might help you.'

'Yes, yes, of course, I'll do anything.' I hear myself lying to her already. I don't actually know if I'm willing to do anything to heal. But I want her to think I'm a good girl. I'm a hard worker. I'm willing. I want her to like me.

'It might be good to try to stop achieving some of the things you mentioned while we work together. To go easy for a while. The running and dieting might need to be left aside for a little while. Just while we work towards understanding and healing.'

Is she suggesting I stop dieting? NO FUCKING WAY. I'll just get fat!

'OK, OK ... I can do that. Can we start working together, then? I would like to. If you think you can help me.'

No fucking way am I working with you because you'll make me fat again.

When I left Máire's house, I was convinced that I would never go back. I could not imagine a world where I was not striving to be thin or fit or both. I had lived all my adult life with the constant hunger to be smaller. Letting go of that seemed impossible. I agreed to another appointment despite my doubts. I had two weeks before I had to see her again – ample time to think this through. *To make my excuses.*

'Mam, will you be OK?' Tadhg looks up at me from his dinner.

'What ... son ... what do you mean?' I answer, confused.

'You can't eat with us any more. You get sick a lot. You just ... don't seem happy, Mam.'

His wide eyes tell me he is scared asking me this question, that he has been thinking about it a lot. I want to snatch his fear away. Erase it from his mind. Not let any part of me affect any part of him. But it's too late. He sees me, and this. I'm not hiding anything, from me or from them.

'Of course I'll be OK. Please don't worry, I'm working on this. I started to see someone last week. I promise you I'm going to be OK!'

I reach over and awkwardly squeeze the hand that's holding his fork. I want to erase his fear, never have my past affect his future.

And, so, the decision is made. I will keep seeing Máire. No matter how hard it gets, I will work to get better for me, and for them. The pain of staying the same and hurting my little family looks far worse than the pain of trying to change.

Despite the trepidation and the doubts, I kept going back to see her. I kept going back to me. I got the band emptied, stopped contacting the clinic. Let go of the idea that it would fix me.

And, with each session, with each week, that passed, the clouds started to lift. I started to talk. About the hunger. The hurt. For the first time, I talked about all of it: about the boys and the men who hurt me, whom I hurt. Things that Dave doesn't even know.

I began to connect my past with the present. To see how my body was stolen from me. When it got hard, I thought of Tadhg and his words. The desire to live a full life drove me on. The desire to change their destiny kept me showing up. Speaking up.

'Why didn't she love me, Máire ... what was wrong with me?'

The air in the room is still; the heat from her radiator fills the space between us, her eyes alight with love and hurt, reflected in mine.

'I was so small and helpless. What did I do wrong? What was wrong with me?'

This is the deepest I have ever gone. The darkest I have ever shone a light. This is the theme tune of my life.

She didn't love you because you did something wrong.

This has underpinned everything. All the decisions. All the hate. I feel it engulf me, the room getting bigger as I shrink into the chair.

'Katriona.' I hear her in the distance. 'You did nothing wrong; there was nothing wrong with you; there *is* nothing wrong with you.'

She is pulling me back into the room. Máire, my new anchor, the person whom I have chosen to tell it all to. I stare at her and cry. No words. Nothing to say.

I know she means it.

I know she means it.

I hope I will mean it one day too,

'I know you don't like all the woo-woo stuff, but I've got you something. I'm hoping you might let me show you her.'

She reaches behind her chair before I have agreed. She pulls out a doll: a beautiful knitted doll with long blonde pigtails and a lovely pink dress. She sits her down on the spare armchair, directly across from me.

'I saw her in a market last week and as soon as I did, I thought of you. She reminded me of you.'

She thinks of me when I'm not here. This makes me feel warm.

'I'm not asking you to do anything, but I would like it if we could sit her on the chair here; if we could invite her into our sessions together. I've called her little Katriona. Would that be OK with you?'

I nod. I can't answer, my voice swallowed whole by my tears.

She sits the doll down gently on the chair and I look at her. My hair was never naturally blonde, I started dyeing it when I was fourteen, but the way she sits across from me, her face, the line of her shoulder, does remind me of me when I was small. I look at her in the chair. Remembering how small and vulnerable I was. How sweet I was.

'I want to talk a little bit more about Tilly, Katriona. If we could go back a little bit to where her life started ... You had told me that she was hurt as a child too, that her dad was an alcoholic who beat her with a belt ... is that right?'

I nod along, picturing my mum being hit by her drunk Irish dad, her little hand scalded red by his belt buckle.

'And then, as an adult, she was so hurt by your dad that addiction was her way out. It made her a shell of herself, unable to love herself – let alone you. Would you agree with that?'

I see my mum sitting on the chair with the can on her knee, snarling at me, waiting to pounce. I see her climbing the stairs with a punter behind her, selling her soul and her body for a bag of gear for her and my dad. I see Tilly. I feel Tilly.

'I'm not saying what she did was right, because it wasn't. I get angry when I hear what she did. What I'm saying is, I don't think she had a choice.'

Tears stream silently as I think of our last day together. She was in a hospital bed, liver failing, yellowed eyes, skin paper-thin. I see her laugh as she tells me she is going to have to cut back on the drink. She thinks she has gone too far this time. I see my mum. My poor mum, who could never find a rope strong enough to pull herself out of the trenches.

Cleaning Up the Piss – and My Body

'Can you pull your trousers down there and lie on your side facing the wall? Just push your backside out towards me.'

She puts gloves on, places the jelly on the tip of her fingers, and I look away.

'OK, pop your trousers back on there now.'

The burn of shame fills my cheeks. Two fingers up your bum on a Tuesday afternoon will do that to anyone.

But Máire said this would be good for me. When I was brave enough to tell her about the pissing and the pooing, when I shared with her the uncontrollable urges that ruin days and nights, she suggested I go to a physiotherapist.

Máire said that healing was more than talking. It was loving my body, taking it to doctors, touching it kindly. It was about trying to restore and reclaim all of it. Coming here today, telling the doctor about the harm, the hurt, the piss, the poo, is part of reaching for myself. It is part of holding the little girl who lay in bed at night and said to herself over and over again, 'I must not wet my bed ... I must not wet my bed.'

Coming here is my way of cuddling in next to the little girl, whispering to her softly, 'It's OK, little one: your body is broken because of the hurt, because of what was done to you. It's not because of you. You did nothing wrong. You don't need to control or cry any more ... I'm here to help you with that. I am here to carry you.'

The physiotherapist is looking at me intently.

'Katriona, I know from your history that you have had some issues with your bladder and bowel since you were younger. Can I ask about the births of your children? Were they vaginal, normal deliveries?'

I overexplain, tears in my eyes. 'Well, with John, I was sixteen. He was facing upwards, so they had to pull him out with forceps. He was nine pounds. I got a bad tear after and an infection and blood transfusions. Sean was ten pounds, and he was a ventouse birth, but Tadhg, he just flew out of me!' I laugh nervously.

'And before that, were there any ... complications ... in your life?'

Tears roll down my face.

'I only ask because the loss of control you have can be related to trauma. I know from your records that you mentioned this to the doctor who referred you. I want you to know that we can work on this together. There are wonderful tools to help with this sort of issue. We can start straightaway. Physiotherapy that's focused on the pelvic floor is great – have you heard of this?'

I wipe my eyes, smudging my mascara. Sometimes, the acknowledgement of hurt hurts more than the hurt itself.

'Yes, I heard of someone doing this recently as they were leaking while playing sport.'

'Exactly – there is so much we can do to help. Please don't worry yourself. I've seen lots of women with these issues.'

It's not the issue I am crying over; it's the indelible ink left on my body by my childhood. It is the 'ick' I feel in my own skin. It is the faint smell of piss that follows me everywhere I go. It is the acknowledgement that I was a victim. That I cannot hide that from her; it's not only ingrained in my psyche, but it is evident in my body.

But I came here for help.

I want help.

I want to reclaim my body.

To stop the shame.

I wipe my eyes again, the tears slowing to their natural end.

'OK ... what do I have to do to fix this?'

I dust myself off and go again.

For her.

For me.

The cost to me and my body of living through poverty, trauma and hurt is long-lasting, and sometimes it feels irreparable. The shame of being a bedwetter has never quite left me.

Even today, I have a hyper-awareness of how I smell or how others smell. Dave and I fight sometimes because he might say, innocently, 'What's that smell?' and I snap.

'What ... ? Are you saying that I smell?'

The remnants of being that pissy kid never leave me. Each time, I have to say sorry to Dave and coax myself on to steady ground. Each time, I realise my past has never left me. Dave has adapted to me and my past over the years. He has learned not to ask that question. He has learned to hold my hand when pissy Katriona emerges.

I know now that bedwetting is a fight-or-flight response. That my poor traumatised body, raped and ravaged by bad men, starved of food, living with the chaos of my parents' addiction, had lost its capability to regulate itself.

The fear centre is right at the back of the brain. Some call it the lizard brain. It regulates our breath, our heartbeats, preparing us for survival. When we experience any sort of stress, there is a flood of neurochemicals into that area. The chemicals wake it up, make it ready to fight or run.

The stress that awakens this area of the brain can come in many forms. It can be a real or imagined threat. It can be a kick or a punch or a slap; a bad man coming into your room at night; prolonged uncertainty; extensive hunger – or it can be all these things and more!

My lizard brain broke from the toxic stress. The warzone that was my childhood put me on constant alert – with a fast heart, sweaty palms, constant awareness of the environment and rapid emptying of my bowel and bladder for efficiency. Bedwetting, or nocturnal enuresis, was a direct result of stress.

The loss of control of my body and my bladder is not unique to me. As I have grown older and more comfortable in my body and myself, I have spoken about my bladder with other women. When laughing hard, my friends and I regularly press our hands between our legs to stop the occasional leak. Sneezing and pissing at the same time is a regular occurrence for most women over a certain age. 'Wee-zing' is what we call it in my friend group. I was listening to Annie Macmanus on her *Changes* podcast, and she talked about starting to play soccer as a woman and the embarrassment of leaving the pitch soaked from pissing after every training session. It's not uncommon for women to have bladder issues. I wonder, though, whether the shame around it is normal.

'Babe, babe ... can you come here for a minute, please?'

He is downstairs watching TV. I lie on our bed, naked from the waist down, laughing to myself.

'WHAT ARE YOU DOING?!' He laughs too, seeing me lying on the bed, sex toys around me, fanny out for all to see. 'Why have you no clothes on? And why have you got all your vibrators out? The kids are in ... and I haven't showered after my run.'

'This isn't an invite!' I grin as I push myself up on to the pillows at the top of our king-size bed. We spent an extortionate amount of money on the bed and mattress when we bought our house back in 2013. Some canny salesman in Harvey Norman convinced us that it would be an investment in our health. Nearly ten years on, it is still going strong. Even if there are a few stains here and there, the structure of the mattress is still good, and our lives are imprinted on it.

'I'm doing my exercises. The physio said the best way to check and see if I'm strengthening my muscles down there' – I point at my fanny laid out in front of him, red hair sprouting in all directions – 'is to have someone put their finger in there as I do my pelvic exercises. She said I could either use a finger or an instrument. I can't tell with these things, so thought you might like to help?'

He is laughing as he sits down next to me; he rolls up his sleeve from his luminous running top. 'Oh, well, no problem. You know I'll do anything to help you, love. ANYTHING!'

He emphasises *anything* so much that we both start laughing. I have to hold between my legs to stop myself from pissing.

'It's not all bad, this healing stuff, is it, babe?'

He leans over to kiss me full on my lips. 'I'm here for it all!'

Unravelling in Turkey

'You are a very healthy woman, Katreena.' The Turkish doctor smiles as he speaks. 'All came back good – kidney, liver, bloods. You are extremely healthy, Katreena.'

He holds my gaze for a second longer than necessary – then begins packing the ultrasound away. Wiping the cold gel from my stomach, I don't know how to reply. I sense the tension in him, his white jacket pulled tight across his shoulders.

Is he saying what I think he's saying?

He stops and sits down next to the hospital bed, putting his shoulders back, as he takes my hand. Tears sting my eyes.

'Do you know questions?' he asks.

'When you say I am very healthy, do you mean I should not have this done to me?'

Seconds tick by. He doesn't answer.

Is he telling me to reconsider this gastric sleeve?

Then he squeezes my hand gently and smiles. 'You are very healthy women, Katreena.'

There it is again: his tone, the way he emphasises my health. I am not imagining this.

He thinks I shouldn't be here.

What the fuck am I doing here?

Back in my room, Dave is waiting. We arrived at 8am and it's close to noon now. The room in the private hospital in the centre of Kuşadası is air-conditioned, protecting us from the baking sun.

We have been coming to Turkey for eighteen years. Dave's mam's house is our summer respite. The kids have grown up here. Swimming, singing and softening over the years, we have spent our lives as a family enjoying this place.

But this year it's been different.

This year, the disgust I have felt in my body has ruined our time, has stopped the sea swims, the loving, the hugging. Days of body-hate have destroyed our once-loved haven.

'All OK, love?'

Before I can answer, the door opens. Another test.

'Katriona, hi. I'm Sarah; I'm the Irish co-ordinator here in Turkey. I'm going to be your go-to person. I'm here for you.'

'Hi ...'

'Now before you say anything, I know what you're thinking. I'm not the skinniest of people to be working in an obesity clinic, right? Well, I'm working my way up to having the operation you're having today. I can't afford it right now. I'm parenting alone, so my work here is about me saving enough money to be able to afford the gastric sleeve, and do what you are doing.'

Please don't do this to me!

This is the moment I know I can't go through with it. This woman, her story, the doctor's words, Dave's face.

I am in here still. Please don't hurt me any more.

My heart beats the loudest it has ever drummed. Calling me to listen. Shouting my name. I try to breathe. I try to speak.

'Katriona, we will have everything ready for you in the next hour. It's going to be so exciting for you!'

I can't even reply. My heart stops me from nodding my head, from smiling, from saying yes. I look at Dave and then her, and then Dave again.

'You OK, babe?'

He is scared now. I am never silent.

'I don't think I should do this.'

The words appear from behind me, from above me, from inside me.

'I don't know if I should do this.'

He sighs with exasperation, hurt. It's an *I-am-so-sick-of-this-shit* sigh. 'You're here now, love. You've decided you're going to do it. You've paid the money – you might as well go through with it now.'

Black-and-white Dave to the rescue.

She stands at the end of the bed, looking from him to me. Unsure what to do.

'I don't think I should do this.'

I repeat it over and over until she stops me.

'Katriona, it's totally OK to be scared. Everyone is nervous. When the doctor comes in, he will help with the nerves.'

'I DON'T THINK I SHOULD DO THIS!'

'Hello ... hello, Máire? It's me, Katriona. I'm sorry ... is this a bad time?'

'No, no, it's fine ... all OK there in Turkey?' she asks.

'I need help,' I say. 'I'm in a hospital here. I booked in to get a gastric sleeve, but I don't want to do it. I know I shouldn't be doing it. But Dave is pissed off that I've come this far. I'm in the gown and everything ... but I know it's wrong.'

'Katriona, Katriona ... calm down, please. It's OK, calm down. First thing to do is tell me how you got there.'

I explain about the body-hate, the holiday, the surgery website, how easy it is to book in, how I ignored my voice, my heart, how hard it was to be away. I cry. And cry. And cry.

'Well, it's a disgrace that they would even think about operating on someone without checking their mental health. You're clearly struggling, and allowing someone to book such a big operation over Facebook Messenger ... don't even get me started on that!'

Despite the situation, I can't help but smile to myself. She really does care about me.

'Now, you are to get yourself out of there, right now! None of this cutting yourself any more. You're allowed to feel shaky after being away from home, that's your safe place, but you are not allowed to hurt yourself. We decided this. Can you do that for me? For little Katriona. Can you get out of there?'

'Yes, OK. Yes, OK,' I say over and over. I am so glad I called her. My anchor. My connection to myself. My reminder of who I really am. I am so glad that I have been given permission to look out for myself. I know Dave tried, but I am a bulldozer. Máire represents something else for me. A real knower, no investment in me other than to see me get well.

She knows what is right for me.

I know what is right for me.

Having an operation to cut away half of my stomach in the pursuit of thinness is not what I or anyone should be doing to heal the way they feel about their body. Lying there in the Turkish hospital bed, talking to Máire, remembering little Katriona – it was like a cloud lifting.

I could say that I snapped, but that would not be the truth. It's more like I unravelled. I could see and feel all the connections. My history, the abuse, the losses, the pain I had inflicted on my body – and I could see me, little Katriona, cartwheeling around the football pitch by our house in Coventry, full of joy, at peace in her body.

I knew deep in my being that this operation – the sleeve – was never going to give me what I was looking for. In the same way that fog lifts on a dewy morning to reveal a beautiful day, the realisation that I was enough, that my body was enough, engulfed me. All the people I had ever been – the five-year-old, the seven-year-old, the fifteen-year-old, the thirty-year-old, the forty-five-year-old me – we all stood there together, finally realising, finally getting it.

I am enough.

We *are* enough.

All the searching, all the hurting, all of it had been focused on the wrong thing. Shrinking my body was never going to give me what I longed for. The diets, the injections, the operations to change my outsides were never what I needed. What I needed was here all along.

She was inside me.

Waiting for me to reach in and tell her, 'It's OK, you are enough ... I've got you!'

Meltdown

'I don't think I can do this any more, Máire. I don't think I have the strength.'

I start speaking before I have even sat down in the chair. I'd decided this was going to be my last session, driving along the dark country lane on the way here. I can't keep this up.

'I am so unhappy with my body. Since starting with you, I'm the fattest I have ever been – not dieting, not running, not chasing has made me fat and unhappy.'

I hold my hand up to stop her interjecting.

'Please let me finish what I'm saying. Every day I wake up planning to eat healthily, reduce my calories, exercise for an hour a day, and every day I fail. Every day. I thought that coming here, talking, getting better would mean I would treat myself better, that I would get skinny, that I would *feel* healthier. I feel so out of control. Like I cannot control myself.'

I'm sweating saying this. I'm sick of talking about my childhood, my parents, the trauma, the abuse – when will this stop? When will I have freedom? When will I be skinny?

'I'm so glad you're telling me all this, that you can trust me with these things. And I love hearing that you're not able to restrict your food and your body, Katriona. I know you don't want to hear that right now, but I'm happy to hear that you cannot hurt yourself any more. We are not here for that.'

She reaches over and picks up little Katriona from the chair.

'Can I ask you to hold her for me?'

I reluctantly take her in my arms. She feels soft and nice to hold. I look down at her.

'There was a time in your life when you needed to control everything, Katriona, isn't that right?'

I nod, suspicious of where this is going.

'When you would hide food and gorge on it, you did that because you were scared and hurt. Those thoughts and feelings are deep, really ingrained in you.'

I nod. Tears prick my eyes.

Don't be nice to me.

Please don't be nice to me.

'I want you to imagine that you can reach yourself back then, that you can talk to yourself back then. Can you try to do that for me ... ?'

Please don't be nice to me.

'OK, so if you can look at little Katriona there – scared, hungry, not knowing who is going to hurt her next – what would you say to her? What words would you say?'

I can see myself.

The darkness of the cupboard is comforting. I still fit.

The bread is still fresh. I unravel the pack and bite down hard and fast. Sugar spills on me and on the airing cupboard floor. I shove it in, fast and hard.

Weightless.

Lifeless.

Painless.

I can't find words. I can't reach her. She is stuck in there – alone.

'I don't know what to say ...'

Máire pauses before she speaks, leaning forward in her chair. 'Would you mind if I tried?' She is soft, kind, confident – present.

'OK,' I whisper.

'Hey, little one, are you doing OK over there ... ?'

She is talking to little Katriona, the doll lying in my arms.

'It's OK to feel sad, you know, and scared. It's OK to be frightened ... I'm here to tell you that you don't have to worry. Please don't worry. I'm here with you, and you are not on your own any more ... I'm here for you now. No one is going to hurt you again. I'm going to look after you. You don't need to hide any more. You don't need to do anything. I've got you!'

My heart breaks open. The realisation hit me that no one ever loved me, no one ever told me it would be OK, no one picked me up, made me safe, told me it wasn't my fault – her words crack me wide open. I cry tears I didn't know I had. I hold little Katriona tight. I stroke her hair while I hold her in my arms. I let the waves of hurt wash over me.

I feel it.
Really feel it.
The loss, the hurt.
I see me, the beautiful, innocent girl I was – I am. I hold myself in a way I didn't know was possible.

Mine – Ours

Summer 2025

WhatsApp:
Hi Katriona, Lee here from *Ireland AM*. We loved your interview last month on the show and wanted to see if you would do a regular slot, a type of agony aunt, wise-woman slot. The audience loves hearing what you have to say!

I re-read the text, delighted to be liked. To be thought of as someone wise, who can be on TV! As a young girl, I dreamed of being on the stage or on TV, of dancing, of singing, of writing books, of telling stories – and now here I am, doing it, living my dreams.

But you'll look fat on TV. The camera adds ten pounds, remember. You should tell him to wait for six months so you can shrink before you start ...

Doubt. Fear. Worry. My inner critic plagues me for a moment – until I hear her. The other voice, the part of me that has grown loud over the past three and a half years, since I started with Máire, since I gave myself a chance.

Katriona, you're a good person. You deserve to speak and be heard. You are so much more than what you look like. You are enough.

I text him back immediately.

Lee, I would love to. When do I start?

When I started writing this book, I secretly hoped that by the end I would be able to unveil a new me; that I would be showing off my new, improved body in a sexy bikini on the front cover. This new body would be the result of all my hard therapy work: being 'fixed', healthy, no longer hungry.

But that would not be the truth, and that is not the point of this story.

The point of my story is to tell you the truth.

That I am still hungry.

That I still strive.

That I still long.

The difference now is that I know my body is not a destination; that there is no solution for how I feel in a 'before' or 'after' photo; that there is no end place for me where body hurt and hate do not exist any more.

After my meltdown in the clinic in Turkey, I gave my body the gift of continuing therapy. I committed to therapy in the same way I committed to WeightWatchers that first time around. And I told Máire everything. I told her my whole story, many times. And I told it in many different ways. I told it from my point of view, my mum's point of view and then my dad's point of view. I blamed me and her and him and them and me. And I cried and shouted.

And I got braver. I told her about Bob and Don and the men who took my shine from me.

I told her that I thought I'd done something wrong.

I asked her if I could have done something different.

And I cried. Hard tears. For my body. Lost to hurt and hunger.

With each session, the distance between me and my body grew smaller. I began to feel myself. Forgive myself. To hear the kinder voice, the one who reminds me of the little girl I was, how she is still here, searching for a safe place to exist.

'Máire, it's me. Can you talk for a minute?'

I hate calling. I am on holiday again. On a big, beautiful cruise ship. Floating around the Mediterranean Sea, Dave, the boys and I, visiting Italy and Spain and France. And I can't enjoy it. Consumed by the shape and size of my body, I can't breathe because the inner critic is so loud. Comparing. Crying. Searching for somewhere to hide.

'Yeah, my love. I can talk. I said you could call any time. Is everything OK?'

I sit on the top deck, looking out at the horizon, and I cry. I tell her I feel so exposed, so naked, without my home, my clothes, my secure base.

'I hate my body ... being half-naked ... the women. Dave is so happy ... I feel like I'm dragging him down. Can you help me?'

This is the first time I have done this – called her when I am in the middle of a spiral. In Turkey, I called Máire after the pain, after the hurt, when I was already reacting, doing something mad, hurting myself more. Now I'm calling her before. During. Not after. She told me this is what I should do when I feel the cracks. But it feels unnatural; the shake inside me is louder than her voice.

'I'm so proud of you for calling me. You're OK now. Let's talk it through. I have loads of time.'

As we talk, I realise it isn't the holiday that is the problem, or my body; it's the change. I feel safe in my home, in my own bed, in the life I've built. Change brings fear, a feeling of powerlessness. It reminds me of days I would rather forget.

We talk it through. I sit on the deck and cry. For the lost girl. For my lost body. I say, 'It wasn't fair, it wasn't fair,' and she listens, stands firm for me, reminds me that it wasn't fair – and that she is there.

And eventually it passes, and the sea calms.

And I thank her with all my heart.

I learned through therapy about my trauma and the way it fractured me. How my centre is sometimes unstable, cracked; how the desire to shrink and achieve and love were natural reactions to a world that hurts girls. And with every call to Máire, every time I talked through, the upsets and the cracks – they got shorter and the space between them grew longer.

And I learned it was OK to ask for help in those moments; how the vibrations of the past do not have to ruin today. How my body isn't the issue; that this pattern of thinking my body is the problem is old, obsolete. That, while focusing on my body helped me gain some semblance of control as a child, I don't need that any more. As an adult, I am safe.

I learned that I am safe.

I learned to talk about my thoughts and feelings. I learned that someone will be there for me if I ask them to be. As a girl, when Bob hurt me so badly, I asked my mum to help me. I did the best I could for me and my body. I told an adult. But she looked away, unable to acknowledge or help me. She ignored my cries for help. The shadow of that experience cast a darkness across my whole life, making it hard for me to ask for help.

Máire taught me how to change that, and she showed me I was safe – that she would answer my call. She showed me how to respond to my own cries for help! I have learned that I may always experience hurt, but how I deal with the hurt can change.

And it has. It has!

Epilogue

When I published my first memoir, *Poor*, in 2023, I thought I had said it all. That that was it for me: no more oversharing, no more stories of my life. But, as time progressed, I realised I had more to say. More to share.

Poor was my call to action; it was my reflection on poverty and education. It was me demonstrating that all children need help; we all need the right conditions to demonstrate our excellence to the world.

But this book, *Hungry*, is as important a story for me to tell as *Poor* was.

When I sat down to write this book, it was to tell the story of my body. So I wrote down all the memories I had about my body, and all the things I had learned about my body from the people in my life. I wrote stories that hurt me and stories that made me smile. And I started to make connections, to see what had made me hate my body.

I saw my hurt mum, Tilly, pulling at her fat, selling herself for drugs, losing her body; and my dad, Tony, so desperate for love that he would ogle women, manipulate me, show me that my value lay in being a good girl, a beautiful girl. I saw Jace, and how his issues and my low self-worth were a recipe for disaster; how I didn't know the value of my own body. I saw me losing my body to sexual abuse, and the fractures it caused. And I saw how the men in the world saw me and my body as an object for their pleasure – and how I internalised this, complied with it.

I saw how these experiences combined and resulted in a deep desire to heal – a desire that went awry because we live in a world that tells us that being skinny equals being healthy, beautiful, worthy. Seeing my body laid out on the pages of this book helped me see that I deserve to be free, to love myself, to heal. To return to that place where I felt myself running through the fields with my brothers, proud of my body, laughing and free.

While telling the story of my body, I have begun to understand something much bigger than my own story. I have learned that I live in a world that *benefits* from me hating my body; that there is money to be made from body-hate, body-hurt, body-trauma. As I've grown in self-love, I have grown angrier and angrier at the billion-dollar industries that benefit from the hate I feel for my body. I recognise that there is a vast machine in train that plots every day to ensure that I continue to dislike myself; there is probably a group of (mostly) men sitting somewhere right now, in fancy offices and boardrooms, scheming to ensure that I continue to hate my body and feel 'fat' or 'wrinkled' so that I will continue to buy the never-ending stream of products and procedures promising quick fixes for my really complex problems.

Hungry is not just about my body; it is about *our* bodies. I wrote this story to shine a light on what happens to women: all women, some women, hurt women, most women. I wrote it to show that when we place unrealistic expectations on our bodies, we are hurt.

When we're relentlessly told that ageing isn't OK, that belly fat isn't OK, that thin lips are not OK, we are hurt.

When we are taught that our worth is tied up in how beautiful we are to men, we are hurt.

When we are told our sexual and emotional needs are not as important as men's, we are hurt.

We need to talk about how the beauty and cosmetic industry is taking advantage of women. How the standards of beauty are inflicted on all women, even those who have no hurt or harm. I see it in my professional life – women encouraging each other to 'stay on track'. 'Let's take the stairs rather than the lift' or 'let's get our steps in' are common refrains. Or, after we eat cake in the office: 'I'll have to work that off later.'

In a recent WhatsApp group, a woman posted: *Purple Snacks are on sale in Lidl* (the best low-calorie chocolate bars in town). The woman who posted about the purple snacks is not to blame. Women are not to blame. We are all susceptible to the pressures and messages of idealised beauty; we're all inundated with images of 'perfect' bodies and flawless looks before some of us are gifted a Barbie doll.

We need to talk about this. We need to fight against it. We need to acknowledge how society inflicts impossible standards of beauty on women – unrealistic standards that hurt all women, but especially women like me, women who are vulnerable, traumatised and poor.

Making the connection between my childhood experiences and my adult behaviours lies at the heart of this story. But the message is for everyone, and it is simple: we learn the value of our bodies through the world we grow in, through our families, our friends, the media, through trauma, through hunger – and these things affect everyone. The message is that, for some women, these experiences result in self-harm, in hurt, and an insatiable hunger to shrink, to be good, to achieve or to connect.

In a world where one in four women have been sexually abused, and 370 million women and girls raped, we need to talk about this. In a world in which thirty-one per cent of children in Ireland and the UK live below the poverty line, and in which children who are poor are nine times more likely to experience sexual trauma, we need to talk about it. We must do better for these women, for these children.

The complexities of what I have done to my body are sometimes difficult for me to comprehend. I look back at that little girl with sadness. I see the woman I was with compassion. When trauma and stress are overwhelming, humans often act irrationally, attempting to survive in ways that make no real sense, looking for the quickest and easiest solution.

My reactions went beyond rational. I was completely broken; I was trying my hardest to live each day in a world that was scary and out of control. Controlling the size of my body, or the drive to control its size, was my way of trying to gain security. Of regaining control, of believing that I could do something for me. That I could be a good girl.

Today, I know differently.

Today, I live in the messy awkwardness of not loving my body but not hating it either. Of having a voice that says, *No one cares about your belly but you!* Today, I live in the arms of a man who loves me, in a home that is peaceful.

Today, I have hope.

Today, I am healing.

Today, I have love.

'Dave … do you ever think about a person or someone from your past, like … the one that got away?'

He props himself up on his elbow.

His eyes still take my breath away. All these years later, and he is still the best man I know.

'Are you thinking about Dylan again?'

He is smiling now. He knows everything, all of me.

He still loves me.

'I can't help it. Sometimes, I feel so bad about Dylan. Like … I never saw him again after I told him about you. He was holding on for me.'

'My luck was his loss.' He is laughing, snuggling into my neck.

'No, but seriously, babe … is there anyone like that for you? You never tell me anything!'

I am always digging. I don't know if it's the psychologist in me or the trauma. But there has to be more to him than this calm, happy man – some dark secret hiding away.

'Well, there was someone ... about a year before we got together ...'

I feel sick now. His eyes are shining. *Why did I fucking ask him?*

'Yeah ... tell me.' I can't help myself.

'I was at a meal in an Italian restaurant in town on the Quays. We were celebrating a lad's year of being clean and sober. I remember this girl came in. She wore this lovely red dress, and ... I remember she just lit up the room.'

Oh, Jesus, I'm going to puke.

'Everyone wanted to talk to her. She was so confident. I asked one of the lads who she was. She was so fit. Not just in the way she looked; it was the way she commanded the room. Everyone knew her. Everyone wanted to chat to her.'

I wish he would stop now; the jealousy is making me sick. *Why did I start this?* The thought of him with someone else is horrifying.

'I wanted her. She was so beautiful ...'

I look at him, his eyes shining into mine. I don't know whether to hit him or hug him. 'So ... what happened with her?'

I have to know, even though I don't want to know.

He stops. Kisses me gently on my lips. Catches my hand and speaks. 'Her name was Katriona – babe, it was you!'

I am stopped dead. My heart, my head and my soul all shine at once.

It was me.

It was always me.

And then it comes to me: the night, the red dress, the feeling I had of confidence. It was one of the rare nights, back then, when I knew I was beautiful. The way I know I am beautiful now.

I didn't even see him then.

I couldn't even see him then.

I wasn't ready.

Thankfully, I am now.

Acknowledgements

The idea for this book began on a train journey, I was sitting across from Dr Richard Hogan on our way home from a book festival and I said to him, 'Richard – I think I have something else I want to say.' He said to me, 'Katriona that sounds amazing – write it!'

I am so grateful for all the people who have said these words to me along the way. To Ciara, Ella, Eleanor, Sophie and all the team in Hachette and Headline – you have encouraged me to no end, reminding me that my words are enough. To Kathryn, my editor, you made sure every thought was mine, every word was mine! You made me feel empowered and safe, and you pushed me to be better. I will always be grateful for the time we had – even if you had never heard of a 'silver seven'.

To all the writers I have met and chatted to over the past year, thank you for being so kind to me, for sharing your journeys, for encouraging me. To Elaine, Edel, Liz, Vikki, Grainne and all the other wonderful people I have met who write wonderful stories – thank you for letting me join this deeply insecure and wonderful club! To the Tyrone Guthrie Centre at Annaghmakerrig for your wonderful residency. To Cian, in Maynooth Book Shop, you have been a constant support this past couple of years – thank you for naming this book for me – 'Hungry' was your best idea!

Dave, you are the love of my life, the man I never knew I needed or wanted – without your soft landing my words, and my life, wouldn't be what it is. I am so lucky I know what matters and what doesn't.

To my entourage, you know who you are, my girls who are there every step, thank you for the love and support. For the laughs. For the kindness. For the coffees and the chats. I love you more than I loved any man!

And, finally, to all the women who have ever felt like they were not enough, that they needed to shrink to fit. This story is for you. Thank you for never giving up on yourself.